Does the Writing Workshop Still Work?

NEW WRITING VIEWPOINTS
Series Editor: Graeme Harper, *University of Wales, Bangor, Wales, Great Britain*

The overall aim of this series is to publish books which will ultimately inform teaching and research, but whose primary focus is on the analysis of creative writing practice and theory. There will also be books which deal directly with aspects of creative writing knowledge, with issues of genre, form and style, with the nature and experience of creativity, and with the learning of creative writing. They will all have in common a concern with excellence in application and in understanding, with creative writing practitioners and their work, and with informed analysis of creative writing as process as well as completed artefact.

Full details of all the books in this series and of all our other publications can be found on http://www.multilingual-matters.com, or by writing to Multilingual Matters, St Nicholas House, 31–34 High Street, Bristol BS1 2AW, UK.

NEW WRITING VIEWPOINTS
Series Editor: Graeme Harper, *University of Wales, Bangor, Wales, UK*

Does the Writing Workshop Still Work?

Edited by
Dianne Donnelly

MULTILINGUAL MATTERS
Bristol • Buffalo • Toronto

Library of Congress Cataloging in Publication Data
A catalog record for this book is available from the Library of Congress.
Does the Writing Workshop Still Work?/Edited by Dianne Donnelly.
Includes bibliographical references.
1. Creative writing. 2. Workshops. 3. English language–Rhetoric–Study and teaching.
4. Writing centers.
I. Donnelly, Dianne.
PE1404.D64 2010
808′.042071-dc22 2010014103

British Library Cataloguing in Publication Data
A catalogue entry for this book is available from the British Library.

ISBN-13: 978-1-84769-269-6 (hbk)
ISBN-13: 978-1-84769-268-9 (pbk)

Multilingual Matters
UK: St Nicholas House, 31–34 High Street, Bristol BS1 2AW, UK.
USA: UTP, 2250 Military Road, Tonawanda, NY 14150, USA.
Canada: UTP, 5201 Dufferin Street, North York, Ontario M3H 5T8, Canada.

The policy of Multilingual Matters/Channel View Publications is to use papers that are natural, renewable and recyclable products, made from wood grown in sustainable forests. In the manufacturing process of our books, and to further support our policy, preference is given to printers that have FSC and PEFC Chain of Custody certification. The FSC and/or PEFC logos will appear on those books where full certification has been granted to the printer concerned.

Typeset by The Charlesworth Group
Printed and bound in Great Britain by Short Run Press Ltd.

Contents

Acknowledgements

I thank all of the contributors to this collection who have devoted their time and expertise to this very important project. On behalf of these contributors, I thank Graeme Harper and Anna Roderick of Multilingual Matters for their support, guidance, and belief that this workshop collection is a vital and timely topic in creative writing scholarship and an exciting addition to the *New Writing Viewpoints* book series. I additionally thank the creative writing teachers who responded to my survey on the writing workshop model. Their insight proved critical to the development of the collection's introduction and to the first 'voice' in this workshop dialogue. I also appreciate the University of South Florida's support and recognition of my teaching, writing, and scholarship, and I am grateful to my colleagues Joseph Moxley, Rita Ciresi, John Fleming, Deborah Noonan, Hunt Hawkins, and Patrick Bizzaro for their encouragement in my professional development.

A special thanks to Rob, Sherry and Constance for their steadfast friendship and love. As always, I express my deepest gratitude and affection to my family, in particular my children, Keith and Julia, who tell me I am the best at whatever I do, even when I know this cannot be true.

About the Authors

Keith Kumasen Abbott

The Things I Used To Do: Workshops Old and New

Keith Kumasen Abbott is an associate professor at Naropa University. Publications include the novels *Gush, Rhino Ritz* and *Mordecai of Monterey*, a 2009 reprint of *Downstream from Trout Fishing in America* and short story collections *Harum Scarum, The First Thing Coming* and *The French Girl*. His works appeared in the international anthology *Rimbaud Après Rimbaud* and *Richard Brautigan: Essays on the Writing and Life* (for which he also chaired a symposium). Ziji Productions optioned his story 'Spanish Castle', and he co-wrote the screenplay. His work is translated into five languages, notably books in German and French, including his novel *Racer*, which was short-listed for the Berlinale Film Conference in 2007. An ordained lay Soto monk, his Zen art and calligraphy were shown at Seoul's 11th International Calligraphy Exhibition and Beijing's China–USA Calligraphy Exhibition.

Mary Ellen Bertolini

Workshopping Lives

Associate Director of Writing at Middlebury College, Mary Ellen Bertolini teaches, tutors writing, and directs the Peer Writing Tutor Program. She has published on Frank McCourt and Sandra Cisneros and has given presentations on Jane Austen, writing and healing, First-Year Programs, blogging, and writing pedagogy. She has held positions as Director of Academic Support, Acting Director of the Center for Teaching, Learning, and Research and of the Writing and First-Year Seminar Programs. She received a BA in English from College of New Rochelle (NY) and has graduate degrees from Bread Loaf School of English (VT) and Wesleyan University (CT).

Patrick Bizzaro

Workshop: An Ontological Study

Patrick Bizzaro has published nine books and chapbooks of poetry, two critical studies of Fred Chappell's poetry and fiction, a book on the pedagogy of academic creative writing, some textbooks, and a couple of hundred poems in magazines. He is a frequent reviewer of his peers' work in magazines like *Asheville Poetry Review, North Carolina Literary Review*, and *Appalachian Journal*, among others. Bizzaro, first Director of the University Writing Program at East Carolina University, is a UNC Board of Governors Distinguished Professor for Teaching and ECU Scholar–Teacher Award winner. He lives quite happily with Resa Crane and their five-year-old son, Antonio, in Indiana, PA, where he is currently a Professor of English in Indiana University of Pennsylvania's doctoral program in Composition and TESOL, after retiring from ECU. During his last year on the ECU faculty, he received the 'Outstanding Professor' award from the ECU Department of Disability Support Services, the ninth award for teaching he has received during his career. His articles on composition studies have appeared regularly in *College English* and *College Composition and Communication*. His co-edited book on poet and pedagogue Wendy Bishop is forthcoming from Hampton Press.

Mary Ann Cain

'A Space of Radical Openness': Re-Visioning the Creative Writing Workshop

Mary Ann Cain is Professor of English at Indiana University-Purdue University Fort Wayne, where she teaches fiction writing and creative nonfiction, along with other writing courses that explore the nexus of rhetoric and poetics. Recent publications include a novel, *Down from Moonshine*, stories in *The Bitter Oleander, The Denver Quarterly*, and *The Hawai'i Pacific Review*, among others. Her scholarly work includes *Breathing Space: Composing Public Spaces for Writing and Teaching* (co-authors Michelle Comstock and Lil Brannon) and *Re-visioning Writers' Talk: Gender and Culture in Acts of Composing* along with numerous articles and book chapters that explore social, spatial, and material aspects of writing and writing instruction.

Dianne Donnelly (Editor)

Introduction: If it Ain't Broke, Don't Fix it, Or Change is Inevitable, Except from a Vending Machine

Dianne Donnelly is the recipient of multiple teaching, scholarship, and writing awards and has published articles and short stories in a number of venues. She is also a frequent presenter at conferences on the subject of creative writing theory and pedagogy and on the emergence of creative writing studies. Her most recent publication is an essay on the intersection of creative writing and composition in the collection, *The Teacher–Writer in English Studies: Starting with Wendy Bishop*. She holds a PhD in English and teaches creative writing at the University of South Florida and Eckerd College.

Philip Gross

Small Worlds: What Works in Workshops If and When They Do?

Philip Gross is a writer of many parts – a poet and writer of thought-provoking fiction for young people who has also published science fiction, haiku and schools opera libretti, plays and radio short stories. His poetry 'The Wasting Game' was shortlisted for the Whitbread Poetry Prize and collected in *Changes of Address*. He has published six books with Bloodaxe, including *The Water Table*, *The Egg of Zero*, *Mappa Mundi*, and *Changes of Address: Poems 1980–1998*. Gross was announced as the 2009 winner of the T.S. Eliot Prize for his collection of poems, *The Water Table*. A new collaboration, *I Spy Pinhole Eye* (with photographer Simon Denison) is due from Cinnamon Press. He is the author of ten teenage novels – most recently *The Lastling* and *The Storm Garden*. His collections of children's poetry include *The All-Nite Café* which won the Signal Award. He has taught in universities for 20 years and since 2004 has been Professor of Creative Writing at the Glamorgan University, South Wales.

Katharine Haake

Re-envisioning the Workshop: Hybrid Classrooms, Hybrid Texts

Katharine Haake is the author of a new collection of stories, *The Origin of Stars*. Her prior works are a hybrid novel, *That Water, Those Rocks*, and the *LA Times* best-selling collection of stories, *The Height and Depth of Everything*. Her first book of stories was *No Reason on Earth* (1986). Her work has appeared widely in such journals as *The Iowa Review*, *Witness*, *One Story*, *New Letters*, and *The Santa Monica Review*, and has been featured in the online journal, *Segue*, as well as in the LA's New Short Fiction Performance Series. Haake is a recipient of an Individual Artist's Grant from the Cultural Affairs Department of the City of Los Angeles, along with distinguished story recognitions from *Best American Short Stories* and *Best of the West*, Editor's Choice Award from *Cream City Review*, and an honorable mention in the Foundation Award for Speculative Fiction. A regular contributor to scholarship in the theory and pedagogy of creative writing, she is also the author of *What Our Speech Disrupts: Feminism and Creative Writing Studies*, and *Metro: Journeys in Writing Creatively* (along with Hans Ostrom and Wendy Bishop). She holds a PhD from the University of Utah and teaches at California State University, Northridge.

Colin Irvine

'It's fine, I gess': Problems with the Workshop Model in College Composition Courses

Colin Irvine is an assistant professor of English at Augsburg College in Minneapolis, Minnesota. He teaches courses in composition, American literature, environmental literature, and English education methods. His research often focuses on the intersection of pedagogy and narratology, and he edited a collection of essays titled *Teaching the Novel Across the Curriculum: A Handbook for Educators*. Currently he is developing a digitized 'Researcher's Edition' of conservationist Aldo Leopold's seminal text *A Sand County Almanac* (1949). This edition will employ technology to determine and develop post-process, para-logic methods for teaching students to do rigorous research and equally sophisticated academic writing.

Anna Leahy

Teaching as a Creative Act: Why the Workshop Works in Creative Writing

Anna Leahy's collection *Constituents of Matter* won the Wick Poetry Prize, and she has published two poetry chapbooks, *Turns about a Point* and *Hagioscope*. Leahy served as guest poetry editor for the second issue of *Fifth Wednesday*. She edited the collection on pedagogy entitled *Power and Identity in the Creative Writing Classroom* (Multilingual Matters), which launched the New Writing Viewpoints series, and contributed to other collections, including *Can It Really Be Taught?* and *The Handbook of Creative Writing*. Recently, Leahy collaborated with an art historian to explore the poetry of Pulitzer Prize-winner Natasha Trethewey; one article appeared in *English Language Notes* and another is forthcoming in a collection about ekphrastic poetry. Additional information about Anna Leahy can be found at www.amleahy.com.

Willy Maley

Workshopping and Fiction: Laboratory, Factory, or Finishing School?

Willy Maley, Professor of Renaissance Studies at the University of Glasgow, is the author of *A Spenser Chronology*, *Salvaging Spenser: Colonialism, Culture and Identity*, *Nation, State and Empire in English*

Renaissance Literature: Shakespeare to Milton, and *Muriel Spark for Starters*. He is co-editor of Edmund Spenser's *A View of the Present State of Ireland*, and of five collections of essays: *Representing Ireland: Literature and the Origins of Conflict, 1534–1660; Postcolonial Criticism; British Identities and English Renaissance Literature; Shakespeare and Scotland; and Spheres of Influence: Intellectual and Cultural Publics from Shakespeare to Habermas*. Willy, along with Philip Hobsbaum, founded the Creative Writing Masters at Glasgow University in 1995.

Tim Mayers

Poetry, F(r)iction, Drama: The Complex Dynamics of Audience in the Writing Workshop

Tim Mayers is associate professor of English at Millersville University of Pennsylvania, where he teaches courses in creative writing, composition, rhetoric, and literary criticism. His scholarly research focuses primarily on the past, present, and possible future states of English studies; more specifically, he explores points of overlap and contention between composition studies, creative writing, and literary criticism. He is the author of *(Re)Writing Craft: Composition, Creative Writing, and the Future of English Studies*. His scholarly work has also appeared in *College English*, *College Composition and Communication*, and *JAC*. He has published more than 20 poems in literary journals and magazines, and he is currently seeking a literary agent for his novel, *Intelligence Manifesto*, which won the 2008 Paradigm Novel Prize.

Gaylene Perry

Potentially Dangerous: Vulnerabilities and Risks in the Writing Workshop

Gaylene Perry is a lecturer in Professional & Creative Writing within the School of Communication & Creative Arts at Deakin University, Melbourne, Australia. She teaches mainly in the areas of fiction and life-writing. Gaylene's book, *Midnight Water: A Memoir* was short-listed for Australia's National Biography Award. She is currently working on a major piece of fiction.

Sue Roe

Introducing Masterclasses

Sue Roe is a biographer, poet, novelist and critic. She is author of *Gwen John: A Life* and of *The Private Lives of the Impressionists*, which has been translated into six languages. Her poetry has appeared in journals and anthologies including *Agenda, The Rialto, New Poetry Quarterly, New Writing, New Poetries III*, Edited by Michael Schmidt and *New Writing: The International Journal for the Practice and Theory of Creative Writing*. A Virginia Woolf scholar, she is Editor of the Penguin Modern Classics edition of *Jacob's Room*. She also works closely with contemporary artists and has published a number of catalogue introductions to exhibitions, with more forthcoming. She runs and teaches the MA in Creative Writing & Authorship at the University of Sussex.

Brent Royster

Engaging the Individual/Social Conflict within Creative Writing Pedagogy

Brent Royster's poems have been published in *Center: A Journal of the Literary Arts, Cimarron Review, Green Mountains Review, Iron Horse Literary Review, Mochila Review, The North American Review, Quarterly West, South Carolina Review*, and other notable journals. He teaches writing and literature at Ball State University in Muncie, Indiana.

David Starkey

The Creative Writing Workshop in the Two-Year College: Who Cares?

David Starkey is the editor of two books of creative writing pedagogy – *Teaching Writing Creatively* (1998) and *Genre by Example: Writing What We Teach* (2001), both with Boynton/Cook – and the author of two textbooks: *Poetry Writing: Theme and Variations* (McGraw-Hill, 2000) and *Creative Writing: Four Genres in Brief* (Bedford/St. Martin's, 2008). He currently directs the creative writing program at Santa Barbara City College and serves as the Poet Laureate of Santa Barbara.

Stephanie Vanderslice

Once More to the Workshop: A Myth Caught in Time

An Associate Professor of Writing at the University of Central Arkansas, Stephanie Vanderslice's essays on the teaching of creative writing have been included in books and journals such as *Creative Writing Studies, New Writing: An International Journal of Creative Writing Theory and Practice, Profession, Teaching Creative Writing (Continuum), and The Creative Writing Handbook*. Her fiction and creative non-fiction have appeared in *Writing-on-the-Edge, Knowing Pains: Woman on Love, Sex and Work in their 40s* and many others. With Dr Kelly Ritter, she edited *Can It Really Be Taught?: Resisting Lore in the Teaching of Creative Writing* and wrote *Teaching Creative Writing to Undergraduates: A Resource and Guide* (2010).

Leslie Kreiner Wilson

Wrestling Bartleby: Another Workshop Model for the Creative Writing Classroom

A writer living in Studio City, Los Angelis, CA, Leslie Wilson teaches writing at Pepperdine University in Malibu where she has directed the MFA program, WordFest, the Fall Literary Arts Festival, and the campus literary magazine *Expressionists*. She also edits the creative writing journal *Review American* and holds a PhD in English from the graduate university at The Claremont Colleges. Her most recent work includes the script for *Fighting Words* (PBS), the script for *Foreclosure* (Fall Literary Arts Festival, Malibu), a novel *The Quilt*, and poetry published in *The Other Voices International Project* anthology.

Foreword
On Experience

GRAEME HARPER

1.

Frequently we humans get it wrong; or, considering the particular focus of this book, we could say that frequently we humans have gotten it wrong in particular instances for particular reasons. That might be our first definition of human experience: 'those situations of getting it wrong and yet continuing, afterwards, less or more aware of those previous mistakes'. Frequently in universities and colleges we have gotten it wrong when we've spoken about creative writing. And yet, as might be expected given creative writing's association with the core human traits of creativity and communication, we have continued nevertheless. By 'getting it wrong' I mean we have spoken about creative writing in one way while knowing, intuitively, humanly, accurately, that it was another.

By getting it wrong, I mean that while we have known that creative writing primarily involves human action – activity, event, movement – we have frequently approached creative writing as if its primary manifestation occurs (and has occurred) in the final works that have emerged from our variety of actions. We have known this is untrue; that logically, intuitively, experientially, humanly, creative writing exists first and foremost as the *things we do*. But we have frequently spoken about creative writing as if it is the *objects we made.*

In this lies only barely hidden a second definition of human experience. That is: 'our own actions, which we consider, and to which we respond'. Those actions, of course, include the event of learning and of teaching. How we respond to our many human actions is determined not only by the recognition that something is occurring or has occurred but also by our capacity (and interest in) critically considering what has occurred or is occurring. In other words, human beings act, more or less (sometimes less, sometimes more) consider their actions, and act further. Such is how we engage with the world. We could even call this our *modus operandi*.

Our natural *modus operandi* informs creative writing. Primarily actions, the human event that is creative writing is imbued with our individual and group, critical understandings. It carries these within it, as a human *activity*; so that when someone is learning creative writing they are not only learning the modes and methods of writerly inscription, they are – all running to plan – also learning key elements of the critical understanding that informs and assists our creative writing.

None of this is well addressed when we begin our consideration of creative writing not as if it is human action, informing our experience, but as if it is a textual manifestation, found in only some of the artefacts that our action produces, and mostly at the end of the event of creative writing (that is *post*-event). In approaching it this way, our actions are reduced to a set of pre-determined reference points established not by creative action but largely by the *post*-event considerations in relation to one or another cultural moment that informs current opinion. Contextual conditions understood fluidly would be productive, but this is not what I'm speaking about here. I'm speaking about the contextual conditions established by monocratic paradigms of academic critical study, *post* the event of creation, *post* the event of creative writing.

In considering how this might conceal knowledge and understanding, a third definition of human experience begins to emerge. Experience in this third case is defined as: 'a discovery, accumulation or gathering of knowledge that is founded in an event and produces further events'. Simply put, experience is not something that exists until we act upon it (or, perhaps we could add, sometimes choose not to act because of it). Indeed, an expression like 'he is very experienced' carries no weight of truth whatsoever unless that experience manifests itself in displayed understanding. It is, otherwise, either a speculative suggestion or it is an ironic statement.

As the writers in this book make clear, the creative writing workshop is itself an event, a significant site of human action. Because creative writing is action the workshop cannot be considered unless it is considered in relation to action. And so it is here. Action imbued with understanding.

And yet, how often have we approached creative writing workshops in universities and colleges as if they are the attendants to knowledge founded primarily on the aims of producing recognised cultural commodities? By this I mean, has it not frequently been the case that the creative writing workshop has been put forward as an addition to the cultural or, indeed, modern academic commodification of human experience; while all the time we have known, have participated in, have recognised, the individual human values associated with our fundamentally action-based creative exploration, creative interaction, human creativity?

Of course, the word 'workshop' has long carried with it the holistic industrial sense of object production, as well as its more specific association with small manufacturing. And why wouldn't it? Whether considered to have etymological links to the 13th-century French sense of a 'forge', or whether (with our educational hats on) we link it to the 19th-century adoption of the term 'homework' (a 17th-century English term meaning 'work done at home' rather than in the factory), the workshop has long been associated with something to be done in order to produce something to be valued. The question, however, is what is it that we value in and about the workshop, and for what reasons?

2.

Value is both a hard-to-grasp ideal and a significant ideal. The value of an experience is even harder to grasp than the value of object. For example, while it is relatively easy to place a value on a diamond (according to regularly published and commercially verifiable mathematics) it is far less easy to place a value on the experience of owning a diamond. And, indeed, it becomes even worse if we ask ourselves to make a comparative judgement – say, between the value of owning a diamond compared to the value of walking on a sandy beach on a warm summer's day. At very least, there are two sets of values at play here; and, indeed, at certain points in our thinking they are closely connected and at other points they are widely disconnected.

The value of education also falls into this mode of connection/disconnection. Certainly there are many who would defend the ideal that education is valuable regardless of whether it has any commodity worth whatsoever (e.g. whether it leads to employment; increases the earning power of the educated individual or community; produces a 'thing'; or, alternatively, provides employment for educators). However, there are others (and there is an array of representations in this regard) who make claims for education as laden with commodity value, with the capacity to generate worth beyond the worth of knowledge in and of itself. The value in, and of, education is thus not without some controversy – and never is this more obvious than when government educational bodies or university administrations consider the viability of particular subjects within their realms, and the ways in which some subjects may, or may not, be deserving of their further investment.

The value of a creative writing in a university or college can certainly be judged in many ways. Some judgements may have a resounding effect on university administrations, some may be more akin to a wondrous tune heard in corridors far away from the bustle of 'hard' administrative decision-making. We see in this book a variety of judgements that display an understanding of the varieties of approaches that might be taken to the question of value – the value of creative writing and, in particular, the value of the creative writing workshop. However, the most important aspect of this is surely that what needs to be valued in the creative writing workshop is *the value of the human experience*.

It would be wrong to say that what I am putting in play in this Foreword is an opposition between object-value and experience-value – with the suggestion that in valuing objects we somehow devalue humanity. Nothing could be further from what I am suggesting. However, I do foreshadow here Philip Gross's statement, later in this book, that 'the workshop ... is not a thing', and I do point readers toward Dianne Donnelly's reference in her Introduction to a 'patchwork of practices', among other comments from the writers published here. I don't reject the suggestions made by those who have focused more on the generally recognised 'final' artefacts of creative writing. These have importance too. And yet we need to be clear that the value of the creative writing workshop, the undertaking of the creative writing workshop, and *all* the attendant physical results of the creative writing workshop are addressed equally and with attention to the sense in which there is a human experience as the primary defining notion.

Since the 18th-century formation of a modern market for the final artefacts of creative writing we have spent far too much time in consideration of the outputs of creative writing (that is, those artefacts that have been released as 'finished' products, under the conditions of modern commodification) and far too little time considering the experience of creative writing as a human activity. For much of the 20th century, informed by this commodity focus (whether commercial commodity or cultural or academic commodity), we gave to education a similar consumerist reference point. But ask the following questions and it soon becomes clear that such a commodity focus does not get us close to the actual event of creative writing, the human experience that is also part of the creative writing workshop.

That is, is creative writing 'literature'? Or is it the creating of works that, in some instances, have been defined as 'literature'? Does creative writing begin when it ends? That is, is creative writing its results or is it its actions, or is it a combination of actions and results of action? Does creative writing only produce end results (i.e. are there artefacts that emerge in creative writing that have not been given commodity value – certainly not commercial commodity value and often not cultural commodity value? Take, for example, a creative writer's rough notes, the gatherings of source materials, doodles, rough draftings). Is creative writing valuable if it produces knowledge that is only of use to the individual creative writer undertaking it? Or does creative writing generate a wide range of knowledge, some of which is individual, some of which is of the group, or of the society, some of which is universal?

3.

The creative writing workshop is not a packaged pedagogic tool set, as the writers in this book recognise very well. Nor is a discussion of the creative writing workshop merely a discussion of the delivery of a subject that has more or less value, as defined by trends or trajectories of contemporary higher education. The creative writing workshop is the site of a human event – an exchange of human experiences, in fact.

If we have come to see the workshop as the 'natural academic mode for creative writing', as Anna Leahy correctly notes in the pages that follow, then it must be in the nature of the creative writing workshop that something about humanity is clearly signalled. Where our consideration of this is thrown off track is where we focus not on what we observe in and around us (as commonsense would suggest we should), but where we focus on outcomes defined by wider historical contexts, socio-economic conditions. Though these relate only partially to the condition of individual human experience, they can have the effect of impacting on institutional or formal representations – and such can be the case of the university creative writing workshop and its popular manifestations. By this I mean let us recognise, and, indeed, even celebrate 'literature'; let us observe, and even tout the importance of certain artefacts produced in creative writing; but let us not forget that creative writing is much more than those things. Creative writing is complex and multi layered in its actions and in its artefacts. It is interactions and it is exchanges.

The creative writing workshop undoubtedly brings to the fore opportunities for getting it right, not only in how we might approach teaching creative writing but also in how we speak about creative writing. Commonsense already tells us what the workshop highlights; and our continued engagement with the workshop as a site of human activity offers us the potential to explore much further the nature of creative writing. In doing so, we will find in the workshop many points of discussion, frequent occasions for debate and numerous avenues of investigation. Such are the ways and means of investigating and extending human understanding. Indeed, it strikes me in concluding that what is at the heart of the misconceptions we have made in the past in discussing creative writing and likewise at the heart of the accuracies, the truths, we have uncovered is how we have dealt with creative and critical knowledge. Working in universities and colleges, sites of higher learning, we are empowered to explore knowledge in all its forms. The creative writing workshop is exploration. In this book that exploration is productively re-visited and the suggestions made, speculations put forward, and conclusions reached offer much potential for genuinely furthering our understanding.

Introduction: If it Ain't Broke, Don't Fix it; Or Change is Inevitable, Except from a Vending Machine

DIANNE DONNELLY

Those of us in creative writing must, *if* we are to move beyond questions of whether the workshop model works or does not work – or to ask instead more utilitarian questions such as the one Mary Ann Cain aptly interrogates in this collection: 'What makes it possible for those in the academe to keep asking, *'Does it work?'* without any real challenge or inquiry to the question itself' – come to better visualize what *else* is possible in this workshop space. Creative writers have answered the challenge generated by some (Ostrom, Ritter, Vanderslice, Bizzaro, Mayers) of whose interests are served by the replication of the workshop model.

Perhaps many of us would agree with Tim Mayers' (2007) suggestion, that as teachers, we are implicated in this answer, in this rationale for the reproduction of the workshop model. Such rationale includes:

- 'creative writing's investment in the notion that writers are born and not made [which] makes the whole issue of pedagogy suspect from the onset';
- the identity of authors as writers first, teachers second, and along those same lines, our 'lack of explicit attention to pedagogy ... creative writers [who] consider themselves writers who teach, rather than teachers who write';
- the replication of the model by tradition – the 'basically unrevised' model as taught by our mentors; and
- our embracing of the Associated Writing Program's (AWP) version of our identity (Mayers, 2007: 8–9).

Randall Albers (Columbia College Chicago)[1] validates a couple of these points when he proposes that 'teachers must totally rethink the way they approach the teaching of writing.' He addresses the time and effort this would take, and suggests 'many, many writing teachers are content to do what they were themselves taught.' He submits faculty 'would rather spend that time writing their own work than taking on the extra reading, thinking, experimentation, and training that new models would take.' Rationales for reproducing the workshop from program to program and laying claim to its workability often edify or rouse those in the field, usually without much constructive forward movement or change. Rather than idle over the question of why creative writing teachers continue to hold fast to the traditional workshop model or whether creative writing can be taught, we need to ask: What might be gained by flexing the elasticity of the workshop model? How might we add texture and rigor to its applaudable merits? In what ways can markers of professionalism in the workshop model set us apart in our scholarship from other university studies? (In the United States, these studies, in particular, include composition studies and literary studies).

My inquiry and research of the writing workshop along with my proposal for a more robust and intelligent model are part of an overarching goal to ascend *creative writing studies*. This study suggests that although the model remains dominant in the discipline's field of practice, there is little agreement as to what constitutes the workshop practice in creative writing classrooms internationally. My research also reveals that more and more teachers are in fact exploring new spaces for the workshop model. I propose that there is significant interest in more radical openness and re-envisioning of the workshop model (to frame Mary Ann Cain's essay title) to warrant a call for further pedagogical inquiry. A study such as this one and those that follow would be helpful to the field of *creative writing studies*, the profession, and our creative writing students.

A Workshop Survey

While there exists some MFA and creative writing PhD students who may turn a 'tin ear' to peer responses after too many workshops taken at the undergraduate and graduate level and while the same students may tend to create stories and/or poems that are workshop-ready (too polished) or suited for workshop approval (too safe) or customized for a teacher's preference (too similar in style), the writing workshop model for the most part, especially at the undergraduate level (as problematic as it may be), is still the heart of the creative writing program and the favorite part of the course.

My recent survey of undergraduate creative writing teachers at programs predominantly across the US, my own personal experience as a creative writing teacher, and much scholarship in creative writing pedagogy inform the basis of my analysis of the workshop. Of the survey, my driving questions prompted responses (to name a few) on the utility of the workshop, its effectiveness and value, and its best practices. Respondents considered student motivations, preparedness, and readiness for the workshop model. Creative writing teachers offered ways to keep the workshop fresh and alive or they lamented at such futileness. Still others shared exciting corollaries to the model in the classroom. One hundred and sixty-seven creative writing teachers replied to the workshop inquiry (five more participated in an initial test collection) from a base of 174 undergraduate creative writing programs (identified for the most part from the Associated Writing Program's database). While teacher response could be anonymous, 105 did identify their comments, and *this* 62% represents a total of 70 colleges and universities.

According to the survey results, nearly 51% of the teachers use a model that is similar to the basic workshop (very *broadly* sketched here as a forum for sharing and commenting on stories and poems by teacher and student readers; with varying rules of operation, the most prominent being the silence of the author during the peer review process) while 39.2% practice a variation of the mode of instruction, and only 10% define their model to be markedly different than the traditional workshop. The model serves as the primary focus or a major component in 80% of creative writing classes. Students can take the workshop-based course as a creative writing requirement (84.9%), as an elective (86.1%), as a writing intensive requirement (35.5%), or for other reasons (enjoyment, outlet for self-expression, general education requirement, and such 32.5%), and in some cases, students can participate in a workshop course to satisfy more than one requirement at the same time. A majority of institutions (60%) do not require prerequisites or a writing sample/portfolio prior to course enrollment, and 24% of programs call for students to complete a previous semester or two of composition. For the most part, creative writing majors take fifteen or more workshop hours in the course of their study.

Overall, creative writing programs still rely on the tradition of the workshop; surveys by Edward Delaney, David Starkey and Wendy Bishop, and my own survey demonstrate this to be the case. It remains, as Delaney says, 'the hub of the wheel.' Nancy McCabe (University of Virginia) who has been teaching writing for the past 23 years claims what we all know to be true: 'students always say on evaluations that the workshop portion of the class was the most enjoyable part.' Karl Elder

(Lakeland College) concurs, that his class is 'almost universally motivated' by the workshop encounter, and this observation has been my experience as well. Perhaps the basis for why the model retains its place at the center of the creative writing classroom is as Phillip Gross says in his essay 'Small Worlds: What Works in Workshops If and When They Do?': 'a workshop is a very human situation.' Or maybe, when all the spark plugs are firing in sync (or synapses, as the case may be), there is nowhere else in academia where students can 'find a rigorous program of study that is also directly personal for them' (Lisa Roney/University of Central Florida).

It might hold true that some will follow the logic of posits put forward in Michelene Wandor's *The Author is Not Dead Merely Somewhere Else* (2008), Dana Gioia's *Atlantic Monthly* essay, 'Can Poetry Matter? (1991), Donald Hall's 'Poetry and Ambition' (1988) or its short story counterpart written by John Aldridge 'The Assembly-Line Fiction' (1990), and John Barr's 'American Poetry in the New Culture' published in *Poetry* 2006. In these polemics, the workshop is either stripped of any rational or purposeful function or the type of writing generated from workshops reportedly has no readership outside the academia. The complaint is that creative writing programs have yet to produce another Mark Twain, Walt Whitman, or Emily Dickinson. What is more, we might find disheartening, the renouncements by those in the field such as poet and critic Allen Tate (1964), who also ran the creative writing program at Princeton. Tate complains about the sameness of teaching modalities (the workshop implied in his argument), noting that 'the academically certified Creative Writer goes out to teach Creative Writing, and produces other Creative Writers who are not writers, but who produce still other Creative Writers who are not writers' (p. 181). Similarly, Kay Boyle, though a teacher for 16 years at San Francisco State's creative writing programs, suggests 'All creative-writing programs ought to be abolished by law' (qtd in Menand, 2009). Some may be familiar with R.V. Cassill's response at a Boston convention, ironically, on the 15th anniversary of the Associated Writers Program to disband the very organization he founded in 1967. In this address, Cassill derided the complacency of writers, the corruptness of the academic system, and the poisoning by departments and institutions. It was time for writers, he insisted, to get out of the university (Menand 2009).

It is hard to dismiss, offhandedly, such cancellations of support by those with respectable histories as Cassill's. He is writer, critic, author of the popular textbook *Writing Fiction*, teacher at Brown University, and editor of *The Norton Anthology of Short Fiction*. Still, despite apologias that shake the workshop at its core, some, like Louis Menand (2009) say that 'in spite of all the reasons why they shouldn't, workshops work,' or some of us may murmur from a position *sans* theory, *sans* standards, *sans* empirical data, 'like Galileo at his inquisition,' like Philip Gross of Glamorgan University: '*Eppur si Muove*. And yet it moves.'

Defining the Workshop Model

When one speaks of the pedagogy or the discipline of creative writing, the workshop is implied in the address. The model might be defined as 'competent but uncompelling' (Myers, 1996: 118) or as a place where we 'teach craft and discourage self-indulgent junk' (Toni Graham, OK State). Philip Roth contends the workshop serves three objectives: 'to give young writers an audience, a sense of community, and an acceptable social category – students' (qtd in Grimes, 1999: 4–5). Our goals for our undergraduates may be lofty as we wish to 'enhance students' understanding of the meaning of art in their lives' (Karl Elder/Lakeland College) or far-reaching as we strive to create deeper, closer, more responsible and creative thinkers, readers, and writers' (Linda Russ Spaar, University of Virginia). Michelene Wandor (2008) likens what we do in the workshop model to the 'academic practice of peer-reviewing (in journals and publishing)' (p. 124). Peter Harris (Colby College) finds the space 'a wonderful place where people's lives open up,' where they 'begin to own their own voices.' The pedagogy introduces vocabulary necessary for the discussion of texts. It also foregrounds writing as process.

For most, the operation of the model often depends on course level and teacher design. I can report that some teachers approach the workshop with a heavy reading list such as the instructor whose workshop syllabus requires students to read 10 books over the course of the semester or the one who assigns long, difficult novels. There are those who view the workshop as a course in craft, a study in how to read poetry, how to identify elements of fiction, how to appreciate the choices writers make, how to imagine ways in which these choices might have been different; how to, as Martin Cockroft of Waynesburg University suggests 'reform student ideas about what *is* poetry, what is possible in the form, and how it can/ought to be written.' In still other classes, the students' work is the center of the course; the workshop functions as the single pedagogy. Some teachers support the practice of free-writing, others prefer invention strategies such as exercises and writing prompts to generate story and poem seeds. For the instructors at Columbia Chicago College, the model differs from the traditional one in that theirs is a process-based story workshop, one that uses 'classic, storytelling forms, along with skills of conceptualizing, abstracting, critical thinking, and imaginative problem-solving' to supplement basic skills (Randall Albers). Most would agree with contributor Sue Roe who claims in her essay 'Introducing Master-classes': 'Workshops are fundamental – launch pads rather than flights, rehearsal strategies rather than the exigencies of polished and finessed performance.' We might also agree with Maurice Guevara (1998) that its design can be 'sin of all sins – unimaginative.'

A Study of the Workshop Model

Before undertaking a defense of the writing workshop it is important to outline a more global assertion on behalf of creative writing as an academic discipline. Briefly restated, in order for creative writing to advance as an academic discipline in its own right, it must undergo an inquiry into its field, much like composition studies did in the middle to late 20th century. This field of inquiry, a factor critical to the development of *creative writing studies*, necessarily explores the pedagogical problems and paradoxes of the discipline. Such internal complexities are typically the impetus that sets a 'programmatic revolution' (Mayers, 2009: 218) in motion, of which *creative writing studies* is situated in its early phase. Kelly Ritter and Stephanie Vanderslice (2007) remind us that 'a field whose teaching practices and theories are relatively unexamined runs the risk of being dominated by an ever more unwieldy body of knowledge and practices, some of which have likely outgrown their usefulness or been misapplied' (p. xv).

The workshop, as the default model of pedagogy in creative writing classrooms, has been, Bizzaro (2004) says, our 'model of instruction [for] over a hundred years' (p. 296), and as Peter Vandenberg (2004: 7) infers, our practice 'is ripe for annexation.' Consider that AWP's 2008 *Guide to Writing Programs* points to a significant rise in creative writing programs. The 79 undergraduate and graduate creative writing programs recorded in 1975 pale to the reported present figure of 822. Of this number, more than 300 are at the graduate level (37 awarded the PhD), and thousands of students are enrolled nationally (Healey, 2009; Menand, 2009). Consider that every program, according to Virginia's Christopher Tilghman, 'devotes 50 percent of its time to the workshop' (qtd in Delaney, 2007). Given these staggering statistics, the workshop's universality, its application at all levels to vitally diverse populations, its differing teacher foci, and its reportedly mixed results, in the words of Ostrom (1994), 'all of us could probably benefit from taking a hard look at precisely how ''the workshop'' functions in our classrooms' (pp. xix–xx). Such an inquiry asks us to consider at a microcosmic level:

> What are our guidelines, and what assumptions underlie them? How explicitly do we probe the criteria for assessing work-in-progress? What is our role in workshops and group work, and how productive has this role been? What other roles might we experiment with? What else should go on in a workshop besides the workshop? To what extent are we 'playing the old tapes' of workshops we took? What do we know about group dynamics, and what should we know? Who gets silenced in our workshops and why? How often do we/should we revise our workshop methods? When are the conversations in our workshops most productive and why? What might be gained by dismantling the workshop model altogether and starting from scratch? (Ostrom, 1994: xix–xx)

On a more macrocosmic grade, if *creative writing studies* is to operate as a more distinct academic discipline, then scholarship at a curricular level should as Katherine Haake suggests 'seek to move beyond our preoccupation with the writer or the text to the role of creative writing as an academic discipline inside a profession that includes, but is not limited to, the production and teaching of imaginative writing' (qtd in Mayers, 2009: 218). This begins with establishing 'markers of professional difference' (Ritter, 2001: 208) to include ways in which the field of creative writing is set apart in its scholarship from composition studies and literary studies. These are significant undertakings, and yet, as Bizzaro (1998) regards 'there may be a great many teachers of creative writing like himself' interested in discussing and debating pedagogy (p. 287). I wish to join that discussion and debate by continuing the field's inquiry and offering not a dismantling of the workshop model or even a simple re-tooling (which would not address more systemic issues),[2] but rather a more enlightened view of the model as an intelligent and robust pedagogy, one we might advance with our emergent field of *creative writing studies*.

Dawson's question: 'Is the pedagogical process [of the workshop model] merely guided by idiosyncrasies of each teacher, the practicing writer able to pass on knowledge by virtue of his or her innate talent and secret knowledge of the craft? (qtd in Ritter & Vanderslice, 2007: xiii) is more than rhetorical, and his question has merit when we consider that the workshop model offers no real standards of measurement. Bizzaro (2004) reminds us that we have practiced this 'basically unrevised' century-old method 'without giving it proper scrutiny' (p. 295). Sharing stories and poems, reading from a writerly perspective, providing helpful feedback, re-envisioning works-in-progress, are at least some of the functions of the traditional workshop model. Its practice has become so deeply-ingrained in our pedagogy that it continues without investigation. Or if it *is* questioned, in the sense that many of us are uneasy with varying degrees of a workshop's artificiality, ethical disparities, multiversity, idleness, singularity, program design, authority, evaluation, absence of theory, and/or its range of student readiness, preparedness, and motivation; we are at a loss as to how to fix it.

If what seems to be a melting pot approach to the model boils down to a little of this and a lot of that, a community crock pot of flavors, it is no wonder that, at times, we are unsure of just what it is we taste in this covered dish – this workshop. And we wonder, how might it sustain us?

For instance, some may suggest that as untrained creative writers (by which I mean as creative writing teachers we have not had any formal teaching training in our field), we are teaching 'by the seat of our pants,' our workshops presumably 'unstructured and friendly' (Leahy, 2007: 20). This relaxed 'we're just chatting' consciousness surfaces regardless of how much planning goes into the class. Others could suggest we operate our workshops in a vacuum, with a separatist view that defers outside reference; certainly, AWP's mission statement supports this position. The majority opinion is that we practice the workshop model as our primary pedagogy, sometimes emulating our own mentors because these are the methods from which we have learned. Or perhaps, the workshop 'has remained,' as Katharine Haake, says in this collection, 'as close to a home as we are ever going to come in the academy.' Even with this thought, the one thing Haake and many of us can say with any certainty about the workshop is 'that's not it, that's still not it.'

To illustrate this patchwork of practices, we could consider some workshop praxes and teacher perspectives. For example, if one teacher supports, encourages even, personal self-discovery (and recovery?) and another endorses the objectification of the text, excluding all outside factors; and the instructor in the neighboring academy focuses mostly on writerly techniques found within the current *Best American Short Stories* with the last 15 minutes dedicated to writing activities, and if a creative writing teacher in Boise, Idaho sanctions the bulk of classroom time to the critique of students' texts, and if the instructor who teaches inner city students refuses to abide by the author gag rule of the traditional workshop because her students' voices have been silenced long enough, then how can the writing workshop be contained within the same pedagogical model? How in fact can it not be paradoxical in nature or contradictory in its aims? Michelene Wandor (2008) addresses such antipathetic purposes when she says:

> If creative writing is training professional writers (those who already have 'talent'), then the great-writers approach privileges the text over the writer; if students are taught that creative writing expresses the self (writing as therapy), then the person is privileged over the writing. The first overvalues the art, the second overvalues the person, and together they confuse the object of the work and its objectives. (p. 128)

To add to this, there are inconsistencies that surface in an egalitarian relationship where both teacher and student assume the role of 'writer.' For instance, Tim Mayers (2007) references the pronged 'Elitist versus democratic' scenario: democratic in the sense that 'newcomers might make significant contributions' to literature and elitist in 'identifying in the end only a select few students who might be worthy of the label "real writer"' (p. 4). Additionally, the 'theoretical egalitarian responses of the peer friendly' workshop create an addling for our students when the postscript to their default response of praise contradicts that of the teacher (known as a 'tutor' in the United Kingdom) who has ultimate authority as evaluator of students' work upon completion of the course (Wandor, 2008: 127). These 'built-in tensions' are reflected in Siobhan Holland's collective response of some of the delegates at the 2001 creative writing conference at the Bath Spa University. Holland argues 'It is not fair to students to find their work praised in workshops and criticised in assessment feedback' (qtd in Wandor, 2008: 127). What is more, an ethical dilemma presents itself when we are faced with the decision to silence the author and her valued intentions and processes versus justifying this traditional silence as a necessary function of minimizing the writer's defense and maximizing her processing of the workshop response. Complicating these paradoxes are the ethics of exposing personal experience in the workshop and the standard of measurements for such writing reflection. Finally, though the list of ambiguities may go on, the traditional workshop may move along the 'consensus' principles of Kenneth Bruffee's collaborative learning theory. It may also butt against 'dissensus' as argued by those like compositionist John Trimbur.

Granted, the workshop is a *process*, and as such, its 'plasticity' conforms to individual manipulation, and its response depends to some degree on the dynamics and preparedness of each particular class. However, if we continue to place such emphasis on the workshop *process* in our classrooms, if we name it our *practice*, our *signature pedagogy*, if we assign it curricular substance for fulfillment of a degree and usher our students out into the workforce and community with diploma in hand; then should we not consider how we manage that which defines the heart of our course?

More importantly, given such variances within our pedagogy, how can the workshop *be* properly scrutinized? If we were in fact to examine it in such regard, how might we determine what happens in the workshop and why? To ask the enveloping question then: how are we to evaluate *if*, indeed, the writing workshop model still works? By extension, as it is implicated in the workability of the model, when those inside and outside our field question whether creative writing can be taught, and if so how is it taught, and who can teach it – questions, by the way, which have been asked long before the new compositionists embodied a constructivist view that 'genius,' 'imagination,' and 'power' were not given but obtainable – is it enough, then, when someone like Mark Winegardner of Florida State counters with 'You can't teach every piano player to be Thelonious Monk, but no piano teacher seems tortured by the question of whether piano can be *taught*'? (qtd in Delaney, 2007). Is it enough to say as John Barth did in a 1985 article in the *Times Book Review* titled 'Writing: Can it Be Taught?', that 'emphatically it can, mainly on the ground that it so emphatically *is*'? (qtd in Menand, 2009, *my emphasis*). Where might one begin this ontological study? The answers to probing questions such as these are, as Shirley Geok-lin Lim (2003) notes in her essay 'The Strangeness of Creative Writing,' 'so nuanced, constrained, interrogated, and indeterminable as to raise more questions' (p. 157). Indeed, I say.

Part of the difficulty in even defining the workshop, let alone re-conceptualizing it as a rigorous and intelligent pedagogy, relates to the elasticity of the model – its ability to morph into variable shapes, to stretch in so many ways, and as such, it is easy, like Saran wrap, to take it for granted. My goal is not to dismiss variances of the workshop model, but rather, I want to explore current practices of creative writing's signature pedagogy as part of an overarching inquiry into the field with a secondary goal to ascend *creative writing studies* as a distinct discipline independent in its own scholarship.

Perceptions and Practice: Our Students

If it were possible to construct our student profile, we would need to consider the vast diversity of all who enroll in our workshop classes, their values and traditions, their motivations, and their preferred method for learning. Not to consider such variables might generate stereotypes and assumptions. However, although as educators, we cannot assemble such a character sketch; it is impossible, really, outrageous even to envision, we *can* appraise the wide range of sociological and cultural research and studies that issue collective perspectives on forces that bear influence on the students we teach in higher education, factors that impact our students' interest *in* creative writing and their ability to learn and respond to our modes of teaching. Teachers *can* assess their students' motivations for signing up for their workshops. They can and should draw on these conclusions and their usefulness as it relates to the (re)construction of their workshop design.

Today, we teach the Google Generation. These 'Tech-savvy "Millennials",' as Scott Carlson (2005) describes them in his *The Chronicle of Higher Education* web article entitled 'The Net Generation Goes to College,' 'have lots of gadgets, like to multitask, and expect to control what, when, and how they learn.' Our students think differently; their attention is scattered, their concentration diffused. We are no longer of the mindset that 'the 100 billion or so neurons inside our skulls are largely fixed by the time we reach adulthood' (Carlson, 2005). Our students have begun to take on the qualities of 'our intellectual technologies' – their brains are 'adapting ... at a biological level,' says writer Nicholas Carr. In his 2008 *The Atlantic* article 'Is Google Making Us Stupid?' Carr complains that 'Immersing myself in a book or a lengthy article used to be easy. My mind would get caught up in the narrative ... and I'd spend hours strolling through long stretches of prose.' No longer is that possible, Carr admits. 'Now my concentration often starts to drift after two or three pages,' he notes; 'I get fidgety, lose a thread, begin looking for something else to do.' For Carr, 'the deep reading that used to come naturally has become a struggle.' These 'troubles' are not dissimilar to the experiences of his friends and acquaintances who are, mostly 'literary types.' Kathryn Tyler (2007), author of 'The Tethered Generation' specifies that individuals born after 1978 tend to have difficulty thinking for themselves without the tethered advice from parents or significant others who are just a text or speed dial away. They struggle with patience, with detail-oriented tasks such as those required for writing and proofreading, and also with attention to social conventions and understanding what it means to focus and work hard.

My students and I have talked about their digital generation and their 'supposed' self-absorption. One student, I'll call Jake, adds one word to the above descriptions that characterize his generation – *isolation*. He says, 'The condition of humanity in which the digital generation exists is one of profound isolation.' Jake speaks of a 'closed bubble,' an 'impenetrable wall of loneliness,' one which 'no light can pass through.'[3] Another insists 'The notion that any individual whose entire existence can be uploaded and stored quite easily on a three inch hard drive could establish a meaningful relationship with any human being is so absurd as to be laughable,' though he is serious. Jake's workshop partner adds that 'the digital generation is not concerned with the world at large; their only concern is studying and analyzing their own personal existence.' She concludes that the loss of barriers, the loss of trials, the loss of ambition and curiosity ('after all, what is curiosity when all the answers are given') have created a culture fueled by self-absorption.

This perception runs parallel to the one which situates our students as self-gratifiers with inflated egos, liberated from oppressed influences, and immersed in an American culture of disposability and commodification. The emphasis on feelings, a fundamental absolute of progressive education persists as a dominant postmodern philosophy in our educational system. As a result, some students come to us with Romantic notions of writing their poems and stories in one long, uninterrupted stream of consciousness. They have ideations of talent – they've been writing their whole lives. Mark Wallace (CA State University, San Marcos), a respondent of my workshop survey, has seen some of these preconceptions play out in his classroom. He notes, 'Students often come into my courses with high expectations about their futures as writers and are sometimes shocked to discover how much time and effort it takes to write well.' Additionally, Monica Berlin (Knox College) contends 'students often misunderstand what our job there is.' She observes, 'They often come into workshop expecting we will disregard all notions of graciousness, and in doing so they often do not take the work on its own terms.'

Problems created by lack of experience are sometimes compounded by a lack of motivation and a lack of talent. One instructor admits 'I don't want to spend time workshopping sloppy, incomplete, last minute efforts.' Lorna Jackson (University of Victoria) asserts 'students are still reluctant to commit themselves to a schedule of practice,' and Martin Cockroft (Waynesburg University) adds 'students tend to undervalue the 90% of the time spent reading and talking about OTHER students' poems and stories.' Because of this perception, he contends 'a few students put very little effort into prepping for workshop (i.e. they write few comments, have lost the poems for that day, or have little of substance to say).' For Gaylene Perry (Deakin University, Melbourne, Au), lack of effort translates to students 'not reading drafts in time for class or the workshopping student not supplying a draft in time.' She considers this 'to be a new problem for us, perhaps partly due to university pressure to let more students enroll in our program. In the past,' she submits, 'the classes were smaller, the skill levels higher, and the commitment and preparedness much greater.'

While I am aware that these comments may generalize students' lack of effort, it is also clear (as some workshop survey responders specify) that a complicated history buttresses students' engagement with their coursework. It is a history that significantly precedes the day students sign up for creative writing courses or the day they enter creative writing classrooms. Concerns of program design and class size, open admission policies, and a long well-documented history by the National Endowment for the Arts (NEA) of poor reading skills and comprehension at the college-level coupled with fewer opportunities for the reading of literature in college, shadows our students' profile. Although there are many more influences, certainly the focus of this section on the Net Generation and all that it bears is a major contributing agent to how well our students perform and learn in the workshop model.

What motivates students to seek out creative writing workshop classes may be because they want 'freedom from an oppressive curriculum that demands too much rote critical thinking, dry textual analysis, and academic prose strangled by thesis statements and Strunk & White correctness' (Healey, 2009: 32). Catherine Cole (2007) agrees, citing a panel of researchers who note that 'society's emphasis on success, instant gratification, the retail/consumer model of education' as well as 'student-centered approaches to learning, lead students to look for easy answers and to count on high grades, to avoid difficult work and to develop inflated perceptions of their abilities' (p. 7). Edmund Hansen and James Stevens implicate our students' 'low tolerance for challenge,' their 'risk averse' posture in our classrooms as products of 'educational consumerism and an institutional focus on assessment' (qtd in C. Coles, 2007: 7).

Others sit in our workshop for reasons still valid in Stephen Minot's 1997 assessment of student motives, some which involve therapy and a childish love of language. They may enroll in our workshops, according to Gregory Light's (2000) study, for an opportunity to write in a structure that provides 'an interactive writing environment with experts/tutors and peers' (p. 4). While they may find a place in the circles of desks creative writing teachers construct for community sake, it may be because they assume their workshops will be fun, engaging, and easy. I would second the response of teachers who note how their students are surprised by how much hard work goes into the practice of writing and how vigorous this coursework can be. But more often, students today recognize, as one of my student writers says, 'Adulation is earned through talent and ability; claims which could be made in the future, but right now the digital generation has not earned that right.'

If this is a fair profile of our students, then how are creative writing educators to connect with students who are preoccupied with a virtual rather than a physical world, students who are more likely to skip lectures and less likely to go to the library and check out a book? Are our writing students among the average college graduates who have 'spent less than 5,000 hours of their lives reading, but over 10,000 hours playing video games (not to mention 20,000 hours of watching TV),' as Marc Prensky (2001) claims in 'Digital Natives, Digital Immigrants'? We do know that our students are among the majority who want technology at the ready. 'The more portable the better,' Carlson notes. After all, 'they are able to juggle a conversation on Instant Messenger, a Web-surfing session, and an iTunes playlist while reading *Twelfth Night* for homework.' Are creative writing teachers prepared to embrace and prepare for changes that suit these Googlers – to construct workshops online, craft lectures on podcasts, which can then be downloaded to students' iPods, becoming portable, rewindable, even pauseable? Should they be?

While this generation may depend on the 'tethering' that Kathryn Tyler (2007) addresses in her article 'The Tethered Generation,' to feel secure in its decision-making, it is also a population which works well in group environments. Tyler contends Millennials are familiar with diversity. Perhaps the physicality of our small class size attracts students to our workshops. They are a creative bunch; experts at multitasking, at thinking out of the box – and their creativity – the 'buzzword of the business world' – has real market value claims Steve Healey (2009) in his essay 'The Rise of Creative Writing & the New Value of Creativity' (p. 34). Healey reports that business recruiters are presently visiting top arts graduate schools looking for candidates for their corporations. This is because, per Daniel H. Pink, author of 'The MFA is the New MBA,' published in *Harvard Business Review*, 'the basic financial skills learned in the MBA program are quickly becoming obsolete ... The tasks that remain ... increasingly involve creativity' (Pink qtd in Healey, 2009: 34). Businesses, looking to distinguish their products and services 'in today's overstocked, materially abundant marketplace' are seeking alternatives, creativity, ways 'to make their offerings transcendent – physically and emotionally compelling' (Pink qtd in Healey, 2009: 34).

Creative writing students are deeply immersed in the digital world and are a part of the historical moment Thomas L. Friedman, author of the bestseller, *The World is Flat: A Brief History of the Twenty-First Cent*ury, coins 'The New Age of Creativity.' Friedman connects communications technology and the occasion for people interested in 'authoring their own content' (qtd in Healy, 2009: 34), particularly, Healey adds, 'in easily manipulated digital format' (p. 34). Creative writing students can make this 'leap,' Healy accurately suggests, from the new authors of the digital networks to the new authors of the creative writing workshops (p. 35) with better pedagogical planning in our workshop-based classrooms.

Much has been written about the holistic purpose of creative writing and the writing workshop and its noble ability to make our students more rounded citizens. These are echoes of the egalitarian principles of Deweyan education, which advance the 'democratization of creative power' (reiterations of Emerson). Healey cites the Romantic mission statement of AWP, Jane Ciabattari's (2005) *Poets & Writers'* essay 'Workshop: A Revolution of Sensibility,' and D.W. Fenza's (2000) defense of creative writing in the academy in 'Creative Writing & its Discontents' as proselytizing these views. AWP adopts the artist as 'outsider, set apart from the standardized triteness of institutions' (Healey, 2009: 32); Ciabattari refers to the 'willed discipline through which students learn to shape and order their perceptions of an ever more complicated world around them'; and Fenza strengthens creative writing's otherness when he says:

> Like other lessons of creative writing – creativity, empathy, persuasiveness, expression, and aesthetic discernment – the artistic experience of the will's efficacy may seem too rarefied a goal for a practical age that prefers to quantify success in patents, cures, sales units, and dollars.

Healey thinks not, and I agree with him. While poems and stories are valued products of the workshop, there is more to be learned through the model's process, more 'front loading' as Henley calls it, pedagogy 'with interventions in the writing process before it begins and while it's happening, instead of the more traditional back-loading – that is, intervening after a written product already exists' (p. 38).

Creative writing teachers miss opportunities to design more vigor in their writing workshops, when they lag behind as a field, Healey and I suggest, a field which also falters in the 'development of a reflexive theoretical framework that would make it more aware of its real social value and its real social effects, and this lag has encouraged further lag in revisions of its teaching methods' (p. 38). Creative writing students may be ahead of educators in the discipline in terms of 'thinking out of the box' if teachers consider that as part of an institutionalized field, they generally continue to think of themselves as still 'inside the box.'

Perceptions and Practice: Our Teachers

Creative writing teachers make efforts to monitor the pulse of the workshop as Karl Elder (Lakeland College) does, gauging the needs of students by offering 'models of strong work that will appeal to their unique sensibilities.' Likewise, my workshop survey indicates that creative writing teachers try to engage with students as individuals rather than abstractions. One surveyed instructor 'finds [students'] issues and challenges' and in this pursuit, s/he discovers 'who they are, their passions and goes from there.' Similarly, Robert Boswell (New Mexico State U) considers the individuality of his students by affirming 'that every student is taught in every class, not just the student whose story is being discussed.' To personalize his workshop course, Keith Kumasen Abbott (Naropa) makes adjustments based on student responses to his first week survey, while Jane Hilberry (Colorado College) dismantles her workshop by teaching 'on a model of improvisation, each course and each class different, depending on what the students bring to the course.'

Some creative writing teachers *are* responding to the 'shifting nature of students' readings in new media, film, and digitized images, music/texts' (Cole, 2007: 7) by adding digital writing workshops. The University of Massachusetts Amherst, for example, transitions students to write in the new digital age by offering courses like 'Telling it Straight, Telling it Slant, Telling it Digital.' George Mason University offers an introduction to digital writing in the genres as part of its creative writing concentration program. Janet McCann (Texas A & M) has a 'section on hypertext poetry and using computers in poetry,' and Valerie Martinez (College at Santa Fe) includes in her course, 'a study of cyberpoetics.' Judith Baumel (Adelphi University) uses 'wikis, blogs, and Moodle to teach the workshops,' and one teacher 'encourages the use of graphics and the material nature of what they are making' when they construct and 'distribute their own books.' What else is possible in the creative writing workshop-based classroom? How might we insert digitalized writing to a creative revision of say, *Macbeth*? Most have witnessed comedic versions of Shakespeare's Romeo and Juliet (*Shakespeare in Love*) in the theater; how would a scene from *Macbeth*, for example, play out in today's techno lingo?

Flexing the Workshop Shape or Opening the Space to Alternatives

The success of the writing workshop and our students' 'success' in the workshop model are relative in terms of standards of measurement because of many contributing factors. In some cases, student publication is still the primary institutional aim, and there is pressure to produce results to sustain program visibility and enrollment, even at the undergraduate level. This more global objective may be contrary for the teacher who uses the workshop as a platform for students to acquire and practice fundamentals, for more risk-taking activities and experimentation, and for opportunities to emphasize process and explore *how* a story or poem unfolds.

On the other hand, department goals may disclaim a teacher's expertise and privilege a workshop space in which student feedback carries more weight than a teacher's technical knowledge. In many institutions, program design is in the hands of administration and guided by bottom line costs and profit margins. The success of the workshop is largely contingent on class size, particularly at the introductory level. Ideally, a workshop class could be well-managed with 10 students. Martin Cockroft (Waynesburg University) has 17 students in his introductory class; some have 18 or more. Given the increased class size, Karen Holmberg (Oregon State) attests, 'if we were to workshop all poems in the class, we would only have time to write 3 poems a term.' Lorna Jackson (University of Victoria) admits that 'as a fiction teacher, at certain times of the semester' she is 'unable to read the volume of work in a reasonable work week.' Furthermore, oversize classes can lead to students spending excessive amounts of time 'reading the works of student writers rather than those of more accomplished writers' (Deanna Kern Ludwin/Colorado State). Course workload and the mix of majors and non-majors in workshop courses are other issues for teachers like Lex Runciman (Linfield College), who notes, 'We struggle to meet student demand, and recent assessment feedback from our creative writing majors tells us they wish we had more "majors only" courses.'

Many suggest entry requirements for enrolling in a creative writing class, particularly an upper level class, would lead to more authentic learning opportunities and more serious student commitment. There are more colleges and institutions that offer creative writing classes without a major or minor than there are BFA or minor tracts or associate degree programs. Wendy Bishop and David Starkey (2006) suggest the 'workshop has led to an unprecedented democratization of imaginative writing in America' (p. 198) In fact, they conclude, 'now that nearly every American high school and community college offers at least one creative writing class, access to basic instruction in the art is widely available' (p. 198). Given the recent expanse of the field that Kelly Ritter and Stephanie Vanderslice (2007) address in their introduction to *Can it Really be Taught?: Resisting Lore in Creative Writing Pedagogy*, such a proliferation of program development should give us pause to rethink creative writing's pedagogy to include the workshop model by 'reassessing specific patterns and practices' (p. xvii). Such rapid program development might also serve to further dilute the significance of a creative writing degree. Imagine, some teachers ask, that anyone can declare himself or herself a creative writing major or that anyone can take a creative writing course with little or no experience. The experience of such indiscrimination, according to one unnamed instructor, leads to a class 'filled with a lot of disinterested, unengaged, untalented students. Not just untalented,' s/he notes, 'but students who actually have significant writing problems; students who need to retake composition, even.'

In fact, the survey suggests that many students can take creative writing to satisfy an elective, and/or to satisfy a creative writing program requirement and/or a writing intensive requirement. To this claim, Juliet Davis (University of Tampa) responds, 'This should not be the case.' She grants that 'one of our biggest challenges is the fact that students can take creative writing to satisfy both a writing intensive requirement and a humanities requirement.' For 60% of the programs surveyed, students are not required to take a pre-requisite to an introductory creative writing course.

There are many influences that complicate the workshop space that range from the teacher's appropriation of student work and/or the presumption of style to the more global call for us to attend to the poor reading and comprehension skills of our students as reported in the latest NEA report. We are now being asked to 'focus our attention and resources on an activity both fundamental and irreplaceable for democracy' (Dana Gioia qtd in Burriesci, 2008: 2). My point in emphasizing factors that bear influence on the workshop model is twofold: first, as Minot suggests, teachers should 'draw on a full range of tastes and address particular student motives for coming to the creative writing classroom' (p. 35), and second, teachers must reconsider their program design, addressing what one teacher in my survey calls 'one of the narrowest educations ... especially if most of its courses are run with the traditional workshop model.'

Students' motives girdle my second point which addresses program design in our universities and at what level, the workshop can best function. To begin, I propose the advancement of two possible workshop trajectories at the undergraduate level. The first path functions as a series of courses under the general education tract for the appreciation of literature through writing and one that centers on a degree program situated for the advancement of writing (and reading) for its own sake (creative writing's early pedagogical goal). Coursework at the general education level might include 'The Craft of Fiction' (or poetry or drama), 'The Writing Process,' 'Reading as a Writer,' 'Form and Technique,' 'Narration and Description'; perhaps, genre writing to include fantasy, science-fiction, digital options, writing to discover; non-fiction studies in memoir, creative essays, nature and travel writing. A course that addresses the lore of creative writing would be illuminating. Considering some of the courses noted above, I see the workshop setting for this track in any number of ways: as a pairing of partners, a small network, a larger writing community, a one-on-one student–teacher conference. The workshop would provide a place for students to experiment, take risks, develop skills, share work, and advance creative and critical thinking.

This program track might also incorporate more panoramic goals to include, among others, an outward attention to public spheres. I see this offering as one open to all undergraduates; perhaps, even as a course option that is required of first-year students as suggested decades ago by Wendy Bishop and advanced by Kevin Clark (1999) in 'Study as Practice: On Creative Writing & the English Curriculum' for the purpose of satisfying 'rigorous standards' set by English departments. This option considers the popularity and growth of creative writing and the workshop model while understanding that the goals of this path are noble in their encompassing nature.

The second baccalaureate program track considers the intermediate and advanced creative writer, one whose placement in the program is dependent on a sample of student work. While not excluding some of the coursework outlined above, the curriculum for this track should be more robust and inclusive. At this level students should understand and apply variable critical approaches to reading and writing. With a secondary goal toward flexing the elasticity of the workshop, students might be exposed to other performative arts in an effort to broaden their expanse of writing. I am not thinking of an appreciation of art (or music or drama) in this regard, or an approach that suggests less rigor, but rather one which introduces more outlets for expression, more venues for creativity, more activity and demonstration, and more synthesis, analysis, process, production. This might mean a sharing of workshops between the arts; perhaps, a dialogue that is acted by drama students, action that is produced on stage, and/or poems expressed in music, painting, sculpture, dance – *more rigor*. Hans Ostrom (1994), in his introduction to *Colors of a Different Horse*, wonders how creative writing might be linked to 'the street.' He asks, 'Who among us is already inviting rap, hip-hop, performance poetry, and other so-called popular sources of compositional improvisation into our workshop?' (p. xxii). Not all instructors agree with the kind of performative art that Ostrom addresses, nor are all teachers interested in employing technological techniques in their classrooms, but there are many creative writing teachers who *have* initiated some movement in other creative arts disciplines. For example, Gaylene Perry (Deakon U) speaks of 'dance studio sessions or visual arts life drawing classes,' where students can 'practice' their work. Donald Platt (Purdue) has partnered with a visual arts class, 'visiting their studio for 1–2 class sessions and writing poems from their work. In turn,' he says, 'we gave them poems that were not inspired by art, and the artists used them to generate drawings and paintings.'

Similarly, Lisa Russ Spaar (University of Virginia) team-teaches 'a poetry/printmaking workshop in which students collaborate (the print-makers write poems, the poets print, and they work together to produce low and high-end books.' Mekeel McBride (University of New Hampshire) asks students 'to invent or make a musical instrument, then write a poem and accompany the poem with the instrument.' She notes, 'People have used Volvo car engines, crystal glasses filled with water, etc.' McBride claims this exercise 'teaches [creative writers] to listen to sound in a whole different way.' In Martin Cockroft's (Waynesburg University) workshop class, students listen to recordings of poets reading. He has shown them 'YouTube videos of slam poets and animated poems (i.e. Billy Collins and others).' Cockroft also introduces his class to useful websites such as '*Poetry Daily*, the *Penn Sounds* poetry archive, online journals, and writers' blogs.' Another teacher plans to establish a web page that she will 'seed' with an opening sentence. She'll permits students 'to add or delete anything at any time and see what we have at semester's end.'

Film clips are used by Deanna Kern Ludwin (Colorado State) to 'illustrate dialogue and the use of metaphor.' She adds '*Il Postino* is great for this.' At the three year MFA program at the University of North Carolina at Wilmington, Philip Gerard notes, that students 'write dialogue, and then see it performed by actors in a black-box theater on campus ... They watch films to learn how to build scenes better. They attend "long-narrative workshops" to try to learn how to move stories beyond short-story length' (Delaney, 2007). Philip Gerard, chair of the UNCW creative writing program suggests students 'need to figure out how to tell a longer story that doesn't peter out.' He reminds us that 'There's a whole generation of writers that didn't learn to do that' (qtd in Delaney). Keith Kumasen Abbott (Naropa) uses media – 'drama and documentary – usually in the opening eight weeks – but very sparingly in terms of length.' He never uses an entire film during a workshop, and introduces 'artists and musicians and their art or music to discuss organizational principles.' I use film to demonstrate dialogue techniques – dramatic and comedic clips in films such as *Before the Sunset* to show how dialogue delves into relationship issues, or a snippet of *Princess Bride* as an example of a dialogue that takes a serious situation and deals with it in a comedic fashion, or a preview of *Doubt* to accentuate how dialogue can convey conflict, urgency, power. We always follow these clips with discussion and writing – prompts that allow *us* (always I experiment with my students) to practice our craft in new ways. Film as a venue can also illuminate scene development and the credibility of details, setting, and atmosphere.

This program course might include more interdisciplinary activity – perhaps a literary studies course that embraces creative projects or a theory course that experiments with the construction of writing. Creative attention to workshop development should also include student and group research and presentations. For example, demonstrations on the different kinds of submissions included in literary journals emphasize critical functions, explore market preferences, and include creativity when exercises which imitate these variable styles – not for entry, but rather for stylistic and experimental purposes – are employed. At this level, working collaboratively in small groups, my creative writing students are empowered to choose stories, facilitate discussions, and design exercises to demonstrate and practice processes in such a way that is different than what students do in literature and composition. We might intersect with ways in which social and cultural hierarchies and contrasting ideologies impact our roles as writer and reader. Deweyan principles of 'doing' are advanced here, not to mention a shifting of master–apprentice assumptions. Moreover, these are the type of activities which Haake refers to as linking with the world, and Argie Manolis (2005) refers to 'outside of academia,' the engagement that occurs beyond the classroom defined as 'teacher, writers whose work is studied, peers, and student author' (p. 149) Deanna Kern Ludwin (Colorado State), for example, takes her class on field trips such as 'campus art galleries to stimulate writing.' This concept is not unfamiliar to Julie Carr (University of Colorado Boulder) whose class writes 'on location together.' Carr suggests that in her class, 'It's never just "write a poem." There are always things to try.' Additionally, a workshop course that includes what our students might do with a creative writing degree would be well-attended – one that offers multiple perspectives, visiting lecturers – real practical exposure. In both baccalaureate tracks we should not forget 'that our aim should be to foster more dedicated writers' (Royster, 2005: 65), a goal Brent Royster claims we often lose as we engage in other pursuits.

Coordinated carefully, a program that includes a series of mini-lectures on relevant topics might interest a large number of students, could defray costs, and might be managed over shorter six to eight week semesters. Workshop breakout sessions might follow these lectures to advance writing and discussion relevant to lecture topics. With such variability, rigor, and relativity, there would be no need to 'abolish workshops' as Eve Shelnutt suggests (1991: 60).

At the MFA level, the same course direction might exist, with pedagogical differences. For example, splitting the MFA track into two paths opens possibilities for the writer who is interested in advancing her writing. The other track might include writers who are also interested in the pedagogy of creative writing, the pedagogy of *creative writing studies*, the pedagogy of composition, the interdisciplinary approach to teaching creative composing practices. A complimentary or overlapping track might include a concentration on creativity in the marketplace. Think of the exciting coursework, internships, and relevancy to such a program design with conscious departures from traditional models. Right now, creative writing certificates and concentrations are provided in some universities for the business major. Why not apply this practice as part of the MFA career track, perhaps inviting corporate recruiters to classes while creative writing staff team-teaches with the business faculty? Craft critics Tim Mayers (2007) and David Starkey (1994), in particular, advocate for the splitting of the MFA into two directions. Finally, the workshop at the PhD level might be more variable than the tired 'shopping' of 'works'. Such a program design would include more critical exigency, teacher training, and relative coursework, all of which are considered in Patrick Bizzaro's (2004) course suggestions: 'Research in Creative Writing,' 'Pedagogy of Creative Writing,' and 'Professional Issues in Creative Writing' as a means of 'connect[ing] research skills typically stressed in English departments with skills stressed in creative-writing instruction' (p. 301).

Rather than pitching a one-stop workshop, or pitting creativity against criticism, or constructing a crustacean shell as Haake admits to doing around her practice, 'stubbornly insist[ing] that we commit ourselves ... to an examination of what happens in the writing moment to let writing take place' (2007: 16), we might get more creative and purposeful with our workshop design to better serve our students, our profession, and our field.

The Collection

The writing workshop stays the same when workshop teachers continue to produce 'their own interpretations of creative writing classroom lore in a field that as a whole rejects notions of itself as an academic discipline' (Ritter & Vanderslice, 2007: xi). Most of us do not want to replicate the tired workshop model, despite David Starkey's claim that much is at stake for some in maintaining the status quo. John Hopkins program director Jean McGarry warns 'If workshops are only about self-expression, then you have literary bums floating in and out' (qtd in Delaney, 2007). Teachers who promote rigor and inventiveness in the workshop model stretch the model's flexibility – and in doing so, they also shape, for the better, our pedagogy, our students, and our profession as an intelligent model set apart from other disciplines in its distinctiveness.

This collection contributes to the timely dialogue on the writing workshop model's effectiveness: Does the Writing Workshop Still Work? It attempts to follow Ostrom's suggestion that we take a harder look at the function of the workshop model. As such, the collection's 16 chapters, categorized into four sections: Inside the Writing Workshop Model, Engaging the Conflicts, The Non-Normative Workshop, and New Models for Relocating the Workshop, cover a gamut of theoretical and pedagogical topics. Stephanie Vanderslice takes us inside the signature model by likening the workshop's iconic tendency to E.B. White's elegy of a lake in 'Once More to the Workshop: A Myth Caught in Time.' Her point is that the traditional workshop model remains unchanged despite the 'new educational landscape' created by the burgeoning of creative writing programs and the variant student population. Because the traditional workshop gives limited attention to invention and creativity, it is no longer an effective pedagogy, and as such, Vanderslice advocates for its revision. Patrick Bizzaro offers 'an ontological study' of creative writing by exploring the 'disciplinarity' of the workshop, its epistemological bases, and the ways in which its practices are different than those in literary studies and composition studies. While the model may borrow from these other disciplines, '[in] the end,' Bizzaro tells us, 'the best workshops will address poems as poems, not essays of the sort written in composition classes, and will work with drafts, not with finished literary products of the sort read for literature classes.' Philip Gross defends the pragmatism of the workshop, unearthing, as he does, some unconventional principles of the workshop model. Anna Leahy draws upon conventions that guide creative writing workshops to explain how the workshop defines creative writing as a profession and how it fosters student learning. Willy Maley considers the workshop from the perspective of the business model, the science model, and the writers-as-workers model.

Section two engages with some of the conflicts within the workshop model. Tim Mayers examines the positive and negative effects of the writing workshop model on students' awareness of and facility with audience concerns in creative writing and composition classrooms. Brent Royster interrogates the subjectivity of the author as one site of theoretical inquiry in the creative writing workshop. Gaylene Perry considers the vulnerabilities and risks in the writing workshop model while Colin Irvine focuses on the problems of the workshop model in the composition class.

The non-normative workshop theme in section three takes shape in David Starkey's heuristic assessment of the writing workshop model in the two-year college. Mary Ellen Bertolini's essay faces the dilemma of conducting writing workshops when the subject matter of the writing is the raw material of students' lives. 'The Things I Used to Do: Workshops Old and New' exposes a contemplative approach to workshop design by Keith Kumasen Abbott, a creative writing teacher and ordained lay Soto Zen monk.

The final section of the collection considers new spaces and new models for the workshop model. Katharine Haake describes the model's evolution and her 'own vexed relationship to it.' She offers the insight of Mary Louise Pratt's 'Contact Zones' as a way to approach 'the kind of workshop that responds to the challenge of writing in the 21st century;' plus, she outlines her design for a hybrid workshop model. Sue Roe introduces the strongly directional masterclasses as a variant of the workshop model. In response to student hesitation and/or resistance to submit work-in-progress to a workshop class, Leslie Wilson offers the 'floating workshop' as a successful pedagogical tool. Finally, Mary Ann Cain drives home the collection's undergirding inquiry into the workability of the writing workshop model, Cain complicates the question of 'Does it Work?' by exploring how that question works within specific social, material, historical, and spatial contexts.

Lastly, it seems fitting that Joseph Moxley, who began the conversation on the theory and pedagogy of the workshop model and creative writing in America in 1989, ends the collection with his present-day thoughts on the disciplinarity and future of the workshop model in the scope of creative writing studies.

Despite the disparity of views on the writing workshop presented in this collection and related survey, it seems important that we

(1) continue to re-examine the model's practices and patterns,
(2) share workshop methods and alternatives to the workshop with our colleagues and with the field,
(3) attend and participate in conferences (crossover conferences, even, to extend our voice through the halls of composition, literature, art and drama),
(4) rethink our pedagogy, by asking 'How often do we/should we revise our workshop methods?' (Ostrom, 1994: xx),
(5) answer Wendy Bishop's call for 'fresh ways of talking about writing that enlivens the workshop,' (1997: 262) and
(6) be open to opportunities by which we can extend and flex the writing workshop model's possibilities.

Notes

1. Included in my text are comments/quotes by creative writing teachers who responded to my survey on the workshop model. To best distinguish these responses from other cited scholarship, I have identified the feedback from surveyed creative writing teachers with in-text parentheses that note responders' names and universities.
2. This was a concept addressed by Colin Irvin in a preliminary draft of his essay for this collection.
3. Student comments that refer to the Net generation were generated from my classroom discussions about how writers in the New Millennium read, write, and learn; and how these students think teachers should/could vary teaching methodologies to reflect the Net generation's needs and special proclivities with new media and technology designs.

References

Bishop W. (1990) *Released Into Language: Options for Teaching Creative Writing*. Urbana: NCTE.

Bishop, W. and Ostom, H. (eds) (1994) *Colors of a Different Horse*. Urbana: NCTE.

Bishop, W. Poetry as a therapeutic process: Realigning art and the unconscious teaching lives. *Teaching Lives* (pp. 252–263). Logan: Utah State University Press.

Bishop W. and Starkey, D. (2006) *Keywords in Creative Writing*. Logan. Utah State UP.

Bizzaro, P. (1998) Should I write the essay or finish a poem? Teaching writing creatively. *CCC* 49 (2), 285–297.

Bizzaro, P. (2004) Research and reflections: The special case of creative writing. *College English* 66 (3), 294–209.

Carlson, S. (2005) The new generation goes to college. *The Chronicle of Higher Education*. <http://chronicle.com/free/v52/i07/07a03401.htm>.

Carr, N. (2008) Is Google making us stupid? *Atlantic* (July/Aug) <http://www.theatlantic.com/doc/200807/google>.

Ciabattari, J. (2005) Workshop: A revolution of sensibility. *Poets & Writers* (Jan/Feb) <http://www.pw.org>.

Clark, K. (1999) Study as practice: On creative writing & the English curriculum. *Writer's Chronicle* (Sept) <http://elink.awpwriter.org/m/awpChron/articles/kclark01.lasso>.

Cole, C. (2007) How the university workshop hinders new writers from engaging with ideas (and what to do about it). *Segue Online Literary Journal*. Miami University Middletown (July), 2–23 <www.mid.muohio.edu/segue>.

Dawson, P. (2005) *Creative Writing and the New Humanities*. Oxford: Routledge.

Delaney, E.J. (2007) Where great writers are made. *The Atlantic* (Fiction Issue) <http://www.theatlantic.com/doc/200708/edward-delaney-mfa>.

Fenza, D.W. (2000) Creative writing & its discontents. *Writer's Chronicle* (March/April) <http://www.awpwriter.org/magazine/writers/fenza01.htm>.

Gioia, D. (1991) Can poetry matter? *Atlantic Monthly* 276 (May), 94–206.

Grimes, T. (1999) Workshop and the writing life. In T. Grimes (ed.) *The* Workshop: Seven Decades of the Iowa Writers' Workshop (pp. 1–25). New York: Hyperion.

Guevara, M. (1998) Out of the ashtray: Revivifying creative writing classes. *AWP* (March/April) <http://www.awpwriter.org/magazine/pastissues/twcmarapr1998.htm>.

Haake, K. (2007) Against reading. In K. Ritter and S. Vanderslice *Can it Really Be Taught: Resisting Lore in Creative Writing Pedagogy* (pp. 14–27). Portsmouth: Boyton/Cook.

Healey, S. (2009) The rise of creative writing & the new value of creativity. *The Writers Chronicle* 41 (4), 30–29.

Hall, D. (1983) Poetry and ambition. Poetry.org. Feb 2, 2009. (originally published in *Kenyon Review* ns 5(4) <http://www.poets.org/viewmedia.php/prmMID/16915>.

Leahy, A. (2007) Creativity, caring, and the easy 'A': Rethinking the role of self-esteem in creative writing pedagogy. In K. Ritter and S. Vanderslice (eds) *Can it Really Be Taught?* (pp. 55–26). Portsmouth: Boynton/Cook.

Leahy, A. (ed.) (2005) *Power and Identity in the Creative Writing Classroom: The Authority Project*. Clevedon: Multilingual Matters.

Light, G. (2000) Conceiving creative writing in higher education. NAWE. <http://www.nawe.co.uk/archive>.

Lim, S.G-lin. (2003) The strangeness of creative writing: An institutional query. *Pedagogy* 3, 151–69.

Manolis, A. (2005) Writing the community: service learning in creative writing. In A. Leahy (ed.) *Power and Identity in the Creative Writing Classroom: The Authority Project* (pp. 141–151). Clevedon: Multilingual Matters.

Mayers, T. Figuring the future. (2007) In K. Ritter and S. Vanderslice (eds) *Can it Really Be Taught?* (pp. 1–13). Portsmouth: Boytin Cook.

Mayers, T. (2009) One simple word: From creative writing to creative writing studies. *College English* 71 (3), 217–228.

Menand, L. (2009) 'Show or tell: Should creative writing be taught?' *The New Yorker* 8 June <http://www.newyorker.com/arts/critics/atlarge/2009/06/08/090608crat–atlarge–menand>.

Minot, S. (1976) Creative writing: Start with the student's motive. *CCC* 27 (4), 392–394.

Moxley, J. (ed.) (1989) *Creative Writing in America: Theory and Pedagogy* Urbana: NCTE.

Myers. D.G. (1996) *The Elephants Teach: Creative Writing Since 1880*. Chicago: U of Chicago Press.

Ostrom, H. (1994) Introduction: Of radishes and shadows, theory and pedagogy. In W. Bishop and H. Ostrom *Colors of a Different Horse* (pp. xi–xxiii). Urbana: NCTE.

Prensky, M. (2001) Digital natives, digital immigrants. *On the Horizon* 9, 1–6.

Ritter, K. (2001) Professional writers/writing professionals: Revamping teacher training in creative writing PhD programs. *College English* 64 (2), 205–227.

Ritter, K. and Vanderslice, S. (2007) Introduction: Creative writing and the persistence of 'lore'. In K. Ritter and S. Vanderslice (eds) *Can it Be Taught?* (pp. xi–xx). Portsmouth: Boyton Cook.

Royster, B. (2005) Inspiration, creativity, and crisis: The Romantic myth of the writer meets the contemporary classroom. In A. Leahy (ed.) *Power and Identity in the Creative Writing Classroom: The Authority Project* (pp. 26–28). Clevedon: Multilingual Matters.

Shelnutt, E. (1999) Isolationism in writing programs: What can be done? *College Teaching* 39 (2), pp. 57–20.

Starkey, D. (1994) The MFA graduate as composition instructor: A self-analysis. *Colors of a Different Horse: Rethinking Creative Writing Theory and Pedagogy* (pp. 248–254). Urbana: NCTE.

Starkey, D. and Healy, E.K. (2007). 'A better time teaching': A dialogue about pedagogy and the Antioch-LA MFA. In K. Ritter and S. Vanderslice (eds) *Can it Really Be Taught?* (pp. 38–45). Portsmouth: Boytin Cook.

Tate, A. (1964) What is creative writing? *Wisconsin Studies in Contemporary Literature*. 5(3), 181–184.

Tyler, K. (2007) The tethered generation. *HR Magazine* 53 (5) <http://www.shrm.org/hrmagazine/articles/0507/0507cover.asp>.

Vandenberg, P. (2004) Integrated writing programmes in American universities: Whither creative writing? *New Writing: An International Journal for the Practice and Theory of Creative Writing* 1 (1), 6–13.

Wandor, M. (2008) *The Author is Not Dead, Merely Somewhere Else*. Houndmills: Palgrave.

SECTION ONE

INSIDE THE WRITING WORKSHOP MODEL

Chapter 1

Once More to the Workshop: A Myth Caught in Time

STEPHANIE VANDERSLICE

> *This seemed an utterly enchanted sea, this lake you could leave to its own devices for a few hours and come back to, and find that it had not stirred, this constant and trustworthy body of water.*
>
> 'Once More to the Lake'
> E.B. White, 1941

In his famous, canonized essay, 'Once More to the Lake', E.B. White (1941) elegizes the lake he visited with his family as a boy, the same one to which he, now a father, brings his son, romanticizing this place of memory until it is utterly frozen in time, an idealized icon. In much the same way, the traditional writing workshop, alternately a site of criticism and rosy nostalgia is also a victim of the cryogenics of iconography. Rather than privilege innovation or reflective practice, in fact, 'though smoking in class is a thing of the past, many things [about the workshop] haven't changed much in the last 25 years (Parks, 2008: E6).

The problem with icons is that they are static, unable, from their brittle pedestals, to respond to sea changes that surround them, to evolve and remain relevant to the society in which they were anointed. Pictures of Elvis, Marilyn Monroe, even Mickey Mouse, dominate our visual memories just like the idyllic lake White romanticizes, but they are dead images, their relevance to society buried at the moment they ceased to grow and change with the rest of the world. If the creative writing workshop is to survive and retain its efficacy, it must resist this iconic tendency and respond to the educational landscape in which it currently exists instead of the one in which it was conceived over half a century ago. It must be revised.

> Some of the other campers were in swimming ... one of them with a cake of soap. Over the years there has been this person with the cake of soap, this cultist, and here he was. There had been no years.

As many scholars have noted, some no doubt in this collection, the workshop method of teaching writing arose in the states, in Iowa in the 1930s–1950s, reaching the height of its influence in the late 20th century, in relatively unique circumstances. As conceived and implemented at the University of Iowa through the vision of Norman Forester and later Paul Engle, its primary intention was to provide a post-baccalaureate incubator where 'young *polished* (emphasis mine) writers could come for a year or two and have their work critiqued' (Swander, 2005: 168). Forester and Engle also constructed the workshop as a place where these 'seasoned' writers could be hardened to the critics, where success could be claimed if a student (usually a female) occasionally and perhaps apocryphally (for we know writers are great storytellers) fainted after a particularly rigorous session. A place Tom Grimes (qtd in Wandor, 2008: 131) fondly muses, whose entrance should be guarded by the signage, 'Abandon all hope, all ye who enter here.'

Known in some circles as the Bobby Knight School of writing pedagogy, so named for the famously abusive, chair-throwing college basketball coach, the workshop was also designed as a kind of 'boot camp,' which would 'toughen' students so that they could withstand inevitable adversity and criticism as an artist (Swander, 2005: 168). Such goals are not surprising, for contributing to the uniqueness of the workshop's origins was the fact that at mid-century, most of the students in the eponymous Iowa Workshop were males, many of them World War II veterans on the GI bill, for whom the humiliations of boot camp and the paint of the basketball court were easily internalized metaphors.

And internalize them they did, as these young writers fanned out to become writing teachers themselves and modeled their own workshops on the only method of teaching they had known, so that the abusive basketball coach school of pedagogy dominated the creative writing scene for many years and still counts a number of enthusiasts today. As Mary Swander (2005: 169) notes, 'Every creative writing instructor must face the Bobby Knight legacy.' Indeed, many teachers feel they must still aspire to it, as is evident when teacher Dan Barden (2008: 87) congratulates himself, in a recent article on his workshop teaching in *Poets and Writer's* magazine, on the fact that 'one of the things that makes me a good teacher, I'm convinced, is that I'm a bastard.' Or when Professor Margaret Mullan (qtd in Parks, 2008: E6) describes her MFA experience as 'very much a guys program, but I kind of needed that. I needed to be kicked around a little bit.'

> On the journey to the lake, I began to wonder what it would be like. I wondered how time would have marred this unique, this holy spot.

The essential problem with this method of pedagogy arises in the ways in which the creative writing landscape has changed since the early days of the Iowa workshop. With the exception of MFA programs, the overwhelming majority of creative writing workshop students bear no resemblance to the cadre of graduate students, the 'polished' writers who populated the workshop as it took hold in creative writing mythology. In fact, in many ways, the creative writing workshop is a victim of its own success. Teacher and writer Brent Royster (2005: 35) recognizes this when he cautions that 'creative writing workshops are growing in popularity,' to the extent that a 'revised notion of creativity and a restructuring,' becomes necessary.

Mary Swander notes, as well, that 'when creative writing became democratized,' that is, as hundreds of creative writing programs, both graduate and undergraduate, sprang up in the last 50 years, the student population changed.[1] 'Poetry, fiction and playwriting [was] offered to students with little *developed* (emphasis mine) literary skill' (p. 168). Moreover, as creative writing programs trickled or gushed, really, down to the undergraduate level, the face of the creative writing classroom changed from the rarefied countenances of more experienced writers to the wide-eyed stares of absolute beginners who felt called to write but who had no idea what this calling entailed, having, for the most part, cultivated their passion for writing outside a classroom (high school creative writing courses are still unusual except in larger or more affluent secondary schools), yet still inside a popular culture that perpetuated, and continues to perpetuate a laundry list of myths about how writers and writing come to be.[2] As many scholars have noted, Associated Writing Program (AWP) director D.W. Fenza among them, the Bobby Knight school of teaching creative writing, in which students learn to write in an economy of scarcity, where the only guidance centers on what *not* to do, ultimately fails beginning writers. Even Barden seems to recognize this as he bemoans the inefficacy of the workshop in educating his undergraduate writers, but nonetheless, as we have seen, he clings to the Romantic myth like a life raft that in order to be a 'good' workshop leader he must maintain his reputation as a 'bastard.'

> There was a choice of pie for dessert and the waitresses were the same country girls ... still fifteen; their hair had been washed, that was the only difference – they had been to the movies and seen the pretty girls with the clean hair.

The necessity of retrofitting the workshop for changing populations, especially for undergraduates, is perhaps best illustrated in the story

Mary Swander tells of her first, undergraduate experience of the iconic 'workshop':

'Write a story for next week,' the instructor told them.

'But isn't she going to show us how to write a short story?' the young Swander wonders. 'There must be parts, components, to a short story, different styles and structures. Is she even going to explain the choices we could make?' (p. 167).

In fact, the traditional, product-centered creative writing workshop gives little to no attention to invention and creativity, to how poems, short stories, essays or plays are actually *constructed*. To this end, Barden characterizes this workshop as 'anything *but* a shop in which writers work' (p. 83). Such workshops, moreover, as Brent Royster maintains, lose sight of their real goal, to scaffold or 'foster more dedicated writers' (p. 27).

Michelene Wandor (2008: 127), in her discussion of the traditional workshop in her book, *The Writer is Not Dead, Merely Somewhere Else*, also notes the paradox that arises in a beginning writing class when 'workshop time (the foregrounded activity) is reserved for student writing . . . completed *outside* of class (emphasis mine). Even if the student thinks it's complete, the fact that it is subject to group criticism renders it conceptually incomplete.' Royster underscores another paradox when he refers to the long held workshop wisdom that the student whose work is 'on the table,' must be silent when it is under discussion: 'the work of the class is the daily practice of writing and the shared process of that practice,' and yet, in the unadulterated workshop, students may be cautioned 'in speaking about their process in favor of listening to peer criticism' (p. 34).

The answer to this workshop dilemma seems relatively clear and yet, perhaps because many creative writing teachers *still* do not avail themselves of the growing body of scholarship on the teaching of creative writing characterized by this book and many, many others, (Mr Barden's essay, for example, demonstrates no awareness of this scholarship) it continues to elude them. Simply put, the workshop must be modified to respond to the varying populations of students who wish – and deserve – to benefit from it. Critically, the workshop for beginning writers, usually undergraduates, must be refocused to include content that enhances skill building and craft. To borrow a term from the British, the undergraduate creative writing course must be more *taught*.

Indeed, Barden hits the nail on the head when he worries that the 'root of the problem is that the way we teach creative writing . . . suggests that there is *no way to teach creative writing*' (p. 83). Even as a 'naïve' undergraduate, Mary Swander observed that in other skill-building classes, 'students were asked to practice the basic steps of the craft, carefully mastering a chunk of knowledge before adding another' (p. 167). Michelene Wandor, further, holds up as an example, the Italian Renaissance art academies where more 'formal ways of teaching fine art developed ... anatomy, life drawing, natural philosophy, and architecture were all part of the curriculum ... the idea was to get away from the empirical haphazard kind of learning that artists had faced in workshops' (p. 132).

Sound familiar? In order to succeed in the current terrain, the traditional workshop must, as all writers-in-training are exhorted to do, *respond* to its audience. Workshops whose students are at the start of the continuum of their development as writers must first of all de-emphasize the *shop* (defined by Royster as the 'daily critique that underscores the weakness in the writer's work') in favor of the work – the aforementioned 'daily practice of writing and the shared process of that practice.'

Such a reinvention can take any number of forms, including de-mystifying the writer's life and creative practice – my own introductory classes always include writers' memoirs through which students will learn that there is no one kind of writing practice any more than there is one kind of writer. It is also heavily exercise-based; students do as much writing inside the class as outside of it. Beginning writers especially, need to know that writing doesn't spring fully-formed from their pens and laptops but is the result of recursive drafting, self-assigned creativity exercises and the like. Finally, it may include substantial reflection on individual process, so that students may discover the creative practices that most support and enhance their development as writers. All of these conditions recreate what Wendy Bishop (1998: 14) termed the 'trans-actional' creative writing workshop, one that puts 'writers in motion.' Moreover, in the hands of those for whom creativity is second nature, reinventing the traditional workshop may ultimately result in innovative forms of teaching we have not even discovered yet, once the necessity of this reinvention is understood as a given in the field.

Throughout 'Once More to the Lake,' E.B. White describes the lake as so frozen in time that he has trouble 'making out which was I, the one walking at my side, [or] the one walking in my pants.' At the end of the essay, moreover, he watches, a late-middle-aged spectator, as his son prepares to swim after a heavy storm. As '[his son] buckle[s] the swollen belt,' of his swimsuit, White's groin suddenly feels the 'chill of death.'

At a 2008 Association of Writers and Writing Programs Conference craft lecture, fiction writer Joan Silber said, 'A story is the rescuer of time like fish from a moving stream.' Unlike E.B. White's intimations of mortality, the death of the workshop is not a foregone conclusion. It can be rescued from the moving stream that threatens to carry it into iconoclastic oblivion, and re-cast, recreated into something lithe and supple. Our students deserve no less.

Notes

1. It is important to add, moreover, that the entire face of the university population in the US changed in the late 1960s and 1970s as the exigencies of the social revolution led to the 'open admissions policies,' at many public institutions of higher education that continue to this day. Such policies, requiring only a high school diploma for entry, meant that entering first year students no longer exhibited homogenous skill sets but came with a vast range of educational backgrounds and skills which needed to brought up to speed to the demands of the university environment. Such policies, in democratizing the US higher educational process, have no doubt also influenced the democratization of creative writing.
2. Many of these myths are more fully explored in *Can It Really Be Taught?: Resisting Lore In Creative Writing Pedagogy*, a collection of essays edited by Dr Kelly Ritter and author.

References

Barden, D. (2008) Workshop: A rant against creative writing classes. *Poets and Writers* Mar/Apr, 83–27.

Bishop, W. (1998) *Released into Language: Options for Teaching Creative Writing* (2nd edn). Urbana: NCTE.

Parks, M. (2008) On the write track: A university of Arkansas program has trained students in the nuts and bolts of producing good fiction and poetry for 40 years. *Arkansas Democrat-Gazette* 3 Apr., E1, E6.

Royster, B. (2005) Inspiration, creativity and crisis: The Romantic myth of the writer meets the contemporary classroom. In A. Leahy (ed.) *Power and Identity in the Creative Writing Classroom: The Authority Project* (pp. 26–28). Clevedon: Multilingual Matters.

Swander, M. (2005) Duck, duck, turkey: Using encouragement to structure writing assignments. In A. Leahy (ed.) *Power and Identity in the Creative Writing Classroom: The Authority Project* (pp. 167–279). Clevedon: Multilingual Matters.

Silber, J. (2008) Association of Writers and Writing Programs Conference, Hilton Hotel, New York, New York. 2 February.

Wandor, M. (2008) *The Author is Not Dead, Merely Somewhere Else: Creative Writing Reconceived* (p. 192). London: Palgrave Macmillan.

White, E.B. (1999) Once more to the lake. *Essays of E.B. White* (pp. 246–256). New York: Harper Collins.

Chapter 2

Workshop: An Ontological Study

PATRICK BIZZARO

Recent scholarship in creative writing has been descriptive. As early understandings of an emerging field, such descriptions enable us to do the important formative work of determining creative writing's place in English studies. These studies have focused chiefly on three areas: classroom activities (Ritter & Vanderslice, 2007; Moxley, 1989), epistemological foundations (Bishop, 1990; Haake, 2000; Starkey & Healey, 2007) and creative writing's indebtedness to other subjects in English studies (Myers, 1996; Mayers, 2005; Ritter, 2001). This last arena of study – influences on creative writing – interests me most because of the uncertainty it has left us with concerning creative writing's place in English studies. The few understandings we have reached about creative writing as an autonomous field have been influenced to a large extent by this uncertainty. In an effort to unravel some of this confusion, this essay begins where other recent studies of creative writing's disciplinary status have thus far ended, with English studies as 'a field divided into *at least three parts* – literature, composition, and creative writing' (Mayers, 2005: 6, see also Myers, 1996: 10–21, my emphasis). Because it elevates creative writing's place in English studies to the same level as literature and composition, this statement differs from other longstanding views of English studies. Susan Miller's (1991) *Textual Carnivals* and James Berlin's (1987) *Rhetoric and Reality* assert the belief that English studies is divisible into *two* parts only, literature (or the poetic) and composition (or the rhetoric). An ontological study of the workshop such as this one intends us to see creative writing as a product of influences from literature and composition but also as a field of study independent of the two. Saying so is no easy task, however, since we are at the start of research in creative writing and must develop methods consistent with the values and emphases of our field. Studies of workshop as a teaching strategy historically linked to creative writing do exactly that: provide a starting point.

After all, if it were possible to simply subtract literature and composition from English studies and use the label 'creative writing' for whatever's left, we would easily complete the task this essay has undertaken, to place creative writing, once and for all, in its proper relation to literature and composition. Unfortunately, such an analysis will not render much useful information, beyond what we already know: that literature and composition, like creative writing, are separate fields of inquiry which address their problems in very different environments and by use of very different data. This statement of difference characterizes 'disciplinarity'. A discipline, from this perspective, is distinguished by what it construes as evidence, and its evidence further clarifies its epistemology. While there is no widely agreed-upon method for a study such as this one, I propose to study a teaching activity historically linked to creative writing, the workshop, and then to determine what its epistemological bases are. As a result, this study of the workshop shows both what creative writers might learn when literary and composition studies are used in a creative writing class but also in what ways literary and composition studies impede learning in a creative writing class. And this examination gives us the chance to further explore creative writing as a discipline. While I believe the connections scholars have made between creative writing and composition have been important and far-reaching, in the end I believe creative writing and composition are separate disciplines, discrete fields of inquiry. A study of the workshop as a method of instruction linked historically to creative writing, with emphasis on what it might profitably borrow from composition and literature and what it must reject, ought to lead us to some conclusions concerning the epistemology from which each discipline in English studies arises. An understanding of the starting points or foundations of creative writing will enable us to better examine the relations that characterize English studies. From this vantage point, then, creative writing is more than a hybrid of literary and composition studies; it is an autonomous field with a right to its own history, epistemology, and classroom activities. A study of the workshop, in particular, will more clearly enable us to see the disciplinary nature of creative writing.

Interpretation in the Workshop: The Literary Emphasis in Creative Writing Studies

For the purpose of exploring issues associated with the workshop method of instruction, I will use a definition forwarded by D.G. Myers (1996: 118) in the following statement from *The Elephants Teach:* 'The method of *communal* making and *communal* criticism is the workshop method' (my emphasis). Such an undertaking must invite participation from students, to be communal. Typically a workshop requires that the community take one of three actions, typifying pedagogical approaches: interpretation, evaluation, or a combination of the two. To make workshop truly communal, then, teachers must consciously prepare their students to perform the two tasks central to workshop: interpretation and evaluation. Creative writing's long association with literary study makes the act of interpretation a natural and even inevitable undertaking where examination of literary texts is concerned, even of unauthorized (that is, unpublished) literary texts. And creative writing's association with composition in recent years has provided creative writing with tools for evaluation. The key question is how, exactly, to make these elements of literary study and composition coalesce in that staple of creative writing instruction, the workshop. And, when they do, what limits must we place on the influences literary study and composition exert on creative writing? For if creative writing is an autonomous field of study, it will differ in some fundamental ways from literary and composition studies and reject some of what is taught in those classes, if not their methods of instruction themselves.

Though there are still very few reliable histories of creative writing, those that exist agree that creative writing came into existence to 'serve' literature. In his institutional history of creative writing, *Creative Writing and the New Humanities*, Paul Dawson (2004: 8) notes that creative writing developed as a response to difficulties in the way literary studies had been taught. Myers makes a similar point:

> Although . . . [creative writing] . . . was founded by writers, it was not created to give them (in Howard Nemerov's words) a quiet life and a fairly agreeable way to make a dollar. Instead it was an effort on their part to bring the teaching of literature more closely in line with the ways in which (they believed) literature is genuinely created.

It is commonly believed that for nearly 100 years, then, creative writing served literary study in most English departments in the United States and abroad as a way of helping students see literature as something immediate, something people actually make, literature treated 'as if people intended to write more of it' (Myers, 2006: 4). Four influences from literary study have served to benefit creative writing teachers, especially those who aim to prepare their students for workshop.

The first is itself ontological. Literature helps us organize creative writing in terms of fields of study. Unlike rhetoric and composition and technical and professional communication, emerging fields in English studies that purport to stress acts of writing, creative writing is understandable in terms of the field coverage model of organization long common in English departments. This model divides literature into time periods and genres, enabling us to envision creative writing, too, as a field with specific areas that must be 'covered'. Our most fundamental notions of creative writing as a field, then, come from literary study, reflecting, perhaps, a hundred years or more of literature's dominance over the shape creative writing has taken, the shape of its container, the kind of influence composition and technical communication have successfully resisted.

As a second and related matter, the study of literature gives us a basis for describing the kinds of texts we write and want our students to write. Efforts to make creative writing a teachable subject, one might argue, were enhanced by the development of the New Criticism; an 'objective' approach to literary study has certainly given teachers language they may use in discussing various features of poetry, fiction and drama (and nowadays creative nonfiction) with students.[1] That language is commonly taught to students in literature courses but it is also often used in creative writing courses so students too can talk about literary texts. These efforts, for right or wrong, tend to make creative writing rule-based and, therefore, teachable; they underscore the teacher's need to find a language for discussing writing. When we assign readings for students in preparation for the workshop, we find ourselves using language that describes literature as literature, descriptions of a genre's elements, most often including, in a poetry writing class for instance, simile, metaphor, imagery, symbolism and other features individual teachers believe students will need to know. Where a literature course is not required as prerequisite to a creative writing course in a particular genre, students should be asked to read and discuss their reading assignments by using this language so that later, in workshop and in describing what they, themselves, have set out to accomplish in their writing, they will have the language to do so. To that end, we should assign readings to elucidate genre, but also to foster understanding of the era in which we write.

Likewise, in selecting texts to be read in preparation for workshop, we should consciously prepare students to write particular types of poems described chiefly for the writing class, what we might call subgenres or pseudo genres. In a poetry writing class, one well known pseudo genre is the 'list poem'. In helping students write one, we are wise to begin with a reading assignment, such as James Wright's (1990) 'Lying in a Hammock at William Duffy's Farm in Pine Island, Minnesota'. When we discuss the poem, we do so in an effort to devise just that set of 'rules' or characteristics that result in a list poem. We then describe the poem as a list of things the narrator sees while lying on a hammock and then similarly choose a vantage point – say a bed in the middle of the night or a street corner in Phoenix or Chicago – from which our students make a similar list of things seen, heard, felt, touched and maybe even tasted. Communal criticism of a list poem, as just one example, will be an active application of 'rules' established for examining that poem, best accomplished by using a procedure called primary trait scoring.

The activity involved in the making of a list poem is fairly typical of what might go on at the 'front end' of creative writing instruction, the portion of the course in which beginning students are encouraged to write with some regularity so that they will have something for examination during the workshop portion of the class. The front end also provides us with time to further prepare students for workshop. For instance, creative writing teachers often employ writing prompts similar to what Richard Hugo calls triggering devices, which help students begin drafts of poems that may be 'workshopped' later. These writing prompts most often employ models, activities, or a combination of the two (Bizzaro, 1983), the Wright poem serving as an example of a model.

The third major influence on the workshop from literary study involves the use of critical theory. It is possible, for instance, to employ methods of reading typically reserved for published literary texts in examining and interpreting student poems (see Bizzaro, 1993). What's more, we should teach students in poetry writing classes how to read using those interpretive tools. What we borrow from literary studies when we prepare students for workshop is a rich and interesting array of reading methods that show them who they may be when they read. These methods help students demonstrate to themselves that their poems, stories, essays, or plays might be read from a variety of perspectives. Vantage points for these readings might include the new criticism, but also reader response, feminist, Marxist, and even psychological perspectives.

Thus, we can teach our students how to carry on the work of interpretation in a workshop and, indeed, we should let *them* do that work once we have taught them how. But my fundamental point is exactly this: teachers must show students how to do the work of the workshop – to interpret and to evaluate. My favorite activity in teaching students how to read from varying perspectives is to use a poem that is amenable to examination from various perspectives. For that specific purpose, I often use 'Everything: Eloy, Arizona 1956' by Ai (1973). I do not ask students to prepare their readings of the poem prior to class. Instead, I hand out the poem during class, face down on their desks. When they turn over the poem, I ask them to cover it with another sheet of paper and then to move the sheet that covers it only as I tell them to. My goal is to address this poem one line at a time. By doing so, I enable my students to predict what will come next, employing in this way a reader-response approach to reading based upon their prior knowledge of subject and form.[2] Once that is done, I provide an oral protocol in order to model for students other types of readings.

But applying critical theories in reading to prepare students for involvement in workshop is, at best, only part of what our reliance on literary theory enables us to do in creative writing classes. Rarely do we study literary periods without reading poetic and aesthetic documents written by authors to explain what they have set out to do (i.e. Eliot's 'Tradition and the Individual Talent,' or Shelley's 'A Defense of Poetry,' or Frost's 'The Figure a Poem Makes'). These documents represent self-reports that the teaching of writing, especially of creative writing, is based upon, though self-reports as such have been summarily devalued in recent years, as I will briefly explain below. But the fact that they continue to help us in creative writing suggests that creative writing is taught from a different epistemology altogether than are courses in literature or composition. By using a self-report, for instance, we might help students determine if they have viable subjects for their poems and do so on the basis of what other writers say they do when they write. William Wordsworth, for one, helps us help students determine if they have a viable subject for a poem since a concern with subject is essential to his explanation of the experiment called *Lyrical Ballads*. And his famous statement provides us with an excellent example of how writers' self-reports might be used in preparing students for workshop. In '"Preface" to *Lyrical Ballads*,' Wordsworth gives us these famous words that affect a poet's search for a proper subject: 'poetry is the spontaneous overflow of powerful feeling.' This advice taken in isolation has rendered some awful poems and stories based upon powerful feelings. But when we let Wordsworth finish what he wants to say, we find that the initial impulse by itself is not enough. No, these feelings must be 'recollected in tranquility.'

What saving words! Some subjects are, indeed, too close to the writer to be profitably explored in poetry. But Wordsworth helps us understand that the experience that generates both an immediate feeling AND, *when recalled later*, generates a second feeling is the experience worthy of a poem.

Why do I value authors' self-reports as I do? Among other things, authors' self-reports help us help our students and bring authority to our responses to what they have written. But there are many other pieces of advice that students should know about. I believe an entire pedagogy could be constructed for teaching creative writing based upon the reports writers have made of their writing processes. What's more, pages of AWP's *the Writer's Chronicle* are filled with such reports in the hopes inexperienced writers will benefit from finding out what experienced writers do when they write. This vital connection between literary study and creative writing, though, is one composition scholars in recent years have tended to deny as useful in the teaching of writing, a point of distinction between creative writing and composition studies. In this particular regard, then, creative writing has more in common with literary study than with composition: cognitivist approaches to research, which studied what experienced writers do when they write, have been rightly rejected as models of research because they are fraught with problems related to race, class, and gender. Nonetheless, composition offers tactics that creative writing teachers have employed over the years to make the workshop an activity that students can profitably participate in by employing innovative evaluation strategies.

Evaluation in the Workshop: The Composition Connection in Creative Writing Pedagogy

As Tim Mayers (2003: 98) points out, the 'composition' referred to in histories of English studies, such as the ones devised by Myers, Miller, and Berlin, is not the field we now know as rhetoric and composition: 'Myers uses the term *composition* primarily to describe a type of course taught in English departments.' Indeed, according to Mayers' account, no one ever intended 'for creative writing to be separated from other activities, such as criticism' (2003: 98). Composition and creative writing seem naturally – maybe even inevitably – allied as fields of writing. But the basis for pedagogies in each discipline differs. But when Mayers and Kelly Ritter argue for institutional changes to coalesce composition and creative writing, their position requires us to view the fields as linked epistemologically; if we cannot make this connection, one field must come to dominate and change the other. My question is whether such an alliance at this juncture in the development of creative writing as a discipline in English studies will do much to help the field's emergence. What's more, making creative writing a subfield in composition studies reinforces the limited view of English studies forwarded by Miller and

Berlin and undermines efforts made by Mayers and Myers, to name but two. In any event, the view of composition's relationship with creative writing is not particularly new.

Wendy Bishop (1990) established the composition–creative writing connection. In *Released into Language*, Bishop claims that academic creative writing has much in common with first year writing. She demonstrates that students in introductory creative writing classes are, in many ways, similar to students in composition classes: 'students in *elective* undergraduate creative writing classes may be more similar to students in *required* composition classes than they are to the graduate students many academic writers would prefer to teach' (p. ix). According to Bishop, most of these students may be unfamiliar with the notion of writing processes but, since they come from very different cultural backgrounds than their teachers, such students should be presented with literature that is an outgrowth of their cultural experiences. As a result, we do not err in our creative writing classes when we stress elements of writing students may (or should) have encountered first in their composition classes. More importantly, we ought to ask students to read literature from a representative range of cultures.

But Bishop went much further than simply noting how students were similarly trained. In my opinion, her major accomplishment in *Released into Language* is her ability to support what writers say in their self-reports, which I have argued have their roots in literary study, by using findings of researchers into composition studies: 'writers' insights can be joined to composition research and theory to further clarify what it means to be a writer and have a writing process' (p. 18). Bishop's goal, then, was to understand writers' self-reports in terms of what researchers found out about the cognitive processes employed by experienced writers. To that end, then, Bishop stressed elements of writing and writing instruction many composition and creative writing teachers have shared ever since. Writing, for instance, is most often discussed as a process in both subjects. Perhaps more significantly, writing largely involves acts of revision. And it is on this final point, revision, that creative writing workshops might best employ strategies developed in composition studies.

We help our students understand toward what they revise if we employ sensible methods of evaluation available to us in writings by composition scholars. Charles Cooper and Lee Odell, in their 1977 study *Evaluating Writing*, name seven methods of evaluation. Of them, I have found the *analytic scale* and *primary trait scoring* to be the most interesting and useful in creative writing courses I have taught (Bizzaro, 1990a, 1990b). An analytic scale is 'a list of the prominent features or characteristics of writing in a particular mode' (Cooper & Odell, 1977: 7). As a strategy for evaluating writing, analytic scales are descriptive. This is how they work: we often define poetry for the purpose of teaching students how to write it in a narrow way in our introductory classes by stressing its 'prominent features'. In an introductory poetry writing workshop, it is common to describe poetry in terms as general as 'show, don't tell'. But there are problems with this generalization; though the statement is descriptive in the way an analytic scale is, the statement is also prescriptive and overly general. We all know that such broad statements only work for so long; we have all read wonderful poems that do an awful lot of telling. 'Show, don't tell' may help us with the lyric poem but not as much with a narrative, for instance. And how do we explain to students the famous last line of the aforementioned Wright poem – 'I have wasted my life' – with a 'show, don't tell' mantra?

Because descriptions made possible by using analytic scales do not always serve the intended purpose (precisely because they generalize), Cooper and Odell identify a useful alternative, primary trait scoring. This method enables us to focus attention 'on just those features of a piece which are relevant to the kind of discourse it is' (Cooper & Odell, 1977: 11). I believe every poem is different and thus employs – or should try to employ – features that are different or in a different combination from any other poem, even by the same author: 'the object in writing poetry is to make all poems sound as different as possible from each other' (Frost, 1972: 439). To describe these variations, even in using the same features (i.e. imagery), evaluative responses based upon primary trait scoring are useful in writing classes. Regardless of what method of evaluation teachers might employ, they should discuss their methods of evaluation with students, with the goal of teaching students how to use those methods in a workshop situation. To participate productively in a workshop, students must employ such methods themselves in evaluating their classmates' writing. Such participation makes workshops the communal activities they were designed to be.

It seems axiomatic to me that if students are asked to interpret and evaluate their peers' writing in a communal environment, teachers must teach their students how to perform those tasks. What's more, the job of interpretation and evaluation does not belong exclusively to the teacher. One symptom of appropriation by the teacher is the teacher's dominance during workshop. To avoid appropriation, we should take advantage of tactics used widely in the teaching of literature and composition. Teachers are not much diminished by acknowledging literature and composition as sources for what they do or by coaching students in how to interpret and evaluate each other's works.

I believe part of any teacher's job in a workshop is to share with students the responsibility for commenting on each other's creative works. Learning how to interpret and evaluate, then, ought to be part of the course objectives. The time has come for all teachers of writing to develop methods of instruction that enable them to empower and authorize their students to reliably interpret and conscientiously evaluate their peers' writing. Creative writing teachers, given their epistemological orientation to the teaching of writing, as I've argued, must take the lead in this emphasis in teaching and, by doing so, assert creative writing's continuing independence from literary and composition studies.

'Constructive Unlearning' in the Workshop: Some Limitations to Creative Writing's Reliance on Literary and Composition Studies

As I have shown, the teaching of creative writing may benefit greatly by employing activities typically associated with the teaching of both literature and composition. Descriptions of creative writing over the past 20 years have been clear on this point though scholars have limited themselves to similarities among the fields. These similarities are not absolute, however; because the epistemologies from which these fields arise are dissimilar, the most we can say is that their teaching strategies sometimes overlap. Creative writing as a whole is more than the sum of its parts, more than the activities borrowed from composition when added to those taken from literature. One of many tasks awaiting new scholars in creative writing studies is the determination of what is uniquely the province of creative writing, for it is only in the study of the differences between creative writing, literature and composition that we will be able to establish what must inform their pedagogies at the level of knowing and lend support to the views of Myers and Mayers with which this essay begins.

In fact, when literature and composition are studied in creative writing classes, students learn writing skills not only irrelevant to creative writing but that ultimately must be unlearned. The workshop is where some of that unlearning must take place. Some techniques taught in composition violate certain premises of instruction based upon what writers actually do, violating then the very basis for knowing valued in creative writing instruction. Nearly 20 years ago, Donald Murray (1989: 103) said as much about teaching students to write fiction: 'the problem is that the students have learned to write. They bring with them knowledge which may be true for some of the writing they have done but which makes the writing of fiction difficult. The better educated the student, the harder it is to return to the natural, magical art of narrative ...' Let us, then, conclude this essay by examining some elements of instruction in literary and composition studies that students need to *unlearn* if they hope to learn how to write in a creative writing class. Murray's observations about fiction are general enough to make room for a teacher of fiction writing, so inclined, to complete a task parallel to this one but to focus on what must be unlearned in a fiction writing class. The same might be done in the case of other genres as well. As a poet myself, I will focus on some of the unlearning that must go on in a poetry workshop.

No doubt, Murray has provided us with one key to teaching students how to write in workshop, 'constructive unlearning'. While literature and composition have become increasingly theory-driven disciplines over the past 20 years, creative writing has remained the realm of writers teaching what they and other writers do when they write. This is the chief epistemological difference between creative writing and more theorized disciplines such as literature and composition. Consider this difference in light of compelling data that come from our classroom activities. In a composition class, for example, students learn that a piece of writing must have a beginning, middle and an end. That is the theory long current in most composition classes, and it comes from a good source, Aristotle. We hate to contradict Aristotle. But it is not similarly true in a poem, for instance, as in an essay that it must have a beginning, middle, and an end. Or that it must have a thesis statement or make a claim. In fact, I doubt that I am alone in my belief that a poem is mostly middle. This belief is sometimes a starting point for me in my evaluation of poems, my own at home and my students' during workshop. That particular 'trick' of response is one I want my students to use in reading their poems and their peers' in workshop. Again, I want to stress that the teacher must prepare students to help their peers unlearn certain habits of writing picked up in a composition class.

This one observation is generative. The most common application I offer, based upon this one very specific view of a poem's probable organization, is that the first stanza might need to be deleted in order to get to where the poem itself actually begins. Often the 'false introduction' is a summary of the poem that follows. The corollary to this view focuses on the way the poem ends. I often hypothesize (just to see what will happen) that the poem, mine or my students', stop a few lines short of where the draft under scrutiny actually stops – that is, get rid of 'false conclusions'. One must be careful with rules, however, especially those that apply to poems; a poem is not one thing, and it is conceivable that every poem follows 'rules' of its own. So what I insist from myself and from my students equally is that these and other comments be offered in the tone of experimentation, in an effort to try things out, as I do with my own writing: 'What would happen if . . .' In short, unlike the teaching I do in my composition classes, my teaching in my creative writing classes often leads me to ask my students to avoid introductions and conclusions in their poems, thesis statements with clear claims, and conclusions with summaries. By contrast I spend a great deal of time helping students figure out how to introduce and conclude essays for my composition classes. An opening of a poem is not necessarily an introduction, and an ending is not always a conclusion.

There is more, of course. The teaching of composition features, to varying degrees, analyses of audience and purpose. These rhetorical elements are of very little consequence in a poetry writing class. Indeed, other than conversations about magazines that might publish individual poems, we seldom deal with audience: 'a poet is a nightingale who sits in darkness and sings to cheer its own solitude,' says Percy Shelley (1967: 1075). And let's get picky. Like my colleague, Marjorie Stewart,[3] 'I do whine about sentence fragments in first year composition and then insist upon them in creative writing.' And how about decision-making in an essay as opposed to the kind of intuitions creative writers most often claim to have? Denise Levertov (1987: 60) makes this very point in her discussion of 'organic poetry': poetry 'is based on an intuition of an order.' I attempt to make this same point when I tell my students in my composition classes that once they figure out which major highway they are on in writing an essay (that is, determine the points they are trying to make), I expect them to stay on that road, no matter how interesting the side streets seem to be. *No deviations!* By contrast, in my creative writing classes, I have heard myself tell my students what I have learned from my own experience: *the real writing is down one of those side streets. Don't stay on the main drag unless you can't find an interesting place to turn.* I believe this must be what Charles Simic (2004: 347) refers to when he alludes to '[t]he surprising outcome' of certain poems.

These statements suggest for me the very point I hope to make concerning the kinds of bedfellows creative writing and composition studies seem to be. The epistemology that gives rise to creative writing is based upon the primacy of the teacher's experiences as a writer or, at the very least, the primacy of other writers' experiences as writers. Composition studies long ago forsook the research direction that would enable scholars to discover the decision-making processes of experienced writers when they write, the cognitive model credited to Flower and Hayes, among others. I believe this model of inquiry was given up for the right reasons; we long for a planet on which people have equal opportunities regardless of race, class, gender, ethnicity, or sexual preferences. But the fallout from the undoing of cognitivist methods of inquiry, in the end, included dismissal entirely of what writers say they do when they write. This particular shift in English studies seems a product of synecdoche: 'expressivism' comes to stand for writers, 'cognitivism' for writers' self-reports. There is hope in the hybrid method of inquiry advocated by Cindy Johanek, which seems to me a move in the right direction. Surely the next generation of scholars will develop research methods designed to figure out how to teach writing based upon what writers actually do when they write. This task is the first, visible necessity for composition scholars if they hope to develop writing programs that place creative writing alongside composition rather than subordinate creative writing to composition.

In the end, we should not be surprised to find elements of literary study useful in our teaching of creative writing. No doubt, Mayers' words are not only encouraging but prophetic of the direction of scholarship in creative writing studies when he writes, 'creative writing can offer unique perspectives on where English departments have come from, and where they might go' (2003: 5). Mayers continues by noting that 'scholarship on the histories and futures of English studies' has been 'written mainly by those affiliated with composition and rhetoric' (p. 5). But there is little doubt that things are changing, that creative writing programs everywhere are adding to their students' requirements a diet of pedagogy alongside the ongoing feast of workshops. David Starkey and Eloise Klein Healy (2007: 38) discuss in some detail the 'pedagogy semester' at Antioch-Los Angeles, which 'requires completing and annotating an extensive reading list, teaching a class, keeping a teaching journal, and writing a seminar paper.' We note with increasing hope the development of creative writing courses not only in the pedagogy of creative writing, but also in the kinds of research creative writers do (see Gerard).

The reason these courses are important additions to the usual series of workshops, seminars and craft courses creative writing students take as undergraduate and graduate students in most writing programs is because they provide students with what Kelly Ritter (2001: 208) wisely calls 'markers of professional difference.' By now, any number of scholars have echoed Bishop's sentiments, that she not only had to learn to teach creative writing but, like the rest of us who entered the classroom untrained, had to learn how to enjoy that teaching. What Ritter means by 'markers of professional difference,' then, are classes that distinguish creative writing graduates from graduates in other areas. Foremost among the skills a teacher of creative writing needs to possess is the ability to run workshops that benefit student-writers. By examining how students might be prepared for participating in workshop, teachers of those workshops will be able to explore that discipline called creative writing in light of what it borrows and what it holds as its own.

More generally, in the space we now believe to be inhabited by creative writing, a space between literary study on the one side and composition study on the other, lies a discipline which only seems a hybrid, a field of study that employs elements of literary study, elements of composition studies, and some elements unique to the field of creative writing that we only find when we unlearn some things learned in literature and composition courses. Teachers can help ready students for workshop by employing strategies historically associated with literary and composition training. What happens when we examine the impact of these two fields on the teaching of creative writing is that it enables us to acknowledge creative writing as a field independent of the two. What we find out when we encounter students in workshops is that some of what they have already been taught, especially in composition classes, needs to be unlearned before students will learn how to write poems and stories. This fact suggests that creative writing is based upon beliefs about writing in some ways different from beliefs that serve as foundation for the teaching of literature and composition. To view them as interchangeable modifies one or all of the fields to a measurable degree. In the end, teachers should be willing to borrow whatever they must from literary and composition studies to help their students become capable writers in the various genres in which students work as creative writers. This requires that students learn to read employing reading skills most useful in literary studies. It requires that students come to understand writing as a process, an understanding they may have reached for the first time, perhaps, in a composition course. In the end, however, the best workshops will address poems as poems, not essays of the sort written in composition classes, and will work with drafts, not with finished literary products of the sort read for literature classes. Once we have established the goals of the workshop, we will continue to find ways to return authority for student poems, stories, creative essays, and screenplays to the students themselves. Doing so is no small task.

Notes

1. See my *Responding to Student Poems: Applications of Critical Theory* for further discussion of the use of the New Criticism as the 'default' theory used in creative writing classes to discuss student writing.
2. See Frank Smith. *Understanding Reading*.
3. I want to thank Marjorie Stewart for her willingness to dialogue with me concerning the unlearning we must have our students to do in our creative writing classes. Stewart is a screenwriter in Pittsburgh.

References

Ai. (1973) Everything: Eloy, Arizona, 1956. *Cruelty*. Boston: Houghton Mifflin.

Berlin, J.A. (1987) *Rhetoric and Reality: Writing Instruction in American Colleges, 1900–2985*. Carbondale: Southern Illinois UP.

Bizzaro, P. (1983) Teacher as writer and researcher: The poetry dilemma. *Language Arts*, 82–27.

Bizzaro, P. (1990a) Some uses of primary trait scoring in the evaluation of student poetry writing. *Teaching English in the Two-Year College* 17, 54–21.

Bizzaro, P. (1990b) Integration and assessment: Some applications of reader-response criticism to the evaluation of student writing in a poetry writing class. In D. Daiker and M. Morenberg (eds) *The Writing Teacher as Researcher* (pp. 256–25). Portsmouth, NH: Heinemann.

Bizzaro, P. (1993) *Responding to Student Poems: Applications of Critical Theory*. Urbana: NCTE.

Bishop, W. (1990) *Released into Language*. Urbana: NCTE.

Cooper, C.R. and Odell, L. (1977) *Evaluating Writing: Describing, Measuring, Judging*. Urbana: NCTE.

Dawson, P. (2004) *Creative Writing and the New Humanities*. NY: Routledge.

Hugo, R. (1979) *Triggering Town: Lectures and Essays on Poetry and Writing*. NY: Norton.

Frost, R. (1972) The figure a poem makes. In D. Perkins (ed.) *English Romantic Writers*. New York: Harcourt.

Gerard, P. (2006) The art of creative research. *The Writer's Chronicle* 39 (2) (Nov/Dec), 50–26.

Levertov, D. (1987) Craft interview. In W. Packard (ed.) *The Poet's Craft: Interviews from the New York Quarterly*. New York: Paragon House.

Mayers, T. (2003) *(Re)Writing Craft: Composition, Creative Writing, and the Future of English Studies*. Pittsburgh: University of Pittsburgh Press.

Miller, S. (1991) *Textual Carnivals: The Politics of Composition*. Carbondale: Southern Illinois University Press.

Moxley, J.M. (ed.) (1989) *Creative Writing in America: Theory and Pedagogy*. Urbana: NCTE.

Murray, D. (1989) Unlearning to write. In J.M. Moxley (ed.) *Creative Writing in America: Theory and Pedagogy* (pp. 103–24) Urbana: NCTE.

Myer, D.G. (1996) *The Elephants Teach: Creative Writing Since 1880*. Englewood Cliffs, NJ: Prentice Hall.

Ritter, K. (2001) Professional writers/writing professionals: Revamping teacher training in creative writing PhD programs. *College English* 64 (2), 205–27.

Shelley, P. (1967) A defence of poetry. In D. Perkins (ed.) *English Romantic Writers*. New York: Harcourt.

Simic, C. (2004) Negative capability and its children. In D. Gioia, D. Mason and M. Schoerke (eds) *Twentieth Century American Poetics: Poets on the Art of Poetry*. Boston: McGraw Hill.

Smith, F. (2004) *Understanding Reading: A Psycholinguistic Analysis of Reading and Learning to Read*. Mahwah, NJ: Erlbaum.

Starkey, D. and Healy, E.K. (2007) 'A better time teaching': A dialogue about pedagogy and the Antioch-LA MFA. In K. Ritter and S. Vanderslice (eds) *Can it Really Be Taught?: Resisting Lore in Creative Writing Pedagogy* (pp. 39–25). Portsmouth, NH: Boynton/Cook.

Stewart, M. (2007) Unpublished email to author. Dec. 4.

Wordsworth, W. (1967) 'Preface' to second edition of the lyrical ballads in D. Perkins (ed.) *English Romantic Writers*. New York: Harcourt.

Wright, J. (1990) Lying in a hammock at William Duffy's farm in Pine Island, Minnesota. *Above the River: The Complete Poems and Selected Prose*. Middletown, CT: Wesleyan UP.

Chapter 3
Small Worlds: What Works in Workshops If and When They Do?

PHILIP GROSS

Case for the Prosecution

The bullying, the blandness and the babble, and the crucifying silences ... All the worst things people say about writing workshops are, or can be, true. Which of us has not sensed that stiffening in the air as the top-dog squares up to a contender ... or felt our hearts sink at the passive-aggressive slouch of the mass who rely on the keen few to make fools of themselves ... or breathed the enervating climate of the group where nothing can be criticized, leaving everyone feeling that the praise they get is not worth much?

A workshop is a very human situation.

When a polemic such as Michelene Wandor's (2008) in *The Writer Is Not Dead, Merely Somewhere Else* tears strips off the workshop, listing models that might ground its practice (apprenticeship? peer review? professional critique? House of Correction?) – when she demonstrates the failure of, or the workshop's failure to live up to, each – it is difficult to fault her logic. Then I find myself muttering, like Galileo at his inquisition (this may be a myth, but still, a telling fiction): *Eppur si muove.* And yet it moves.

Is this self-serving, this response of mine – the state of denial of a writer/educator whose twenty-year journey into academic life has been through the practice-centred, sit-them-in-a-circle, dialogue-not-lecture group? (I am starting from 'I' in this chapter, as I would invite my students to ... *on condition* they offer the reader the means for assessing their evidence. *Own your responses.* Don't hide behind a passive-voice-third-person guise of objectivity. The discipline of the workshop, as of the creative writer, is paradoxical: to be observant of, then to report, to gain an objectivity about, your subjectivity.)

My writing life has been fed by relationships – the timely writer-friend's questions, or involvement in a workshop group. Some groups were led, some 'unled', some frankly mis-led, but still ... Some lasted a weekend, some years. I know how, at best, it can be sunlight and oxygen, that stringent and attentive reciprocity. It can give shifts of perspective one could have taken years to arrive at alone.

Equally, I know the subtle blights and downright poisons: the creeping conformities, the harm done by exposing raw work at wrong moments, or by failing to gauge the state of readiness in a learner–writer's life. Also the play of favour and of faction, the brittleness of the apparently confident, the covert arrogance of the shy ... Naturally. All human life is there.

It is this blend of the best and the worst – sometimes with a hair's-breadth between – that makes workshops a rich field for experiment. (*Experiment?* There are no control groups or double-blind trials. The allusion to scientific method is a metaphor, as is the word 'workshop' itself. Another telling fiction ... This is how creative writers think.) As a means of instruction – delivering professional guidance or conceptual analysis – most workshops will seem half-baked, amateur. But if even the mistakes we make responding to each other's work are part of the material, if (as in our science metaphor) a negative finding can still add to knowledge, then the workshop is an unusually productive place to meet.

The Management of Selves

That hair's-breadth between what goes wrong and what goes right in workshops may be between delivering the same critique to a laboured-over draft as to an initial foray into raw material. This distinction, acknowledged and examined, brings to light the practical, experiential intricacies of composition. There are stages where the right creative move is to be guessing and making mistakes; wrong turnings are to be explored, because each is evidence of an appetite, an apprehension, or maybe an avoidance – whichever, it is material. At other stages the insistence on a mannerism points to ingrained habit, and Quiller-Couch's (1916) maybe-over-quoted 'Murder your darlings' applies.

In one-to-one tutorials, a teacher would or should be scanning for such sensitive distinctions – not soft-pedalling on judgment but being precise in knowing what a certain draft is being judged *as*, and what *for*. This is the sort of discrimination a writing workshop needs and has to teach – for each participant to learn to apply to him or her self, as much as to the others. The attendant risk is neither a failure nor a side effect; it is a condition of the opportunity to learn.

The guardian of that learning is the tutor – guardian, rather, of the means by which, the space *in* which, it can be learned. The tutor might be in the spotlight, as ring-master ... or might be the coach on the sideline. He or she might not (that too is a pedagogic choice) be in the room. By the end of the course, a good tutor hopes to become superfluous, as his or her students internalise the working disciplines all writers need ... just as a good parent counts it a success when a child leaves home.

Practical self-knowledge, self-*management*, is one of the things creative writing teaches, whether it figures in our learning outcomes or not. This dealing with the self is not an indulgence, and it is not 'therapy'. Like many writing teachers, I am drawn to the job partly by sheer interest in people, but what we do for our students is not about their happiness or health. (Writing-as-a-healing-art, cousin of music-, art- or drama-therapy, is an honourable discipline of its own.) In its learned-on-the-job evolution, the workshop tradition has absorbed techniques from group work, often founded in the humanistic psychologies. This may or may not be conscious; for me the word 'experiment' carries the sense used by Perls et al (1951) in Gestalt therapy; Teich (1987) applies Carl Rogers' 'active listening' to rhetoric and composition. But if anything is up for therapy, it is the writing, not the writer. The various selves we walk around in, and our writing selves (the professional ego and that less tangible thing, the *writer's voice*), are simply some of the means we have to work with, tools of the trade.

The Naming of Parts

What, though, *is* a workshop? The term can sound pretentious. I can hear my engineer friend snorting with disdain. But take the metaphor for what it was meant to convey. It alludes to practicality, to process, and to craft. It implies skills to be learned and tools to be maintained.

The term has a formative place in the history of our subject. (In the UK, courses like those run by the Arvon Foundation have informed the experience of most writing teachers as well as many students.) The workshop has been around so long we can slip into thinking (without thinking) that we know what 'a workshop' *is*. We need a dash of cold water like Michelene Wandor's now and then.

A workshop is, for a start, not a *thing*. The real thing is a group of people, brought together in a time and place. They will have some agreements – if not ground rules and guidelines, then an unspoken culture, or at least a tutor's face to scan for clues. What makes a group a 'workshop' is the conventions that shape what participants expect, what they see as up for question, what they will or will not do.

Let us not assume there is only one set of conventions, one *game*, in the serious, psycho-/socio-logical sense. Some instances ...

(a) *The Open Workshop*. No agenda, except that participants bring work-in-progress; no assumptions about audience or context, or stage of development. Each piece is critiqued as if finished work.

(b) *The Set-Agenda Workshop*. The work brought relates to input given and a task set previously; the tutor has described, and the class discussed, the technical or other challenge. They have terms and concepts ready to assess in each case how that challenge has been met.

(c) *The Writing-And-Sharing Workshop*. A stimulus or task in class leads to immediate writing, then sharing of drafts, however tentative, unformed or even not to their writer's own tastes they might be. The tutor's interest is as much in the questions raised as the work produced – though this kind of workshop may also 'surprise' new and promising work out of students hampered by their habits or their expectations of themselves.

(d) *The Ideas Workshop*. The material might not be a written draft at all but, say, a chance to pitch a set of possibilities for future writing, for development and exploration in the group. The tutor's agenda might well be to explore the different roles we play as readers, the conscious choice between them, and the skills appropriate to each. I might respond to your pitch as fellow writer (*If I was writing that piece, I would ...*); as reader (*Hmmm, I wouldn't buy that but my grandma might*); as publisher or agent (*I can see an opening in the market for that option, provided that ...*); as critic (*Look, here are the ways this project will be hampered by the limitations of the genre; here are the almost-invisible ideologies concealed in it*) ... Where there is a choice, there is potential learning.

It can come as a surprise to learner-writers to learn that *a workshop is as much a reading as a writing group*. The distinction between this reading and that of a literary–critical seminar (however much their terms might overlap ... and writers *need* to test out concepts from across that border) is that this is *reading in the service of the writing*. By their fruits ye shall know them. Any understanding that does not tend towards widening the possibilities for composition, with more productive questions and experiments, is, in common-parlance language, *academic*.

Questions, Questions

The variables above are only the start. Will work-in-progress come from volunteers or conscripts? Will the session give air-space to everyone's draft, or a few? If more than a few, will we have time to go deep enough into any? Will slots be booked or assigned in advance, giving students the experience of deadlines? And there are more.

Will work be available to read beforehand? (Between the words 'available' and 'read' can fall the shadow. What will we do about that?) Will there be reading time, with copies, in the session? Will pieces, or extracts from them, be read out loud? (If so, are we judging the performance, not words as on the published page? If not, are we missing a chance to develop a facility most writers will, professionally, need? Or is reading aloud a useful preparation for the skill of silent close reading which 'hears' the words in the head?) If read aloud, what are the different merits of hearing it read by the writer, or a first-time reader-volunteer, or by the tutor who does it as part of his or her job? What are the different dynamics unleashed (or inhibited) if a text is anonymous?

There is not one question here which does not raise deeper questions about writing and the reading process, and the interdependence of the two. On the way it points to the techniques of speaking and listening – incidentally, the most transferable skills any future employer could wish a graduate to have.

There are many groups we might assemble from these variables. What makes them all *workshops* is (in practical terms) their relatively small scale – small enough numbers to allow a sense of direct address between any member of the group and any other in a way the whole group can be party to, equally. (Leave aside, for now, the issue of the *online* workshop – whether and how the 'workshop' feel can be reproduced where our bodily presence, rich in non-verbal communications, is reduced to affectless words on a screen.)

More fundamentally, it is the belief that each and every person's contribution will be part of the learning experience for everybody else. (As a learning style, it is superbly student-centred, in a way that other disciplines find themselves urged to emulate.) This does not, naively, mean that opinions expressed are of equal value; it is the tutor's job to see that even a frankly flawed contribution is received and opened out in useful ways. Any writing tutor who opts for the workshop style in the hope it will be less demanding work than lecturing should be guided to a different job.

And for first-time participants in a workshop, a friendly caution: *Don't mistake the apparent informality of the situation for it being 'natural'. It is anything but.* Rather than see a workshop as a free-form, free-expression, even free-for-all zone, conceive it as a complex culture that demands alertness. There will be rules. The tutor might declare these bluntly or (more to my personal taste ... but the tutor's personality is one of the creative variables) explain what they are for and negotiate the group's consent.

A workshop is not ... a group of friends; a committee; a trial; an encounter group; a casual conversation; an audience; an inquisition. Whatever it *is*, it has to be aware of *what* that is, and why. The questions implicit here happen to be pertinent to any reading process, performance, or response. They point directly at the reasons, and the ways, we write.

Putting Words in the Mouth of the Workshop

If experiment and self-examination are the heart of the workshop, then we need our heads: we have to think. As creative writing stakes a place in universities, as a discipline among disciplines, we are volunteering not simply to write, and to make writing happen, but to reach understandings, to have concepts, of how this is done. (The fact that literary and cultural studies already claim to have the tools to account for literary texts is one of the interesting complications of our subject's birth. Our locus is the writing, not the written. Our identity hinges on a subtle change of tense.) For writers at university even more than any working writer, the whole process is to be handled with knowledge, to *become* knowledge ... even when that knowledge consists of consciously manipulating certain 'known unknowns'.

Some writers, some good writing educators, will feel wary here. Like myself, many teachers of creative writing come to the job through their practice as working writers – sometimes in parallel with, sometimes apart from, other academic work. Most writers report, in a way that need be neither precious nor 'Romantic', that the experience of composition is complex, lived-before-conceptualized, sometimes simply more 'sudden' – in the sense of rapid intuitive thinking, as investigated by Magee (2008) – in its operations than those of logical, abstracted thought. A vital part of the writing occurs, to borrow from Wandor's title, *somewhere else* from much of academic life.

Because this experience is formative, partly sensual and full of emotional tone – in plain terms, it is where we feel most alive – writers can resist conceptualizing it, because concepts simplify, and it is the complexity of the experience that gives it life. Our allegiance to the down-to-earth term 'workshop' may code that resistance. If the arguments in this chapter are even partly true, then the workshop group is where we will see that (hopefully creative) tension played out. We may see just if and when the apparent clarity of concepts, of making our process explicit, starts to distort or stultify the only-partly-conscious fuzzy-logic which is (at a certain stage, not every stage, of composition) one of our working tools.

Because the workshop process is so closely geared into that of composition, with some of the same immediate, rapid-response quality, we might fear that too much self-awareness could become self-consciousness, an inhibition. But the workshop is communication between people; at the very least, misunderstandings are reduced by the ability to give names to the experience. A few early 'clumsinesses' in a workshop are enough to show the need for a practical-critical *lingua franca*. Skilled writing tutors have always addressed this need, sometimes unconsciously, by modeling the use of terms and concepts. Set books, reference sources and maybe an organically-growing glossary of this language built up through the years are ways of making the enrichment and refinement process visible.

The search for appropriate language makes us stand back from our process – take it less personally (whilst giving us the means to acknowledge the role of the personal in that response). Considering the interpersonal business of the workshop leads to making its culture visible, accountable – in other words, an *etiquette.*

A Toolkit

To develop these thoughts into practical detail, then: a starter-kit of dicta for the student writer coming to the workshop process ...

- What is being workshopped' is not *you*, the writer, but the writing.
- Any poem, prose piece or drama has a hidden life of possibilities not currently visible in this draft on the page.
- For you, the writer, to find my criticisms useful, it is up to me, the reader, to demonstrate to you that I 'get' what this piece is doing or trying to do. There is no use in criticizing anything for not being what it never meant to be.
- Therefore, I must *acknowledge* it, to your satisfaction. Point to what is working, before criticizing what is not.
- Point specifically. Give precise examples, for positive points as well as negative.
- Learning writers often need to be told (specifically) what they are doing right. They often do not know.

- At some stages, practise Rogers' (1961) 'active listening': each person has to restate what someone has said to them, to his or her satisfaction, before responding.
- 'Writer' and 'reader' are roles that everybody in a workshop plays.
- The workshop is a test for the reader much more than it is for the piece being read. Everybody is answerable for the quality of his or her response.
- That quality is not measured in its 'rightness' but in its ability to show objectively what one's felt-and-thought reactions are, and to what, and where, and when.
- The workshop is not about judgment but about cause-and-effect: If you do *this*, *these* are the responses (right or wrong) that it elicits. If you do it differently, then *these* ...
- And with this knowledge, in the end, the author (not the workshop) has to choose.

In a university context, of course, work will be assessed. A responsible teacher in a class will not conceal the principles that she will use in marking. The student may well use, or try to use, that as a major factor in his final choice. This is not very different from the power relations in the world of publishing. And, in a course where reflectiveness is given credit, this too is available to be discussed.

No one is born equipped to make good use of workshops. Most undergraduate students come without previous experience. A realistic goal for a three-year course, following the common pattern of instruction leading towards self-reliance, is for students to learn the process and some trust in year one; to experiment with the workshop under close guidance in year two; to arrive in their third year confident and skilled enough for workshopping of works-in-progress to have become the main tool; and to graduate with those skills internalized to reproduce in new groups elsewhere and/or to apply individually to their own work. We learn to be observant readers of our own writing by collating the twin experiments of watching ourselves reading others' work, and others reading our own.

That learning can come in some very deliberate ways – for instance, a tutor might face a group with writing guaranteed not to be any of theirs. In other words, fair game. First, she tests out the range of responses that come 'naturally', then takes the experiment further, e.g. asking some participants to play the 'hard cop', some the 'soft' ... then to swap places. When the best and the worst have been said, she reveals that the piece *was* written by somebody present. After the shock and protest, she says: No,

I didn't lie; the piece is by me, the tutor. Then, objectively, and without putting anyone in the wrong (they were, after all, playing roles she gave them) she says which of the comments she as a writer found most useful, and precisely how and why.

In Praise of Impurity

Deliberate procedures can expand the *lingua franca* of a group. Change and experiment keep that language open for enquiry, as well as resisting the build-up of habit and assumptions in a group. So at any given time 'workshop' might mean:

(a) The whole group, free-for-all, saying whatever comes, in any order.
(b) The whole group, giving feedback with a little structure: naming positives first, then moving on to criticisms, questions and what-if suggestions.
(c) The whole group, but with a pause for everyone to write notes of what they would say *if* they spoke first. (This way you don't lose your own first reaction if somebody else speaks first and 'sets the agenda' in a different way.) In one version of this, you hand the writer of the piece your first-thought comments at the end.
(d) Hard-cop/soft cop: in the whole group, some people are assigned to look out for the positive points in the work, others for the challenges and questions. (This way, you can't take it personally.) Now and then, we swap roles.
(e) Small groups, workshopping each other's work – usually after listening to one piece being workshopped in the whole group, with the tutor suggesting helpful approaches. At the end, the small groups report back to everyone else.
(f) Goldfish bowl: a small group of volunteers give the writer feedback, with the others watching quietly, thinking what *they* would say if it was them (and maybe, offering advice); from time to time, the 'interviewing panel' changes, until everyone has had a go.
(g) Masterclass: the tutor gives a few writers' work intensive feedback. Then the listeners can contribute questions and reflections of their own. Equally important is that they discuss what they've just heard. The tutor's contribution is there to be tested, in terms of how far it addresses the writer's felt needs, and how it connects with those of others in the group.

Call this a *smorgasbord* if you will. It is pragmatic, eclectic and proud of the fact. It is only a start. Some of these strategies came into my own teaching as expedients, trying to reproduce what matters in the workshop for groups of larger than the ideal (between 12 and 20) workshop size. They turned out to be valuable whatever numbers we had in the room. In the last 10 years, widening opportunity had drawn increasing numbers of less academically confident students into UK universities. Methods like these, and the workshop in general, address the need to make participation active, engaging, almost unavoidable.

All this is fallible. We could search for principles and procedures to prevent the failings of the workshop. That search would be the wrong search. For teacher and learner alike, the workshop setting involves skill. Skill develops by practice, by trial (and error), by reflection and repeated new trials over time.

A workshop is a small world, which reflects and refracts worlds outside. It is impure, a hybrid of several models, not quite faithful to any one. It is a species of play, in the sense that all creative art is – and that Opie (2007) contends that research can be positively seen as – *play*. It continues the developmental business begun in childhood where wide possibilities (some of them risky or absurd) get tested with thought and imagination, within boundaries.

A workshop is never the whole world. Most creative writing students will be studying other subjects, most commonly literary studies, alongside. Most creative writing courses use the workshop as a strand in a mixture of modes: direct instruction, set reading, seminar discussion, practical assignments, online interaction, directed research, presentation, pair or small group work of many kinds. The fact that the workshop holds a special, iconic, place among these methods is partly historical, partly an acknowledgment that it embodies something distinctive, something not and maybe not-to-be formulated, about what creative writing is. Jogged out of complacency by bracing attacks like Wandor's, and by our continuing questions, the workshop is there for the learning. It demands that we, the teacher and the student, do that work together. And so ... and yet ... humanly, it moves.

References

Magee, P. (2008) Suddenness: on rapid knowledge. *New Writing: The International Journal for the Practice and Theory of Creative Writing* 5 (3), 179–296.

Opie, G (2007) Play: the root of all research. *Text*. Vol. 11 No. 2 October <www.textjournal.com.au/oct07/opie.htm> [17.04.09].

Perls, F., Hefferline, R., Goodman, P. (1951) *Gestalt Therapy: Excitement and Growth in the Human Personality*. New York: Dell.

Quiller-Couch, Sir A. (1916) *On the Art of Writing: Lectures Delivered in the University of Cambridge,1913–1914*. Cambridge: University Press, Bartleby.com, 2000 <www. bartleby.com/190/> [17.04.09].

Rogers, C.R. (1961) *On Becoming a Person*. Boston: Houghton Mifflin.

Teich, N. (1987) Rogerian problem-solving and the rhetoric of argumentation. *Journal of Advanced Composition* 7 (1/2) <www.jacweb.org/Archived–volumes/Text–articles/V7–Teich.htm> [17.04.09].

Wandor, M. (2008) *The Author is Not Dead, Merely Somewhere Else: Creative Writing Reconceived*. Basingstoke and New York: Palgrave Macmillan.

Chapter 4
Teaching as a Creative Act: Why the Workshop Works in Creative Writing

ANNA LEAHY

Introduction: The Primacy of the Workshop

The Association of Writers and Writing Programs (AWP), which boasts hundreds of academic program members and thousands of individual members attending the annual conference, reports that 'surveys conducted periodically since 1978 indicate that most teachers of writing find they are most effective in the workshop format' (*The Director's Handbook*, 2008: 5). I now count myself enthusiastically among these teachers, in large part because I have come to understand the workshop as an overarching pedagogical outlook and learning environment. While it can be all too easy to think of the workshop as the natural academic mode for creative writing, only with investigation and awareness have I become truly effective in this pedagogical approach. Only now, having taught for many years and having begun to document creative writing pedagogy, do I see how successful the workshop is and can be for decades to come. By investigating and discussing our primary pedagogy, as the authors of this collection and of other recent pedagogical scholarship are doing, we can understand its value and cultivate it.

Eve Shelnutt, in *The Writing Room* (1989: 317), recognizes the effects of this common teaching purpose and pedagogical approach when she discusses judging an undergraduate poetry contest:

> 'Who taught these students?' came to mind because the poems demonstrated that the young writers had been guided to consider carefully a range of formal devices that would help them lift ordinary experience out of the banality and into whole, unique poems that spoke of their authors' particular respect and appreciation for daily occurrences that most of us would fail to linger over, much less transform into poems.

uniformity of product?

> It was gratifying for me as a teacher of writing to observe so clearly that far across the country in another university professional writers and student writers were engaged in a process similar to that my own students and I pursue. (p. 317)

I share Shelnutt's sense that we are doing similar and highly effective things across workshop-based creative writing courses and programs in the United States. While our creative work – the poems, stories, essays, and so on that we publish – defines creative writing as the equivalent of a scholarly field within the larger academy, the workshop – our dominant pedagogical approach – defines us as an academic field in relation to our students and student learning. Though not every creative writing student will go on to publish something, the work our students do – both the process and the product – is evidence of the workshop's effectiveness.

The criticism of workshop pedagogy is familiar, however, as Madison Smartt Bell (1997: 4) notes at the beginning of *Narrative Mind*: 'To say that a book smacks of the creative writing workshop has become a sort of reviewer's cliché, a shorthand expression for the idea that the work in question is trite, hackneyed, stale, spiritlessly mechanical, mediocre, myopically self-involved, and so on and so on.' These criticisms, which Bell goes on to discuss with greater complexity, reveal the assumptions that the classroom is an early stand-in for the editorial process, that the workshop punishes risk-taking or novelty, that true art must stem from entirely individual effort, and that mentorship, a community of peers, and even the literary tradition easily overwhelm the individual imagination. In practice, though pedagogical missteps and teaching failures certainly occur in any field or individual teaching career, most of us – creative writing professors and students alike – likely find the opposite: workshops foster creativity.

Creative writing has successfully established itself in the academy without sacrificing creativity and aesthetic values, in large part because of the workshop. In addition, our courses contribute to students' learning. I'd like to think the workshop has strengthened contemporary literature as well, though this is beside the main points of this essay. Here, I explore how the profession and students benefit from workshop pedagogy and how the workshop's conventions form an adaptable model for the future. While there are other ways to judge the effectiveness of creative writing pedagogy, including looking at how it has influenced contemporary literature and aesthetics, it remains important to analyze it as part of an academic field. From this perspective, the workshop is good for the profession, and it's good for student learning.

Why It's Good for the Profession: The Workshop as Signature Pedagogy

Those academic fields we consider professions – law, engineering, medicine – have what Lee S. Shulman (2005: 54), president of the Carnegie Foundation, calls 'signature pedagogies'. Creative writing, if considered a profession, is no exception, and its signature pedagogy is the workshop. These signature pedagogies 'define how [a profession's] knowledge is analyzed, criticized, accepted, or discarded' (p. 54) so that its structures are recognizable. Using Shulman's definition, the surface structure of creative writing is the workshop itself, usually that ongoing discussion of student work with revision in mind. The deep structure of the workshop, however, is the theories and practices that are being taught and learned through the workshop experience. So, while workshopping may appear, to outsiders or even participants, to be freely flowing discussion, it is a methodology that allows students to learn and deeply understand the theories behind and practices of the writing process. Finally, the implicit structure of this signature pedagogy involves students' growing understanding of the field's expectations for behavior as well as for written work; student writers come to understand their roles in relation to the product and the process of creative writing. As Wallace Stegner (2002: 59) puts it, 'one function of a writing class is to lift students out of classroom amateurism and bring them into contact with professional aims and attitudes.' In these ways, the workshop can be considered our profession's signature pedagogy.

A signature pedagogy, then, positions teachers as builders of an ethical professional community and as mentors who guide students to discover for themselves through problem-solving. In doing so, a signature pedagogy, such as the creative writing workshop, addresses some of the most difficult aspects of teaching. The 'emphasis on students' active participation reduces the most significant impediments to learning in higher education: passivity, invisibility, anonymity, and lack of accountability' (Shulman, 2005: 57). Also, '[t]hese pedagogies create atmospheres of risk taking and foreboding, as well as occasions for exhilaration and excitement' (Shulman, 2005: 57), which seem to be essential for sustaining creative endeavors. While I reward students for what might be considered content acquisition or less active learning, especially in my introductory courses, students in a workshop become enmeshed in the risky and exhilarating creative writing process, too. We are all actively *in* the workshop together. So, one of the great benefits of a signature pedagogy is that 'once they are learned and internalized, we don't have to think about them; we can think with them' (Shulman, 2005: 56). Perhaps, this explains why the field has resisted defining, analyzing, or critiquing the workshop very explicitly. While I have long advocated more aware and informed pedagogical choices in creative writing and while Shulman recognizes the dangers in not questioning the limitations of a given signature pedagogy, that the workshop becomes deeply internalized, likely allows us – both as individual teachers and as an academic field – to think very effectively *with* it.

Because creative writing is a relative newcomer to the academy and because the question of whether creative writing can be taught lingers, a signature pedagogy makes creative writing less an outsider in the academy than it might otherwise be, without compromising creativity and the individual author. As Cary Nelson and Stephen Watt (1999: 281) discuss in their definition of *teaching*, 'there is an astonishing level of collective wisdom and knowledge' in any classroom. The workshop – not merely as a classroom activity but as a signature pedagogy – allows this collective wisdom to flourish. So, as with any academic course, the syllabus, textbooks, assignments, and other elements establish common goals in skill development and content acquisition for all students in a creative writing course. However, in writing poems and prose and discussing each other's work with revision in mind, collective wisdom emerges. Individual members of the workshop contribute to the collective wisdom and also benefit from it, ultimately distinguishing their individual written pieces in relation to the common conversation. Far from homogeneity, the workshop environment teaches students to think of themselves as writers in relation to the literary tradition, readers, and other writers and to develop skills that allow them to create distinctive work in those contexts. To be a teacher in the workshop is an exciting, rewarding proposition for fostering collective wisdom as well as nurturing individual efforts.

In practical terms, talking about the workshop as our signature pedagogy is an argument for much-needed sabbaticals and small classes. A lecture, in the most traditional sense, shows students how an individual mind works its way through material (Nelson & Watt, 1999: 282), but the lecture functions in much the same way whether there are 15 or 500 listeners. The workshop, on the other hand, depends on the mentorship of a practicing writer, on a class size that allows for all students' work to be discussed regularly, and on the time necessary for complex interaction with individual students. In addition, aligning creative writing with law or engineering in its pedagogical approach elucidates the collapse or at least entanglement between theory and practice for creative writers. What might be considered creative writing theory – what Tim Mayers (2005: 33) calls 'craft criticism' – already exists in a variety of texts, such as Stegner's (2002) *On Teaching and Writing Fiction*, but is inextricably linked with practice; *doing* is central.

If we think of creative writing as a profession and the workshop as a signature pedagogy, creative writing professors are able to contribute to and benefit from the academy that supports so many of us. In addition, defining our field as a profession with a primary or foundational pedagogy that collapses theory and practice establishes that a body of theory exists in our craft criticism and a body of practice exists in the poetry, prose, and drama we produce. In all of these ways, the workshop functions positively for our field and for individual teachers.

Why It's Good for Students: Creativity, Community, and Self

That the workshop is good for students is supported by cognitive science as well as the craft criticism of writers themselves. While the question '*can creative writing be taught?*' still lingers, the field has largely moved beyond that question and accepts that creative writing can be learned in an environment that values creativity, establishes a community, and respects the individual. Like whether creative writing can be taught, the question of talent also lingers but is no longer central. Neurologist Alice Flaherty (2004: 52), in a book about writing and the brain, asserts: 'The consensus [. . .] seems to be that drive is surprisingly more important than talent in producing creative work.' The role of internal motivation such as 'curiosity and enjoyment' and a sense of purpose garner the attention that talent used to claim (Flaherty, 2004: 55–27). The workshop allows for talent but decenters passé questions through its pedagogical structures. The workshop shows students how to be curious as writers and how diligence and effort – practice, bum in the seat, revision – matter more than talent.

It should come as no surprise, then, that, while the act of writing requires isolation and individual effort, community is often especially important for creative production. In *The Creating Brain*, Nancy Andreasen (2005: 127–231), who holds both a PhD in literature as well as an MD, asserts that 'five circumstances must be present to produce a cultural environment that nurtures creativity': intellectual freedom and novelty, other creative people, a fair but competitive atmosphere, mentors and supporters, and economic prosperity. While the workshop cannot ensure general economic prosperity (though the academy provides economic stability for many writers), it does offer other crucial environmental conditions that foster creativity: the academy is generally a place of intellectual freedom in relation to the culture at large, creative writing courses reward novelty and innovation, the workshop surrounds the individual writer with other creative people who value creative work, these other writers offer both support and competition, and the professor serves as a mentor. Rather than stifling creativity, 'a model of the comprehensive stylist will be presented to everyone in the room' (Nelson & Watt, 1999: 282) when stories or poems are discussed among creative people who value innovation and push each other under the guidance of a nurturing expert. In other words, the workshop *community* cultivates *individual* creative work and achievement.

A recent article in *Scientific American Mind* also suggests long-term benefits of the sort of collaborative learning that workshops employ, even though individual students author their own pieces. The article 'The Science of Team Success' (2007) asserts three ways to build better teams, each of which the workshop encourages and which prepares students for various future work (they will not all become published writers) by building skills as well as knowledge. First, a group of people who can contribute to 'the right mix of knowledge, skills, tools and other resources' (Kozowlski and Ilgen, 2007: 56) is important. While many workshops cannot control group selection through an instructor-permission requirement, such aspects as prerequisites and self-selection by students often ensure a good mix of perspectives and motivations. The course's organization and content, including required reading, can further work toward and be adapted to increase the chance for the right mix of knowledge, skills, and resources. Second, 'face-to-face meetings, social interaction among members and a leader who establishes a good relationship with every worker help a team make the best use of its expertise and create a cohesive mission' (Kozowlski & Ilgen, 2007: 56). Certainly, the workshop with an informed, engaged teacher orchestrates this social interaction among individuals with varying expertise working toward cohesive goals. Last, elements 'such as setting goals, adapting to change, resolving conflict and providing feedback allow teams to learn from each challenge and continually improve their performance' (Kozowlski & Ilgen, 2007: 56). So, it's crucial for the creative writing teacher to set guidelines, often in the form of a syllabus, which most academic institutions require, and perhaps with portfolio requirements. In addition, the teacher must be ready to adapt, able to guide her students through unexpected circumstances, including conflict or missteps, while keeping the course stable and moving forward; this is no easy task and reasons we should document what we do. The workshop, finally, embodies the kind of feedback that fosters challenge and improvement as well.

The act of workshopping – the sharing of written work, the offering of comments, and the receiving of critique – can be extraordinarily difficult for students. As my workshop-based courses have become more effective, I have realized that it is just as important for my students to be proud of their workshopping skills as they are of the revised writing they include in their portfolios. At its best, the workshop, therefore, fosters collective wisdom, or that 'ability to access and use this distributed expertise efficiently' (Kozowlski & Ilgen, 2007: 58), so that the community becomes more than the sum of its parts. To see community – as well as quality poetry and prose – as a central element and goal, as a means and an end of the workshop, benefits students, whether or not they continue to pursue creative writing in years to come. Students in a well-conceived workshop – future employees, entrepreneurs, and writers – can revel in shared success as well as individual accomplishment.

Concepts and guiding principles of teamwork are also important in creative writing because the so-called self is treated, per writer–teachers like John Gardner (1983) in *The Art of Fiction*, as an inevitable side effect or as a factor always already involved. As I previously explored in 'Creativity, Caring, and The Easy "A"' (2007), the role of self-esteem is unclear and, perhaps, contradictory; I argue there, 'Focusing on the task, on the process and the product, rather than on the self, is a better alternative for becoming more successful teachers and students' (p. 62). J. Gardner states his view even more bluntly, 'None of these writers (Daniel Defoe, et al), ancient or modern, sat down to write "to express himself." They sat down to write this kind of story or that, or to mix this form with that form, producing some new effect' (p. 21). Likewise, Stegner asserts, 'The internal part is the student's own business. Only he or she knows what is intended; only he or she can perform or realize it. A teacher should understand that intention, but not try to control it' (p. 52). As David Citino (2002: 203) puts it in 'Tell Me How it Was in the Old Days', 'There is a way of life that a poet can pursue in which he or she looks at the world as opportunity. "What do I have to write about?" the poet asks. "My self. And therefore, everything," should be the only acceptable answer.' Self is not a goal but a means, perhaps a method, an instrument, or a path. While the self is not absent from the creative writing classroom, the task of writing is the focus of the workshop.

The workshop is good for students, then, because it not only guides them in the production of good written work, but also because it fosters creativity and builds skills they can employ beyond the creative writing classroom and the academy. Though I cannot be sure, student comments lead me to think that, by the end of the academic term, my students place a bit less emphasis on the grade itself and are very much focused on their own writing, what they can accomplish by the end of and beyond the course, and how they might encourage their peers' success as well. Students' attention, in the workshop environment, moves toward the experience. The workshop, then, provides an environment in which students learn, working both toward common learning outcomes and individual goals.

Workshop Conventions and the Adaptability of the Workshop

Importantly, when I refer to *the workshop*, I do not mean that it is a cookie-cutter or monolithic approach. My first creative writing professor at Knox College, Robert Hellenga, told us to go write stories; as a first-year not-yet-declared major, I sometimes lacked the skills and knowledge that my classmates had, but I grappled with character and plot right along with them. My first poetry-writing professor, Robin Behn, provided assignments for our workshop poems and, in individual conferences with me, focused on the importance of specificity. Robin Metz brought a jug of wine to weekly marathon discussions in which stories were vigorously re-envisioned together in various ways. At Iowa State University, Jane Smiley required three versions of three stories each semester, and Mary Swander required book reviews and self-evaluation. At the University of Maryland, Stanley Plumly asked students to read John Keats and Wallace Stevens and to write sequences of poems; Michael Collier brought in essays by Robert Frost and Louise Glück to shape discussions; Phillis Levin had students read work by poets outside the United States. Each workshop I took as a student was different, influenced by the published stories or poems and by the craft criticism we read or didn't read, the exercises or lack of exercises we were given, the long-term and current obsessions of the workshop leader, and the teaching persona of that professor. Moreover, even if every workshop had incorporated the same textbook, the same set of exercises, and the same emphases on, say, plot or image, each workshop experience would have been different because the students bring to the classroom their own original texts for discussion and come to the discussion at various stages and with various new and long-standing questions and obstacles.

Because of this built-in variety, *the workshop* is a genre of pedagogy, just as the Western is a genre of film. We recognize a television series like *Firefly* as a Western even though it is set in a futuristic *verse* because we are familiar with rebel characters with hearts of gold grappling with the frontier where civilization meets wilderness; even at the edge of the universe we recognize a critical mass of conventions like the guns, the saloon and the whorehouse, the cattle, the contraband, and even the spaceship as the equivalent of the trusty steed. Workshop pedagogy, too, is shaped by a set of conventions – not a checklist or rubric – that allows for the building of common knowledge and experience while encouraging original iterations. As Robert Pinsky (1999: 7) says of poetry in the introduction to *The Sounds of Poetry* (1999), there are no rules, only principles. Just as the poet composes within or against a tradition and employs a variety of principles in a variety of combinations, the creative writing professor employs workshop conventions, always adapting the pedagogy to form a distinct iteration. Workshop pedagogy positions teaching as a creative act. From the examinations of how the workshop benefits the profession and students emerge a short list of conventions that guide creative writing workshops.

Any signature pedagogy, for instance, involves a teacher who practices in the field. AWP asserts, 'the writing teacher will be effective as a teacher only insofar as he or she is active and engaged as a writer' (*The Director's Handbook*, 2008). With pressing demands from students, colleagues, and the institution, a professor's own creative writing may be difficult, but essential, to manage. As Audrey Petty (2005: 84) writes near the end of 'Who's the Teacher?', 'What is more difficult than honing my syllabus, conferencing with students, or creating dialogue during workshop is going to my desk regularly and working on a piece of my own. I now believe that this role is crucial to my effectiveness as [a] teacher.' Looking at the importance of the writer–teacher from the other side, Bin Ramke (2006), in a tribute to Stanley Plumly at the 2006 AWP Conference, credited Plumly's mentorship and teaching – or, rather, mentorship as part of teaching – to changing Ramke's brain. The teacher is crucial to the workshop; writing is crucial for the writer–teacher. The workshop, then, is not writing without a teacher, nor without a tradition. The workshop teacher orchestrates the learning environment, models the writer as practitioner, and mentors students individually as well as collectively.

Writerly reading is another convention of the workshop. AWP advocates that courses include published texts that offer students models, and Francine Prose (2006) devotes a whole book to *Reading Like a Writer*. Citino, too, makes a strong point about reading literature as akin to mentoring: 'When we need advice, if we're smart we go to someone with more experience than we have [...]' (2002: 174). The literary tradition, as well as the workshop instructor, is the site of this experience that the emerging writer seeks. In the introductory course I teach, I delay the sharing of student work until students have begun to learn together to read as writers and to use common vocabulary to talk about writing concepts. In addition, I require written responses, first to a published text and then to a student text, so that students receive my feedback on their writerly reading abilities as well as feedback – my own and that of peers – on their creative work. In this way, students become not just stronger writers themselves by reading but also stronger participants in discussions. Also, students, especially those who fear they lack talent, appreciate this more overtly academic responsibility of becoming a writer. The workshop, as a signature pedagogy, depends upon the teacher as expert and guide and upon the literary tradition, including contemporary writing, to steep students in the field's customs and reveal possibilities. Writerly reading, instead of imposing limits on students, opens them to ideas and literary devices they might not otherwise have considered or understood.

In addition, if there is an essential convention for the workshop, the sharing and discussion of student work is likely to be that convention. The article on teamwork in *Scientific American Mind* indicates that face-to-face discussion is important for effective teams (Kozowlski & Ilgen, 2007: 56). While acknowledging that the teacher's role is important, Stegner claims, 'the best teaching that goes on in a college writing class is done by members of the class, upon one another' (2002: 35). Though discussion by writers of each other's writing is probably the most central convention, discussion can be orchestrated in various ways. Discussion, for instance, might begin with pointing out what's working in the piece under scrutiny, or the teacher might pose questions that require students to apply concepts from craft criticism reading to the student work at hand. Students can be asked to prepare for discussion with marginal comments directly on the work to be discussed or with a typed response that addresses particular concepts on which students are expected to work during the course, or the work might be read aloud by the author on the spot for spontaneous oral comments. The author might remain silent, so that the temptation to explain or defend is diffused and does not interrupt responses to the written work as it stands, or the author might be encouraged to provide guiding questions before discussion begins or speak at the conclusion of a session. Even a basic convention like discussion, then, is not a cookie-cutter and, instead, is in flux from classroom to classroom, perhaps from one class meeting to the next.

Discussion is intertwined with another workshop convention: revision. Numerous scholars indicate that revision is crucial to creativity, an argument that not only buttresses workshop pedagogy but also supports a portfolio component. Howard Gardner's (1993: 33–34) study of creative people represents that view: creators often revise their work over extended time. Specifically, he claims, for creative leaps, 'a seemingly local solution needs to be abandoned in favor of a far more extensive reorientation or reconceptualization.' Revision is indeed a common part of the creative process and, in the case of the workshop, encourages the divergent thinking and experimentation necessary for innovation. We encourage divergent thinking – making new connections and finding new paths to solving problems – whenever we incorporate exercises, experimentation, and revision into our courses. Flaherty summarizes the view of cognitive scientists that divergent and convergent thinking alternate in five stages: defining the problem, learning as much as possible, incubating when an impasse is reached, discovering an idea that moves the process forward, and testing the ideas (2004: 62). Rethinking and seeing one's work from new perspectives is essential. Robert Frost (1972: 353) articulated this understanding in different terms: 'And then to play. Play's the thing. All virtue in "as if"'.

Revision as re-envisioning and play can be especially challenging for students. The portfolio and its deferred grading work to force experimentation that students can learn to appreciate, and discussion that moves the author beyond her original intentions or habits, supports that learning and appreciation. Wendy Bishop (2005: 110), in her essay 'Contracts, Radical Revision, Portfolios, and the Risks of Writing' foregrounds revision in various ways, with the portfolio an essential feature:

> I teach revision by offering a course schedule that *demands* revision, by offering revision instruction and opportunities; by requiring an experimental, radical revision assignment; by orchestrating community-response sessions that encourage revision; by nurturing a class attitude that revision is worthwhile; and by insisting on class publishing that illuminates the benefits of revision.

Time and the interpretations and suggestions of others allow varied perspectives to emerge in the author's own mind. Flaherty reminds us, 'Often the editing talent is not the writer's own. An outside eye and hand is usually essential [...]' (2004: 54). In addition, the portfolio permits 'the brain [to continue] to work on a problem once it has been supplied with the raw materials. [...] A little relaxation and distance changes the mind's perspective on the problem – without us being aware of it. This change of perspective allows for alternative insights and creates the preconditions for a fresh, and perhaps more creative, approach' (Kraft, 2005: 23). Flaherty agrees: 'a healthy person solving a creative problem may need to step back from the problem, by taking a shower or a vacation, in order to solve it' (2004: 72). Because revision is part of the writing process and because it encourages the divergent thinking necessary for creative leaps, the portfolio is one way the student can achieve some separation from the draft, find time to play with the work, and be rewarded for skills and learning in addition to being rewarded for the quality of the written work itself.

The foundational conventions of creative writing pedagogy, then, include a teacher who is a practicing creative writer, writerly reading, a writing community that engages in discussion of its creative work, and revision, often embedded in the portfolio and its deferred grading. Not all of these aspects must be equally emphasized or even present in each iteration of a workshop, and numerous additional conventions could surely be added to this basic list.

Such conventions are not rules, but are, rather, principles by which the creative workshop functions. Can a workshop exist without employing the portfolio? Yes. Can a workshop be founded on reading sonnets of centuries past instead of contemporary poetry? Yes. Can lecture, student presentations, and other activities be incorporated into a workshop? Surely. And there are various ways that even those conventions I have included can be realized. Conventions can be mixed and matched, all the while remaining part of the workshop model. Hence, instead of beginning this essay with conventions, I drew from the examination of how the workshop defines creative writing as a profession and of how the workshop fosters student learning. As long as a given iteration is formed with attention to ways it benefits the profession and benefits the students, our primary pedagogy can continue not only to function well as workshop pedagogy but also to grow.

Conclusion

When I began teaching creative writing, I had experience as a student and as a composition teacher from which to derive my pedagogical approach. I had learned a great deal from the vigorous and varied workshops in which I was a student; I knew, through experience, that the workshop can beautifully balance guidance and innovation. I also understood the responsibilities of teaching, from writing a clear syllabus to grading final work. Embarking on my professorial career as a creative writing professor, I felt well practiced in what I would need to do. So, a dozen or so years ago, without much documentation available about how the creative writing workshop functions, I thought the successful workshop would just naturally blossom in my classroom.

Workshop pedagogy is deceptively simple once you have practiced it for awhile as a student, but it's actually rather complicated. If the creative writing teacher defines the workshop as a classroom activity – as a discreet task, like peer editing in composition courses – one has less than an overarching pedagogical ethos and cannot take advantage of the workshop's power to encourage great strides in students over and beyond an academic term. In fact, AWP's *The Director's Handbook* includes *'Peer Review or Workshops'* as one of 12 instructional methods recommended for undergraduate programs (2008: 19). When I look back on my first few years of orchestrating a workshop classroom, I can see that I didn't blend seamlessly the understanding I had of it as a student and the approaches I had to teacherly tasks. My students learned even then; I taught well enough. In those first few years, though, I was sometimes barely keeping ahead of students, and also scrambling to figure out how what we did one week in class prepared us for the next week; the class was making good enough progress, but didn't have momentum. I struggled with simple questions that had nothing and everything to do with the workshop environment: *how best to hold students accountable for turning in work on time, how to reward both experimentation and improvement, how to make sure all students offer comments, how to grade when some creative writers throw up their hands, how to circumvent classroom cliques, how to work with the autistic student who doesn't comprehend metaphor or with the mentally ill student.* Especially with new responsibilities like advising and meetings of all sorts, I couldn't think holistically about the workshop right away – and I didn't run across many books or colleagues who suggested how I might do that.

When I recognized the workshop as a signature pedagogy and as a pedagogical genre, possibilities bloomed, and questions were answered. With that recognition comes responsibility to become adept at acknowledging and employing the workshop's conventions and options. That's no easy task, in part because, like the poetry or fiction writing we do, we must learn, at least in part, from practice, and workshop teaching is never mastered once and for all. Occasionally, like the gift poem that unfolds on the page with little effort, a workshop flourishes with little overt exertion. Like that gift poem, though, it is likely that the effortless workshop is a happy result of the teacher's thoughtful practice aligning with the right mix of students and cannot be depended on the next time around. Sure, it gets easier to teach well, and each of us finds particular conventions or tasks that work especially well for us. In fact, thinking of the workshop holistically helps me manage niggling questions and unexpected circumstances with relative ease, reason, and consistency.

When the parts and the whole work together – when one really understands how a pedagogical genre offers both stability and flexibility – everything falls into place, and even the unexpected, seemingly out-of-place finds a spot among the opportunities of a comprehensive approach. The creative writing workshop is a principled, focused, inclusive methodology for teaching creative writing that is finally being documented in ways that leave a useful, healthy legacy for future writer-teachers. The workshop keeps us engaged in teaching in ways similar to writing itself. Employing workshop pedagogy in creative writing courses positions teaching as a creative act, with all the risks and exhilaration upon which we can thrive and grow.

References

Andreasen, N. (2005) *The Creating Brain: The Neuroscience of Genius.* New York: Dana Press.

Bell, M.S. (1997) *Narrative Design: Working with Imagination, Craft, and Form.* New York: W.W. Norton.

Bishop, W. (2005) Contracts, radical revision, portfolios, and the risks of writing. In A. Leahy (ed.) *Power and Identity in the Creative Writing Classroom: The Authority Project* (pp. 109–220). Clevedon: Multilingual Matters.

Citino, D. (2002) Tell me how it was in the old days: In search of the poet. *The Eye of the Poet: Six Views of the Art and Craft of Poetry.* New York: Oxford UP.

The Directors' Handbook. (2008) Association of Writers and Writing Programs. 24 February <http://www.awpwriter.org/membership/documents.htm>.

Flaherty, A. (2004) *The Midnight Disease: The Drive to Write, Writer's Block, and the Creative Brain.* New York: Houghton Mifflin.

Frost, R. (1972) Introduction to Robinson's *King Jasper. Poetry & Prose.* New York: Holt, Rinehart and Winston.

Gardner, H. (1993) *Creating Minds: An Anatomy of Creativity Seen Through the Lives of Freud, Einstein, Picasso, Stravinsky, Eliot, Graham, and Gandhi.* New York: HarperCollins.

Gardner, J. (1983) *The Art of Fiction: Notes on Craft for Young Writers.* New York: Vintage, 1991.

Kozlowski, S.W.J. and Ilgen, D.R. (2007) The science of team success. *Scientific American Mind* (June/July): 54–21.

Kraft, Ulrich. (2005) Unleashing creativity. *Scientific American Mind* 16 (1), 16–23.

Leahy, A. (2007) Creativity, caring, and the easy 'A': Rethinking the role of self-esteem in creative writing pedagogy. In K. Ritter and S. Vanderslice (eds) *Can it Really Be Taught?: Resisting Lore in Creative Writing Pedagogy* (pp. 55–26). Portsmouth, NH: Heinemann.

Mayers, T. (2005) *(Re)Writing Craft: Composition, Creative Writing, and the Future of English Studies.* Pittsburgh: University of Pittsburgh Press.

Nelson, C. and Watt, S. (1999) *Academic Keywords: A Devil's Dictionary for Higher Education.* New York: Routledge.
Petty, A. (2005) Who's the teacher?: From student to mentor. In A. Leahy (ed.) *Power and Identity in the Creative Writing Classroom: The Authority Project* (pp. 77–26). Clevedon: Multilingual Matters.
Pinsky, R. (1999) *The Sounds of Poetry.* New York: Farrar, Strauss and Giroux.
Prose, F. (2006) *Reading Like a Writer.* New York: HarperCollins.
Ramke, B. (2006) A tribute to Stanley Plumly. Association of Writers and Writing Programs Conference.
Shelnutt, E. (1989) *The WritingRroom: Keys to the Craft of Fiction and Poetry.* Atlanta, GA: Longstreet Press.
Shulman, L. (2005) Signature pedagogies in the professions. *Daedalus* 134 (3), 52–29.
Stegner, W. (2002) *On Teaching and Writing Fiction.* New York: Penguin.

Chapter 5

Workshopping and Fiction: Laboratory, Factory, or Finishing School?

WILLY MALEY

Writing Business: Art for Art's Sake?

In the romantic comedy *Teacher's Pet* (dir: George Seaton, 1958), hard-bitten newspaper editor James Gannon (Clark Gable) enrolls under an assumed name in a journalism class run by college professor Erica Stone (Doris Day). There ensues a debate around whether a subject like journalism can be taught. Can Stone teach Gannon to suck eggs – or sell stories? Is it all in the nose or the nurturing? Journalism courses are more recent imports in the UK higher education system, as are courses in creative writing. Both have had to face criticism as to their effectiveness and practical application.

The Creative Writing Masters at Glasgow was launched in 1995. The Glasgow course grew out of extra-curricular work that Professor Philip Hobsbaum had been doing (at Belfast and London, then Glasgow), working from home in his own time with writers in a group context. Philip acted as a mentor for writers over a period of 30 years, working with a wide range of emerging authors, many of whom went on to become well-known, including Seamus Heaney and James Kelman. This is something Philip did in addition to his academic commitments. Philip finally persuaded the University of Glasgow in 1994, the year of my appointment and five years before his retirement, to support a Creative Writing Masters degree. Philip believed passionately in the value of a group approach to creative writing – he was the author of 'The Group Approach to Criticism' (1970) – and group meetings remain an important element of Glasgow's Creative Writing Masters.

In practice, the Glasgow course has been taught through a variety of means: one-to-one tutorials; workshops which take three forms, prescriptive, work-in-progress, and in-class exercise; critical forums on craft; editorial groups (student-led discussions of work-in-progress); critical seminars ('semshops' or 'worknars') on writing and theory; visiting writers, agents, publishers; reading parties (open mic sessions); and writers' retreats.

Back in 1995, Philip remarked that one day we would see a Glasgow Creative Writing graduate win the Booker, and we came close within five or six years when Rachel Seiffert's (2001) debut novel, *The Dark Room*, written while she was a student on the course, was shortlisted for that prize. Philip did not think writers could be made, but he believed they could be mentored, and they could work with other writers in a supportive environment with constructive criticism, define and refine their work, and pick up pointers towards publication and performance.

The course of creative writing never did run smooth, and we have a constant and vigorous debate every year about the nature and context of the course at Glasgow. Creative writing as a new subject can be seen to be located between areas such as art and music on the one hand, and journalism and publishing on the other. A creative writing course can be both a finishing school for professional writers and a laboratory where aspiring literary artists can experiment without the pressure to publish or perform. Academics and professional writers do not always see eye-to-eye on the best way to foster creativity. At Glasgow, we try to offer a range of teaching styles and contexts. We also offer a range of tutors. Which brings me to my next point:

Is the Creative Writing Tutor a Mentor, Agent, Editor, Facilitator, Reader . . . or Teacher?

This raises the question of the balance between academics and practitioners on the teaching team, and whether both kinds of tutor – professional academic and professional writer – need to extend their skills base in order to function as a mentor on a creative writing course. It raises the question of costs too, as paying professional writers properly may be the key to sustaining a successful creative writing course. And it feeds into the prospects for a PhD programme that is both 'creative' and academically credible in the eyes of Universities and funding bodies. As of 2008–9, at Glasgow, we have around 45 Masters students and 10 PhD students (we get over 100 applications per year). On our tutoring team, we have a balance between new and established writers and academics. The English Subject Centre's *Guide to Good Practice in Creative Writing* points out that it is a labour-intensive subject area and a lot of energy goes into making the course work (Holland, 2003). What do students get out of it? Different things: craft, criticism, confidence, context and contacts.

Success Stories: Measuring Achievement

How do we judge the success of a course? By the number of publications or prizes? Or by the number of students who improve their craft? What are the differences between poets and prose writers when it comes to measuring success? Here we come back to the business and professional side. One distinguished Scottish poet and Creative Writing Professor has spoken of the risk of producing 'MFA clones' – which I think is a problematic expression, and intentionally provocative, but a good point for debate. Individualism and elitism have been the twin pillars of the British system for a long time. The purpose of the group approach to creative writing pioneered by Philip Hobsbaum is to counter such a standpoint, itself the likely cause of the production of 'clones'.

Philip Hobsbaum saw the need for a group approach as a bulwark against individualism and elitism. He notes:

> In 1955 I founded a creative writing group in London: its procedure was based very much on the practice of [F.R.] Leavis. All discussion derived from texts of poems or prose fictions, read by their authors, turn and turn about. These were duplicated and circulated the week before the work in question was to be read. This meant that members were able to acquaint themselves with the subject of discussion, and, with the text before them, could comment upon the poem or story and not upon something less relevant – the author's life, or philosophy, for instance. No effort was spared to find recruits for this Group. It was the reverse of a clique; the only criteria of entry were intelligence and seriousness . . .There have been other gathering of writers before, from the Mermaid Tavern to G.S. Fraser's soirées in the fifties; none, I think, so selective in clientele or so systematically devoted to close perusal and discussion of the text. Art length, in 1963, the Oxford University Press published a selection from the work of this Group – called, modestly enough, *A Group Anthology*. (Hobsbaum, 1970: 165)

To understand why Hobsbaum and others felt it necessary to create a school of criticism that was also a seedbed of creativity, it is necessary to understand what a closed system the world of publishing could be in this period. Muriel Spark, herself a minor player on the publishing scene in London at the time, has recalled this world in interviews and in her autobiography, and most tellingly in *A Far Cry from Kensington* (1989), a novel that takes Spark back to Kensington in the 1950s and the world of bedsits and literary aspirations. The narrator, known as Mrs Hawkins until she sheds a few pounds, and Nancy thereafter, lies awake at night at the opening of the novel, pondering on her insomnia and the possibilities of imagination:

> You can put your mind to anything most of the time. You can sit peacefully in front of a blank television set, just watching nothing; and sooner or later you can make your own programme much better than the mass product. It's fun, you should try it. You can put anyone you like on the screen, alone or in company, saying and doing what you want them to do, with yourself in the middle if you prefer it that way. (Spark, 1989: 5)

Nancy has a lot to think about. The publishing world is one that has given her more than her fair share of memories, and the life of the city in those years when she was struggling to make her way has left its mark.

One viperish and base figure that casts a shadow over Nancy's world is the *pisseur de copie* (the French always have a word for it). The *pisseur de copie* is one of Spark's finest creations, but he was clearly a character waiting to be written, and indeed the type is familiar in the literary world, someone ambitious, talentless, and vicious with it. Ullswater and York, though a struggling concern, prove susceptible to the pushiness of such pen-pushing wannabes, 'the hangers-on who now got round Martin York to agree to publish their frightful books' (Spark, 1989: 44). Nancy is aware that social snobbery is at work in making her employer a soft touch for haughty hacks. Publishers are posh, and hence posh would-be writers of modest ability are in with a shout:

> Sometimes, I think, his desire to sign up these books for his publishing house was not due to a lack of discrimination so much as to the common fallacy which assumes that if a person is a good, vivacious talker he is bound to be a good writer. This is by no means the case. But Martin York had another, special illusion: he felt that men or women of upper-class background and education were bound to have advantages of talent over writers of modest origins. In 1954 quite a few bright publishers secretly believed this. (Spark, 1989: 45)

Publishers move in social circles as well as literary circles and sometimes the two get entangled: 'Publishers, for obvious reasons, attempt to make friends with their authors; Martin York tried to make authors of his friends' (Spark, 1989: 45). It is here that we meet the book's most viperish figure, the aspiring, perspiring, toxic Hector Bartlett:

> At this point the man whom I came to call the *pisseur de copie* enters my story. I forget which of the French symbolist writers of the late nineteenth century denounced a hack writer as a urinator of journalistic copy in the phrase '*pisseur de copie*', but the description remained in my mind, and I attached it to a great many of the writers who hung around or wanted to meet Martin York; and finally I attached it for life to one man alone, Hector Bartlett. (Spark, 1989: 45)

The devil will find work for idle hands, and since the *pisseur de copie* has no interest in developing his craft and no inclination to accept that his limited talents might be best put to editing and mentoring others, he has plenty of time on his hands to make mischief. Talent takes time; viperish hackdom requires only venom. Nancy is onto Hector like a mongoose: 'He had a small but full baby-mouth as if forever asking to suck a dummy tit' (Spark, 1989: 47). When he tells her, 'Mrs Hawkins, I take incalculable pains with my prose style', she thinks:

> He did indeed. The pains showed. His writings writhed and ached with twists and turns and tergiversations, inept words, fanciful repetitions, far-fetched verbosity and long, Latin-based words. (Spark, 1989: 46)

Nancy has tried to help Hector in the past, but he never took her up on her generous offer:

> I had once, some years before, put him in the way of a job that would have suited him very well: door-to-door encyclopaedia-pushing in the suburbs. He would have been able to blab and enthuse about the encyclopaedias, and impress the housewives. (Spark, 1989: 48)

The *pisseur* has many unpleasant scenes and speeches in this book, but the *piece de resistance* is the scene in the bar when the *pisseur* is standing having his pint and eating a sausage roll. A spaniel comes up and has a bite. The other customers laugh. Not the *pisseur*. Talentlessness rarely comes with a sense of humour or irony. The *pisseur* puts mustard on the sausage roll and lets the dog eat it. Writhing on the floor, it has to be given water at Harriet's urging by the barman (Spark, 1989: 105).

Is the North American model one that Scottish – and European – institutions would want to follow? Or is a slower, quieter, less commercially savvy approach more suited to this side of the Atlantic? Is the making of clones or drones really an issue? I think clones were what we were more likely to get when writers tended to be from the same backgrounds, and even then I think writers are by their very nature resistant to an attack of the clones. My own feeling, watching writers pass through Glasgow over the past 15 years, is that there's always been a commercial and even a class factor to writing and publishing. I firmly believe – and students tell me this is the case – that the Creative Writing Masters at Glasgow, and more broadly in the UK, boosts the confidence and self-belief of writers from non-professional backgrounds who have the talent but not the connections and contacts that go towards making a professional writer. On Glasgow's Creative Writing Masters, we've never asked for publication as a prerequisite for applicants to the course, but my own view is that publishing ought to be compulsory for students once they come on the course and after they graduate. Publication is a measure of success, not the sole measure, but the most obvious and public one. Publish or perish. That's the business end of the story.

In the few short years since Glasgow's Creative Writing programme got underway we've had a whole posse of students picked up by publishers. But we can't take all the credit for the writers who pass through our portals because often they've come to us prepared and polished from writing groups they've participated in or even ran outside of the University, in the wider community, or they've been mentored by established writers, a thing that many writers in this country do out of a spirit of generosity and shared creativity. We in the University have got more to learn from writers than to teach them.

Suturing the Future

I think English literature will be transformed by creative writing in the next decade or two as much as it was by literary theory in the 1970s and 1980s. Literary theory energized and galvanized a generation of students and staff working in English literature departments as they opened up to the broader domain of cultural studies. Interdisciplinary studies were the order of the day. But the object of criticism did not change. Then, in the 1990s, and into the first decade of the 21st century, creative writing emerged as a new and vibrant area of rapid growth that engaged and inspired. The role of creative writing in the so-called 'culture wars' is still to be determined. It has some bearing on debates around the organization of writing into genres and periods; the vexed question of influence; the politics of canon formation; the place of new writing in institutions and in the profession – academic and artistic; and the problematic issue of what exactly counts as 'literature'. How well placed are universities to nurture new writing, and what will the spread of creative writing courses do to the ways in which literary art is taught? Whatever the answer to that question is, it's an exciting time to be involved in a new subject.

Can Creative Writing Be Taut?

Can creative writing be 'taut'? I had a lecturer once who wiggled his fingers a lot, just above his ears. At the time, I had no idea what it meant. I assumed it was a nervous twitch. Maybe he saw a giant rabbit, like that film with James Stewart. That was it. His imaginary friend was a six-foot rabbit called Harvey. Maybe I was the only one who could see Harvey?

When I graduated, the tutor with the twitch, Harvey's friend, suggested I forget about the groves of academe and go live in a garret and write. I had to go and look up 'garret' – which means 'wretched room' – a writing pad for the used-to-be-fragrant, or wannabe-vagrant. Beckett syndrome. I decided it wasn't for me. I'd roughed it enough already. So I did a PhD and became an academic, a critic, a 'twitcher'. A friend of Harvey: Homo Academicus. Then one day I realised I was living in a garret and writing after all. Except it wasn't 'real writing', it was 'academic'.

When I came back home to Glasgow 15 years ago I was starting out on what I like to call my 'career' just as Philip Hobsbaum's time here was coming to an end. Philip had been meeting with and mentoring writers for 30 years, informally, largely in his own time. Philip championed the group approach to creative writing. I liked that, the ganging up idea, much better than the garret approach.

I had been teaching a course called 'Working with Language: Creating a Text' at Goldsmiths College, University of London, for a year. I remember meeting a close enemy in Glasgow around this time, and my close enemy saying, all smiles: 'Oh, I hear you got a job lecturing at London Uni?' Then, a look of pained concern passed over his face, 'But they've got you teaching creative writing!' It was like, 'Poor thing, they've got you doing origami!' Creative writing was the new sociology – popular but carrying the taint of the frivolous.

Between us, Philip and I hatched a plot, concocted a story. We called it the Glasgow Creative Writing Masters. We were two characters in search of an author. What I admired most about Philip, and tried to emulate, was his boundless generosity with new writers and his assiduous editing of their work. To be able to open doors and push people through them just as they're hesitating on the threshold is a privilege. When I gave my essay this sub-heading there were no scare quotes around 'taut'. Harvey was nowhere to be seen. A bad pun should never draw attention to itself. 'Can creative writing be taught?' Answering that question would make for a very short talk, because the answer's yes, of course, end of story.

In fact, that question – 'Can creative writing be taught?' – is something of a tautology, because creative writing can only be taught. It can only ever be taught, because 'creative writing' is the name given to writing courses at Universities and Colleges. It's an academic invention, and a relatively recent one. According to my favourite novel, the *Oxford English Dictionary*, a tautology means 'saying the same thing twice over in different words', especially as a 'fault of style'. It also means stating the obvious. The only sensible reply to the question 'can creative writing be taught?' is, 'You've just answered your own question'. Which is not to say that 'creative art' hasn't been around a long time, at least as long as criticism, just that 'creative writing' is something bound up with teaching, bound up first and foremost with teaching in the United States, and in a particular period, the 1920s or 1930s onwards, but now increasingly bound up with new developments in universities and colleges across the UK. So although the *OED* draws a distinction between creative writing 'exhibiting imagination as well as intellect, and thus differentiated from the merely critical, 'academic', journalistic, professional, mechanical, etc., in literary or artistic production', the entry goes on to add that 'creative writing' is a term first used in the United States to denote a 'course of study'.

In *The Business of Writing: A Practical Guide for Authors* (1922), Robert Cortes Holliday and Alexander Van Rensselaer claimed there was 'comparatively small demand for creative writing', by which they meant that the number of magazines was 'fairly limited' (pp. 100–201). But by 1930 the *English Journal* was listing 'courses in creative writing' and in 1934 the *New Republic* announced that the poet Conrad Aiken, a Pulitzer prizewinner, held a Guggenheim fellowship in creative writing. Is there a tension in the very phrase 'creative writing', and in the way it connects institutions and writers? In 1958, the *Oxford Magazine* declared that 'In America ... established, or at any rate committed, writers have been absorbed, permanently or temporarily, into the apparatus of creative writing workshops'. So, let's get this straight, while good old-fashioned English artists starve in garrets, or live off inherited income, their American cousins get accommodated in educational institutions. Except, let's not kid ourselves, it's all about class, in and out of the classroom. Writing is class-ridden. Academia is class-ridden. The publishing industry is class-ridden. The Arts Council is class-ridden. Professionalism starts at an early age. Access, social inclusion, merit – these are important for writers, and especially for writers who can't get that training from family, school, peers, for writers who lack the cushion of a privileged background. Some writers might want to be absorbed. Bring on the blotting paper.

The question, 'can creative writing be taut?', is a different question from 'can creative writing be taught?' Can creative writing be taut, without the scare quotes, in the sense my subtitle implies? Can it be firm and fraught? Can it be – the *OED* again – 'tight, not slack'? Can it be 'in good order of condition'? Can it be 'tense'? Can it be 'strict or severe as regards duty'? I like what film and journalism do to fiction, the pressure they put on words. Maybe poetry's always done that, but the vice-like grip of near-fatal deadlines and dialogue pared to the bone can make sentences sing off the page. Tightness is all, and one of the advantages of being on a creative writing course is having opportunities to tighten up, not just on your writing, but on your approach, even on your identity. Flights of fancy – like flights of other kinds – are most at risk, most vulnerable, during take-off and landing. Cruising at 40,000 words is the easy part. Starting off and getting interest from agents and publishers is harder. Writers need to fly business class, and pay close attention to the final approach. Writers need to mean business if they want to get noticed and get read. Doing a creative writing course is a statement of intent, a declaration of purpose. A 'few good men-tors' can work wonders, and the best mentor is a tormentor.

Creative writing can be taught in three ways, all interlinked, which I like to call PIP! By PIP I mean Prescription, Imitation, and Practice. First, prescription – there are rules, dammit! Don't do this, don't do that. Wage war on quotation marks. Attack those apostrophes. Kill your darlings. Hand over Harvey to the bunny-boiler. Second, imitation – read the best there is in the form or genre you've chosen to follow and try to aspire to those heights. I know Philip Hobsbaum was always keen on individually tailored reading lists that encouraged new writers to make themselves familiar with the 'best in class', to know what had been done before they came along. Third, practice – forget the fussing about and just write. The editing, revising, redrafting will come through practice. Blank page. Biro. On you go. These approaches are all intertwined because imitation is a form of prescription and prescription is a kind of practice. The creative writing workshop can take at least three forms: in-class exercise, writing and rewriting-on-the-spot; a slow trawl through work-in-progress, taking a writer or two at a time and having the group look at a single long-ish piece of work; or a session structured around homework, assignments in advance that are discussed in class. The second option was Philip Hobsbaum's, but I've watched them all work.

I prefer to think about writing in business terms rather than in (purely) aesthetic terms. Creative writing courses might be looked at in at least two ways. They can be seen as schools for success, finishing schools for aspiring authors whose business is writing and who are well on their way to professional status, with publication – or public performance – as their main goal. All they need is a bit of a polish, a tin of gloss over the undercoat, some assistance with those little bridging texts – synopses, treatments, and covering letters – the short pieces of prose that can connect the new writer with an agent or editor or publisher, the type of short prose non-fiction that enables a writer to navigate the system.

Or, alternatively, putting the emphasis on the 'workshop', creative writing courses may be seen as laboratories, artists' studios, improvisatory spaces, places of experimentation and invention, angst and exertion, where serious writers try things out free from any immediate pressure to publish, perform or produce. If it were to come down to a choice between 'art for art's sake', a sacrosanct space of reflection and invention, or the business of writing, 'the writing business', where work is produced with a view to publication, I know which side I'd be on. I tend to see creative writing as cognate with journalism and publishing more than with music and fine art.

In any case, the finishing school versus artist's laboratory opposition is a false one. No writer writes in order not to publish. Personally, I like the practice part of PIP and the prescriptive workshop – that is, homework – and I see the creative writing course as more finishing school than anything else. I want to see students succeed. If that's a crime, cuff me. I want students to sell out. Sell out in Borders, sell out in Waterstone's, sell out on Amazon: sell out everywhere. Other tutors see it differently, and that's fine. Between us I feel students get a good mix.

Creative Accounting Versus Developing the Wolf

The Finishing School (2005), Muriel Spark's last novel, is as challenging and chancy as anything she's written. Published when she was in her 86th year, it shows her to have lost none of her savage wit. If Spark's autobiography, *Curriculum Vitae* (1993), is one of the best books about the making of a writer and a brilliant blueprint for aspiring authors as well as a sparkling portrait of the artist as a young woman, then *The Finishing School* is a satire on the schoolish writing-by-numbers approach of creative writing courses. Spark's ruthless exposure of the hypocrisies and hang-ups of budding authors is hilarious. The novel features a Swiss finishing school, College Sunrise, where five students, hardly *la crème de la crème*, take a 'popular class' in creative writing. The teachers don't inspire confidence, and the fees matter more than the fiction. Nina Parker, wife of the school's founder, who teaches Etiquette, or '*Comme il faut*', informs her pupils:

> When you finish at College Sunrise you should be really and truly finished … Like the finish on a rare piece of furniture. Your jumped up parents (may God preserve their bank accounts) will want to see something for their money. Listen: when you eat asparagus in England, as everyone knows, you take it in your fingers, but the secret of exquisite manners with regard to asparagus is to eat it held in your left hand. Got it? (Spark, 2005: 5)

They get it. Nina is a poor woman's Miss Jean Brodie, but then she gets them when they're a little older and less impressionable. Her husband, Rowland Mahler, failed novelist turned creative writing tutor, has his high opinion of himself shaken by the emergence of a writer of real talent from his class. Rowland is good at publicity, though: 'This year's literary seminar pulls no punches investigating ideas of power and literature' (Spark, 2005: 8). Chris, a 17-year-old precocious redhead is writing a historical novel. When Rowland asks him how useful he finds the creative writing classes Chris replies: 'They're beside the point, in fact, but quite useful in many other respects' (Spark, 2005: 9). This is not the answer Rowland was looking for. The historical novel Chris is working on deals with the life of Mary Queen of Scots and is thus – like many of Spark's works – a piece of genre fiction with ideas above its station. When Rowland reads the first 15 pages 'he experienced a choking sensation'. The teacher cannot bear to be bettered by the pupil:

> No, no, this could not be, this is good, very expert. It can't be Chris's work – the logic doesn't hold that he could set such a scene. Something will have to go wrong. Root it out, stop it. And 'Oh, my God,' thought Rowland, 'what am I thinking?' (Spark, 2005: 12)

Green being one of Spark's favourite colours, she does a wicked line in jealousy and professional envy. She had learned through her editorship of the *Poetry Review* (1948–29) and reactions to her early success how petty and perverse the world of writing and publishing could be. As it transpires, Rowland's high opinion of Chris's work, shared by its precocious author, fails to impress the publisher whose services are called upon: 'The book itself,' said the publisher, 'is actually a lot of shit' (Spark, 1993: 124). It takes one poor author to praise another. Chris and Rowland eventually do publish books. Rowland's is entitled *The School Observed*, 'published satisfactorily, as was Chris's first novel, highly praised for its fine, youthful disregard of dry historical facts ... After a year they engaged themselves in a Same-Sex Affirmation Ceremony, attended by friends and Chris's family' (Spark, 1993: 155).

In a poem entitled 'The Creative Writing Class' (2003), Spark played with the 'he said, she said' clichés of dialogue, reducing it to absurdities like '"Miss Universe," he emoted', '"The signature," she ventured', and '"Develop the wolf," he demanded' (Spark, 2006: 12). Spark has certainly developed the wolf in her own writing, and, in taking the high road she separated the sheep from the goats along the way. But lest we think Spark too much of an individualist and against the teaching of creative writing in any simple sense – in fact she is an expert in dealing with groups, her fiction rarely revolving around a single consciousness – we ought to recall that she did attend a writing class, at least after a fashion. Upon leaving school, Spark took a course in précis-writing in Edinburgh, where her love of the kind of poetic economy exemplified by the ballads was further enhanced:

> I inscribed myself at Heriot-Watt College (now a university) to complete my education in English Prose. I was particularly interested in précis-writing, and took a course in that. I love economical prose, and would always try to find the briefest way to express a meaning. (Spark, 1993: 102)

At Heriot-Watt, Spark found an environment far removed from the romance of her school days. Her best-known character, Miss Jean Brodie, would confidently declare, 'Art is greater than science', but the young Muriel saw things differently: 'The idea of a more scientific atmosphere in general, and a more scientific approach to English, in contrast to the broad, humane, poetry-loving approach of Gillespie's, appealed to me when I started attending classes at the college' (Spark, 1993: 103). This love of plain, pressed language carried forward to her novel-writing career: 'I find "managerial" speech unpretentious, direct, quite expressive enough. One doesn't need sermons, figures of speech, drawling cadences and sonorous poetics in modern parliaments, congresses or conventions'. To be fair, Spark saw the virtue of experience in the making of an author:

> But in order to learn about life as I intended to do, I felt I had first to live. From about this time the essentials of literature were, to me, outside of literature; they were elsewhere, out in the world. (Spark, 1993: 103)

There's no substitute for experience, except, that is, the experience of reading and writing, the experience of the study and the workshop.

Harvey Gotham is not a six-foot rabbit; he's a writer wrestling with what he sees as 'the only problem', one posed by *The Book of Job*. Harvey's musings can tax the reader's patience at times, but among his ruminations is a key passage on the value of his own work, and, by extension – since Harvey is ever prone to enlargement – the nature of study more generally. They also serve those who only sit and study, or as Harvey puts it:

> We all need something to suffer about. But *Job*, my work on *Job*, all interrupted and neglected, probed into and interfered with: that is experience, too; real experience, not vicarious, as is often assumed. To study, to think, is to live and suffer painfully. (Spark, 1985: 153)

This is the key to Harvey's reading habit, and to his apparently uncaring or emotionally cold response to the actual death of a police officer, or his apparently blasé attitude to his wife's alleged criminal activities. Harvey's observations on love and death and marriage, though readers will respond in different ways to them, smack of wit and irony arising from deep study.

Conclusion: Pulling Rabbits out of Hats and Hutches

Creative writing is a developing area of academic activity, like deconstruction and post-colonialism, which threatens or promises, depending on one's perspective, to transform the privileged space of teaching and learning. The development of Creative writing as a new subject area is a fresh and forceful challenge to, from, and for the university, which has issued forth in recent years, and one in which I've been lucky enough to be involved. Scholars as diverse – *perhaps* – as C.S. Lewis, David Lodge, Terry Eagleton, Angela Carter and Lorna Sage have taught us that criticism and creativity can go hand-in-hand. For too long the lip service paid to literary art by literary theory was just that, lip service on the surface but business as usual otherwise. That's changing, and it's increasingly clear that forms of assessment, approaches to pedagogy, and the very idea of 'research' are having to be stretched in order to accommodate this new (inter)discipline. J.R.R. Tolkien, worrying away underground at *The Hobbit* while on a Leverhulme Fellowship, worried that his fellow dons at Oxford might think he had misused an academic award. Those days are gone, one would hope, now that the funding bodies take creative writing into account, as well as creative accounting. Those (mainly male) academics who fiddled with fiction or pottered about with poetry on the side tended to keep their creative work away from the body of their critical writings. Now, with the spread of creative writing undergraduate options and postgraduate courses across the UK, more and more academics are coming out as writers, more and more students are signing up as aspiring writers, and more and more writers are finding employment within the university system. Creative writing may, like deconstruction in its Anglo-American guise, have originated in English studies, but it has begun to go beyond the bounds of that discipline, and to exert leverage on the wider world of the university, rethinking, reorienting and rewriting the lines between authorship, authority, and institution. creative writing is something of a 'Cinderella subject' at present, but when the university takes its next tentative step, the glass slipper may just fit, at which point all the frustrated novelists-turned-critics can have a ball. Philip Hobsbaum's group approach aimed at transforming not just literary production, but critical inquiry: 'Criticism, then, as a mode of discussion, not dogma, is called for' (Hobsbaum, 1970: 186). From the standpoint of criticism, the greatest impact of the development of creative writing in the university may be the ways in which it changes how we think about precisely teaching and assessment, the very areas that initially had issues with adjusting to this new subject of inquiry. The group approach – the workshop – is at its best a challenge to individualist and elites modes of thinking and working. That's my story and I'm sticking to it. I leave the last word to the late Philip Hobsbaum. In an interview, Philip recalled: 'George MacBeth said to me critically once, "All your geese are swans." I said, "Well, it's just the reverse of reviewing and criticism: when it comes to books, treat the book as no good, until it proves itself otherwise. With students, assume they're good: let them prove they aren't"'. And Philip did give the benefit of the doubt on his first meetings with students. His was a democrat intellect, the kind that flourished in workshops, and the kind committed to the culture, critique and conversation of the group approach, in other words, to the passionate engagement of the workshop.

References

Hobsbaum, P. (1970) *A Theory of Communication*. London: Macmillan.

Holland, S. (2003) *Creative Writing: A Good Practice Guide* (Report Series #6). Egham, Surrey: English Subject Centre.

Holliday, R.C. and Rensselaer, V.A. (1922) *The Business of Writing: A Practical Guide for Authors*. New York, George H. Doran.

Spark, M. (1985) *The Only Problem*. London: Granada Publishing.
Spark, M. (1989) *A Far Cry from Kensington*. Harmondsworth: Penguin.
Spark, M. (1993) *Curriculum Vitae: A Volume of Autobiography*. Harmondsworth: Penguin.
Spark, M. (2005) *The Finishing School*. Harmondsworth: Penguin.
Spark, M. (2006) *All the Poems*. Manchester: Carcanet.

SECTION TWO
ENGAGING THE CONFLICTS

Chapter 6

Poetry, F(r)iction, Drama: The Complex Dynamics of Audience in the Writing Workshop

TIM MAYERS

One undeniable fact about the writing workshop model is that it brings student writing in front of an audience. For this reason, it often undoes – at least partially – an unfortunate aspect of many other models of writing pedagogy: that is, that the teacher is the only audience the student's writing ever has. Or, at the very least, the teacher (the one who assigns the grade) is the only audience that ever seems to matter. This teacher-as-audience dynamic has a number of potential drawbacks, as I will explore later in this chapter. But the writing workshop model seems at least to harbor the potential for moving beyond this dynamic. Has it actually done so? That question is difficult to answer in a general sense, and is perhaps best directed toward the analysis of concrete and specific situations. My major argument in this chapter will be that the question driving this volume – that is, the question of whether or not the writing workshop model is still working – is fundamentally a question about how we teach writers to think about (or not think about) real or potential audiences, and how writers go on to put that thinking into action in their own writing processes.

It is crucial to note, however, that the writing workshop model often operates quite differently in composition classes than it does in creative writing classes. There are a number of reasons for this. Primarily, though, the differences can be attributed to the different institutional positions of composition and creative writing within the universe of English studies. Composition is most often figured as remedial or semi-remedial work for students deficient (or at least insufficiently experienced) in writing; creative writing, on the other hand, is most often figured as advanced or specialized work for students already proficient (at least to some extent) in writing.

The Celebrated and Troubled History of the Workshop in Creative Writing

Virtually since the advent of creative writing at the programmatic level in US colleges and universities – especially as represented by one of the oldest and most highly-regarded programs, the Writers' Workshop at the University of Iowa – the workshop has been the dominant, if not the exclusive, pedagogical model. Apparently, it has long been thought that presenting student writing to an audience of peers and the instructor for verbal critique constitutes the best way to help apprentice writers improve so that their work might quickly become publishable. And while the workshop model has undeniably worked for many aspiring writers (the roster of well-known graduates from Iowa, for example, is particularly impressive), there has long been a sense of discontent simmering within the creative writing workshop culture. Consider, for example, this comment from Bruce Dobler (qtd in Wilbers, 1980: 130), who was enrolled in the Iowa Writers' Workshop from 1966 until 1968:

> I sensed that a great many students did not come to Iowa with an open spirit and a desire to apprentice themselves to journeyman writers. They came full of themselves (a charitable way to put it) and wanted only to be appreciated for what they already knew. They were resistant to learning and teaching – self-expressers for the most part who were only looking for uncritical love. Since they didn't get it, they poured invective on their fellows in class.

Public expressions of this kind of discontent, as we will see below, have seemed to multiply in more recent years.

Anyone who has ever taught workshop-based creative writing courses can probably recall at least a few horror stories in which something goes seriously awry: the majority of students are effusive with praise about a piece of work the instructor believes is seriously flawed or even patently offensive; students hurl harsh, unwarranted criticism at a piece of work the instructor believes is quite good or demonstrates a great deal of potential; students divide into warring aesthetic camps that operate much like high school cliques; student writers get defensive about their writing, lashing out at other students, or even the instructor, for not being smart enough to understand their brilliant work. When the workshop does not go well, there is little poetry but much friction and much drama (in the most negative sense of that word). At the same time, most teachers can probably recall a number of workshop success stories as well. For some students, seeing how others read their work is truly eye-opening and productive. At its best, the writing workshop model can provide aspiring writers with insights about their own writing that would have taken a long time, and perhaps much wasted effort, to realize otherwise.

Aside from individual teachers' experiences, though, there has been an ongoing dialogue about the efficacy of the writing workshop model in recent years. To put it bluntly, the workshop model has received a considerable amount of 'bad press'. One particular brand of this bad press can be found in polemics aimed at the alleged ill effects of creative writing programs (especially MFA programs) on the production of contemporary literature. Every so often, it seems, a prominent publication like *Harper's*, *The Atlantic*, or *The New York Times Book Review* publishes a piece by a noted author or editor decrying the proliferation of bland, homogenized 'workshop poetry' or 'workshop fiction'. This type of discourse has enjoyed a certain vogue now for a couple of decades – at least since Donald Hall opined that the workshop model in MFA programs had led to the production of the 'McPoem'. Other prominent examples of this style of lament include John W. Aldridge's (1992) *Talents and Technicians: Literary Chic and the New Assembly-Line Fiction* (the title alone provides an ample preview of the book's argument), and, more recently, John Barr's (2006: 434) 'American Poetry in the New Century', where we can find the following:

> The effect of these [writing workshops and ... MFA] programs on the art form is to increase the abundance of poetry, but to limit its variety. The result is a poetry that is neither robust, resonant, nor – and I stress this quality – entertaining; a poetry that both starves and flourishes on academic subsidies.

Barr asserts, as do many others, that the creative writing workshop leads to the production of poetry and fiction estranged from 'real' audiences; writers write only for each other, and no one else pays attention. Young writers who once harbored the ambition of becoming the greatest poet or novelist of a generation now compete merely to be the best writer in the classroom. The persistence of this line of argument does not seem deterred by the fact that many of its proponents have spent a great deal of time as students and teachers in writing workshops. This present chapter is not the appropriate place for a sustained critique of this type of discourse, though I believe one is certainly possible. What is important, instead, is that one of the commonplaces in this culture of complaint is that writing workshops create an *audience* problem. Perhaps the workshop's greatest strength – that it provides apprentice writers with a responsive audience – becomes, ironically, its greatest weakness as well.

Another line of criticism – and perhaps this one should be more troubling – comes from a group of creative writing teachers who focus not on the alleged ill effects of 'workshop writing' among the reading public outside academia, but rather on the pedagogical deficiencies of the workshop model. (These scholars also consider the strengths and advantages of the workshop model, but in light of the current discussion, their critiques are most relevant.) Unlike the critics mentioned above, these teachers and scholars tend to focus most on the effects of the workshop in the *undergraduate* classroom. The late Wendy Bishop pioneered this line of inquiry by evaluating creative writing pedagogy in light of some of the scholarship produced by compositionists and rhetoricians. Bishop's (1998) most extensive analysis of creative writing pedagogy through the lenses of composition scholarship can be found in *Released into Language: Options for Teaching Creative Writing* (published originally in 1990 by NCTE, republished in 1998 by Calendar Islands Publishers). Bishop, while keeping in mind some of the important differences between the kinds of writing done by students in creative writing and composition classrooms, argues that creative writing's traditional neglect of pedagogy – based perhaps in the notion that a great writer always makes a great teacher – had proven detrimental to a great many students of creative writing, especially in undergraduate classrooms. Because creative writing teachers most often came from MFA programs where the workshop was the default pedagogical model, they tended to employ an all-workshops-all-the-time model in creative writing classes at any level. In her research, Bishop discovers that '[U]ndergraduates will find it difficult to participate in public sharing of their work, especially if it is done in the competitive atmosphere often found in the undergraduate workshop' (p. 52). While not disavowing the workshop entirely for the undergraduate classroom, Bishop argues that creative writing teachers, like many of their colleagues in composition had already done, needed to attend to their own pedagogy in both scholarly and practical ways. Indeed, it would not be hyperbolic to contend that Wendy Bishop – at times working against the grain – legitimized the scholarly study of pedagogy in creative writing, and in so doing, she also helped to establish the foundations of a new field of inquiry: creative writing studies.

Bishop's critique also, in one important sense, focuses on audience; that is, students in undergraduate creative writing courses have proven, in the experience of many teachers, not to constitute the type of audience that might allow the workshop model to work to its fullest potential.

Many students are not ready to offer the kinds of observations, questions, and feedback that will help their fellow students improve works-in-progress. Improvement of the workshop model, then, necessitates a thorough consideration of audience and, because creative writing does not yet have a rich history of such scholarship, compels the interested teacher or scholar to cross the border into composition studies.

Audience Theory in Composition Scholarship

Scholars in composition studies have engaged in lively and theoretically sophisticated debates about the nature of audience in the writing process and the proper place (or non-place) for audience in writing pedagogy. During the past 20 years, however, that debate has waned.[1] The major terms by which audience has been discussed in composition theory can be discerned by looking at a couple of landmark essays from the time period during which the audience debate raged: Walter J. Ong's (1975) 'The Writer's Audience is Always a Fiction' and Andrea Lunsford's and Lisa Ede's (1984) 'Audience Addressed/Audience Invoked: The Role of Audience in Composition Theory and Pedagogy'.

Although Walter J. Ong was not exactly a composition scholar (he might best be described as a literacy theorist), his essay on audience has been frequently cited by composition scholars. Ong argues that the concept of audience, borrowed largely from classical rhetoric, is not particularly well suited to writing because the audience for a speaker is generally present (i.e. listening to the speaker) whereas the audience for a writer (Ong actually thinks the word 'audience' is somewhat misleading in relation to writing) is usually not present. Thus, the writer cannot 'know' an audience the way a speaker does (pp. 9–20). Ong then illustrates that writers tend to fictionalize, invent, and call audiences into being. An effective text positions readers in specific ways; it asks them, in effect, to be particular kinds of people, at least temporarily. In one important passage, Ong writes:

> A well-known novelist friend of mine only laughed when I asked him if, as he was writing a novel, he imagined his real readers – the woman on the subway deep in his book, the student in his room, the businessman on a vacation, the scholar in his study. There is no need for a novelist to feel his 'audience' in this way at all. (p. 10)

And later, Ong asserts, 'What has been said about fictional narrative applies ceteris paribus to all writing ... the writer's audience is always a fiction' (p. 17).

In the context of James A. Berlin's (1988) well known taxonomy of 'rhetorics' – here understood as the articulated or unarticulated clusters of beliefs about what writing is, how it works in the world, and how it can best be taught – this theory of audience is most closely aligned with the 'expressionistic' camp.[2] For expressionists, Berlin explains, writing is fundamentally regarded as an expression of the writer's true self or inner vision. Society most often functions as a corrupting influence upon the writer, an influence that must be escaped. Thinking about how specific readers might react to a piece of writing, and trying to gear a piece of writing toward such readers, is folly for expressionists. They believe a truly great piece of writing will *find* its audience without conscious or specific intent by the writer (1988: 484–287). If creative writing can be said to have a dominant, operative theory of audience, perhaps this is it. Alternatively, it might be argued that the dominant theory of audience in creative writing involves a vaguely-defined and largely intuitive sense of 'publishability' developed through long and careful acquaintance with what gets published in those venues most valued by professors of creative writing.

Ede and Lunsford, in what might be regarded as the most important and authoritative article yet published on the concept of audience in composition studies, find Ong's theory, though interesting, flawed in some important ways. Likewise, they find flaws in the theory that most often stands in opposition to Ong's. 'To many teachers,' they argue, 'the choice seems limited to a single option – to be for or against an emphasis on audience in composition courses' (p. 155). Ede and Lunsford see audience theorists in composition as divided into two major camps: those who prefer to view audience as 'addressed' and those who prefer to view it as 'invoked'. They describe the difference as follows: 'The "addressed" audience refers to those actual or real-life people who read a discourse, while the "invoked" audience refers to the audience called up or imagined by the writer' (p. 156). Ultimately for Lunsford and Ede, the choice – both for 'real world' writing and writing done by students for classroom purposes – is never a simplistic one between audience addressed or audience invoked. Every writing situation involves both, though in varying and complex ways. Some writing tasks clearly must involve serious and careful consideration of the known audience, the audience addressed, even if the writer wittingly or unwittingly also attempts to invoke certain kinds of responses among those readers. Other writing tasks begin with the writer intending to address a very specific audience, but seem to evolve over time in such a way that they invoke a different kind of audience, an audience that might become the audience addressed for the 'finished' piece of writing. Still others involve the writer never really thinking specifically at all about audience, though the resultant writing manages to 'find' a real audience.

The Writing Workshop and Audience Awareness in Student Writing

I have been a teacher of both composition and creative writing for nearly two decades now, and so I have had the opportunity to experiment with the writing workshop model in a wide variety of its possible incarnations. Over the past five years or so, however, my thinking about the relationship between audience and the writing workshop has begun to crystallize. Surprisingly – at least for me – the roots of this new thinking come more from the composition classroom than the creative writing classroom, though the ideas I have been struggling with are relevant to both.

In my composition classes, student inquiries about grading practices – and the professional self-reflection these inquiries have engendered – have led me to realize first that audience-related concerns figured quite heavily in my evaluation of student writing; and second, that I needed (at least at times) to conceptualize more clearly what some of those concerns were. As much as I might emphasize audience in my written commentary and in my discussions with students, the students themselves tended (consciously or unconsciously) to think of *me* as the audience and to try to figure out what *I* wanted to see in their papers. Although I felt I was making a significant effort in my written commentary on student writing to identify myself as *a* reader, and to indicate that different readers might respond differently, students virtually always thought of me as *the* reader. My way out of this unfortunate dynamic was to require students to write (or at least imagine they were writing) for audiences other than me, as illustrated by the following sample assignment:

> Write a 'definitional' argument that provides (or at least attempts to provide) answers to the following questions: What is *good writing*? What is a *good writer*? What are the most important things for a good writer to know (or to be able to do)? Can these things be taught in school? Why or why not? In most cases, you will find it helpful not only to *describe* what good writing is, but also to provide *examples* which will help to illustrate your definition.
>
> AUDIENCE: Beginning college students who are apprehensive about whether or not they will be able to write well enough to succeed in school.

This type of assignment, combined with a grading rubric that clearly emphasizes the importance of audience concerns, has allowed me to address audience – both with individual students and with entire classes of students – in more productive ways. In the assignment described above, for example, student writers often try to illustrate the principles of good writing by using examples from their favorite authors; yet the work of these authors is often not at all representative of the kinds of writing the imagined audience is likely to be assigned in college, especially during the first couple of semesters. The assignment thus provides a context for illustrating how so many aspects of the writing situation, including the kinds of evidence that will be most effective and the manner in which such evidence might be woven into the overall argument being made, require the writer to consider what is known about the intended readers. This kind of pedagogical tactic is not new, nor is it without its critics. More than a quarter of a century ago, Russell C. Long (1980: 223) argued that assignments that ask students to imagine very specific groups of readers invite 'noxious stereotyping ... we would not tolerate ... in any other context.' I must concede that this is a valid concern, but that perhaps like any other aspect of writing, audience awareness is learned by making mistakes, coming to recognize them as such, and moving beyond them.

In Ede's and Lunsford's terms, my assignments (at least at first glance) tend to stress 'audience addressed' over 'audience invoked,' rather than striking a balance between the two.[3] It could also be pointed out, however, that my assignments create an extraordinarily complex rhetorical situation that invokes and addresses audiences, since I and their peers, as opposed to the audiences specified by the assignment instructions, are the 'real' readers. Yet considering how many of my students – the vast majority of them college juniors and seniors – report that they have never before been asked to think of audience in quite this way, I am convinced that such an emphasis at this point in their writing careers is not only helpful but in many cases long overdue.

Writing workshops, in conjunction with these kinds of assignments, have proven to be a particularly rich site for exploring audience-related issues. In most cases, the formal writing assignments in my advanced composition courses go through a one-week peer review cycle before they are due for grading. That is, one week before the paper is due to me, each student must exchange drafts with two other students and respond in writing to a series of questions about the effectiveness of the paper. These written reviews are returned to the papers' authors before the assignment due date, and students have the option, and a bit of time, to revise their papers before handing them in to be graded. This procedure usually allows for two class meetings in which workshops can be conducted on a voluntary basis. Students who wish to have the 'peer review' versions of their papers discussed by the class – either with or without the author's name noted on the paper – submit their paper drafts to me, and I distribute these drafts electronically to the rest of the class. In the ensuing workshops, I almost always ask students to begin their discussions of the papers in question by focusing on audience issues: *What do we know about the audience the writer is trying to reach? Given what we know, how well does the paper's opening paragraph establish a relationship between writer and audience? Are there any places where the language used, or the type of evidence employed, is particularly appropriate or inappropriate for the audience?* Not only does this help the class avoid simplistic 'I liked it/I didn't like it' responses to their peers' writing, but it also roots students' thinking about their peers' writing (and, by extension, their own writing) within the context of the primary category through which their papers will be evaluated and graded.

The general success of writing workshops in my advanced composition classes has helped me to rethink how I might use workshops in creative writing classes. Very few creative assignments lend themselves to the specific sort of audience designation I have used in composition classes, but I began to ask, 'How *can* notions of audience be profitably integrated into creative writing classes and workshops?' There are numerous possibilities. One is to address audience after the fact, so to speak – to ask what kind of audience the text seems to invoke, in Lunsford's and Ede's terminology. In one creative writing workshop several semesters ago, a student was working on a novel and the class was discussing an early draft of the first chapter. One of the novel's main characters, an FBI agent, was constantly described in the text as displaying his badge, stating his name, and identifying himself as a federal agent. Several members of the class said they found this both repetitive and distracting. The student writer defended his practice by noting that he had actually spoken to two FBI agents and asked them about interviewing procedures. He wanted to make sure, he said, if any of his eventual readers were actually federal agents, or familiar with the protocol such agents followed, they would find his representations accurate and believable. I asked the student if he expected any significant portion of his readers to be federal agents, or if he hoped perhaps to reach a wider audience of readers who might be interested in mystery stories or crime dramas. The student said he hoped to reach the wider audience. This allowed the class to begin a discussion about how the description of events in a narrative might be crafted to seem both accurate and unobtrusive to a wide, but nonetheless bounded, group of intended readers. In many other cases too, I have found that the question of which audience a text seems to invoke is a profitable one in workshops. Sometimes this question is very difficult for students to answer, and sometimes it leads to rather simplistic or excessively abstract answers. But even this difficulty is sometimes instructive. If no possible audience can be identified – not even a potential one – the student writer may need to ask whether the text in question is ever likely to have any readers outside of the workshop.

Another possibility for incorporating audience awareness into creative writing workshops involves the study of particular publication venues. One of my favorite assignments for creative writing classes – and it invariably turns out to be a student favorite as well – is to divide the class into small groups (three to five students in each) and have each group engage in research about a particular literary magazine: its circulation numbers, the name(s) of its editor(s), its stated editorial preferences (if any), the genre(s) it publishes, etc. The assignment requires the careful reading of at least one issue (and preferably more than one issue) of the journal in question. Each group completes the project with an oral presentation to the class about the journal they researched. Sometimes I find it helpful to follow up one or more of these group presentations with an impromptu assignment something like the following: 'Write a poem that you believe would be appropriate for *The Minnesota Review*.' This assignment, in turn, can lead to a workshop in which several student poems are discussed not in terms of any general or abstract aesthetic qualities, but rather in light of the specific things the class knows about the journal in question, based on the group project. Although this kind of assignment might seem perverse to some creative writers who prefer to write by following the poem or story idea where *it* seems to want to go and worry about possible publication later, I have found it to be particularly helpful in getting students to think (even if only at a crude and basic level) about how editors, as a potential audience, might be likely to view their work.

In composition as in creative writing then, I might argue, the writing workshop model can still work *if* it is used within meaningful and enabling contexts, *if* writing workshops are clearly linked to other kinds of classroom assignments and activities, and *if* the workshop can be exploited as a site for highlighting the variable and complicated ways in which writers think (or do not think) about the readers they one day hope to reach. In fact, the writing workshop may be the most fertile available site for such considerations, involving many complex layers of real and imagined, invoked and addressed audiences.

Notes

1. A perusal of article titles in *College Composition and Communication* illustrates this trend. In the period from 1965 until 1987, *CCC* published 16 articles with the word 'audience' in the title; the bulk of those articles appeared between 1975 and 1985. Since 1988, *CCC* has published only one article with 'audience' in its title: a 1996 piece by Ede and Lunsford that provides a critical re-reading of their 1984 'Audience Addressed/Audience Invoked' article.
2. Most subsequent composition scholars have used the slightly different terms 'expressivist' or 'expressivistic' to designate these ideas, but Berlin's description of this rhetoric remains authoritative within the field even though some scholars and teachers have argued that Berlin's characterizations are inaccurate.
3. Not every writing assignment in my advanced composition classes entails such explicit and specific consideration of audience. Students are also required to compose numerous un-graded reading responses in which audience is specifically *not* a consideration.

References

Aldridge, J.W. (1992) *Talents and Technicians: Literary Chic and the New Assembly-Line Fiction.* New York: Scribner's.

Barr, J. (2006) American poetry in the new century. *Poetry* 188 (5) (Sept), 433–241.

Berlin, J.A. (1988) Rhetoric and ideology in the writing class. *College English* 50 (5) (Sept.), 477–294.

Bishop, W. (1998) *Released into Language: Options for Teaching Creative Writing.* Second Edition. Portland, ME: Calendar Islands Publishers.

Ede, L. and Lunsford, A. (1984) Audience addressed/audience invoked: The role of audience in composition theory and pedagogy. *College Composition and Communication* 35 (2) (May), 155–271.

Hall, D. (1987) Poetry and ambition. In H. Lazer (ed.) *What is a Poet?* (pp. 229–246). Tuscaloosa: University of Alabama Press.

Long, R.C. (1980) Writer-audience relationships: Analysis or invention? *College Composition and Communication* 31 (2) (May), 221–226.

Ong, W.J. (1975) The writer's audience is always a fiction. *PMLA* 90 (1) (Jan.), 9–21.

Wilbers, S. (1980) *The Iowa Writers' Workshop: Origins, Emergence, and Growth.* Iowa City: University of Iowa Press.

Chapter 7

Engaging the Individual/Social Conflict within Creative Writing Pedagogy

BRENT ROYSTER

Having been trained as a writer, I've come to relish time spent at the computer, especially when the work I do is impelled ('inspired') rather than compelled ('forced'). Whether making notes in a journal, fiddling with a poem draft, or trying to work through an essay, my mood is often at its healthiest when I'm composing. Sometimes when I'm writing, I even sense that time has vanished, and during these timeless episodes, my thinking sharpens. If I'm working on a poem when such a sensation arises, my judgment about word choices, sounds, connotations and structures seems finely tuned and natural. During such periods, I've drafted page after page of work, and have been driven to a frenzied state while pounding keys, pacing, and reading work aloud. Psychologist Mihaly Csikszentmihalyi (1999) calls such periods autotelic experiences. By his definition, the autotelic experience is a flow state, in which a person's performance and mood have peaked. For me at least, the sensation of 'flow' might be likened to romantic narratives pertaining to inspiration, and that feeling is a palpable experience, which benefits the writing process. Certainly other writers have achieved this pleasurable, almost addictive state, and so, it's no wonder that dramatic, even romantic narratives of the writing process are so prevalent.

But a story detailing the flow state represents only one version of the writer's work. And since I've failed to mention the host of cultural influences governing such an experience, recent composition theorists might refute my own process narrative as overly romantic. Their criticism is valid, and has served composition pedagogy by taking the writer out of the lonely garret. By recognizing the writer as an agent within a social setting, and within an historical moment, writers and teachers may investigate the processes through which composition is accomplished. Creative writing teachers must acknowledge the several subjectivities within themselves, as well as within their students. The goal, then, is to recognize the many subjectivities artists embody, while also giving credence to the roles of teachers and students in the work of exploration through language.

The *Craft, Critique, and Culture* conference at the University of Iowa is specifically aimed at theorizing these notions of creativity and writing. In September 2000, I participated in the conference, with a panel entitled 'Creativity, Authorship, and the Workshop' with Paul Dawson, another creative writer involved in continued academic study. Theorists such as Dawson offer an interesting account of how theory becomes integral to the writer's workshop; his research illustrates creative writing's dependence upon literary theory, and though he recognizes the specialization of creative writing within academia, Dawson (1997) also contends that the practice cannot be 'conceptualized as a body of knowledge outside literary theory because it is one that is fashioned within literary theory' (p. 70). With this, he argues that creative writing should be seen as 'an intellectual work characterized by a dialogic engagement with literature and literary theory' (p. 71).

With this goal in mind, the following chapter serves to examine and interrogate the subjectivity of the author as one site of theoretical inquiry specifically fruitful for the creative writing workshop. If a Romantic narrative of the writer is a prevailing trope – one that reflects the dominant activity of the creative writing workshop – this Romantic mythos is damaging because it sidesteps any number of other additional narratives that may inform the writing practice of students. Additionally, the self is much more complicated than has been narrated by any number of countless practitioners; the self, rather, is multiple, is fluid, and is constantly new with each writing situation. Finally, this discussion assumes that all critique is often monologic, a style of criticism that creates a uniform type of product based upon an in-house aesthetic. Creative writing, as an artistic preoccupation wholly disassociated with academia, has been seen as an 'unteachable' craft. My own experience as a poet rooted in academic and theoretical pursuits, is that creative writing can be taught, but only if teachers re-examine assumptions concerning the self involved in a writing practice. For example, 'creative' writing emphasizes the autonomy of the individual, and views the process of writing as an inner-directed molding of consciousness in the service of art, of beauty, of truth. On the other hand, composition studies recognizes that the individual author does exist, but that writing takes place in response to any number of socio-cultural influences. What's more, the 'individual' is constructed in a variety of ways in response to her environments, so that writers can no longer view the self as a sort of fundamental wholeness, but rather, as a reciprocal hole to be emptied and filled.

One might assume that the self is not the solid rock upon which our identity is built; rather, it is fluid, like magma, and formed and reformed over time, through accretion. While conversations about the self are ultimately important, composition theory also suggests that writers construct an aesthetic – a groundwork on which the composition of the self is founded. This is in direct opposition to the conventional creative writing workshop's assumption that artists create by calling upon a wholly given and already constructed aesthetic. Finally, contemporary views in composition suggest that writers of all stripes are engaged in a lifelong process, an evolution, and these writers are always involved in a larger socio-cultural dialogue; rather than enacting an isolated, autonomous, individual author. In other words, the contemporary writer composes in response to her several environmental influences.

Unfortunately, the 'self' that we so often refer to can be slippery and tangential – when we attempt to define it, we find that it dissolves, or rather, disappears behind numerous inexplicable versions. Specifically, two theorists in composition studies shed light on a revised notion of how the self is constructed through writing. First, as Mary Louise Buley-Meissner (1991) puts it, 'every act of writing can be seen as an act of self-representation . . . "who we are" keeps changing, keeps complicating. Our understanding of "who we are" is always incomplete' (p. 30). What's more, there is an ongoing dialogue between self and audience, an interaction between the subject and the world, and these two loci are bound, are constantly forming and reforming. 'At any given point,' writes Robert Brooke (1991), 'our identity structure, both as we ourselves and others understand it, is composed of a conglomerate of stances we take towards the role expectations that surround us' (p. 17). Students are asked, in essence, to play a role, and that role is inaccurately specified. In the composition classroom, as well as in the creative writing workshop, this means students must attempt to embody a way of speaking, or writing, which depicts a self to his or her audience, and deciding on how this portrayal is enacted is one very difficult step in the composition process.

Several cultural studies approaches, such as those proposed by James Berlin, Lester Faigley, and others, incorporate this conversation concerning the self, and by extension, voice and style, by examining how the writer-as-individual is socially constructed. For Kenneth Bruffee (1986), social constructionist thought 'offers a strikingly fruitful alternative to the way we normally think and talk about what we do' (p. 776). In contrast to the subjective, Cartesian, I-centered metaphors for the self, the social constructionist view 'accounts for the fact that so much of what we normally say about knowledge, scholarship, research and college or university instruction is confined within a frustrating circularity oscillating between "outer" and "inner" poles of "objectivity" and "subjectivity"' (Bruffee: 776). The idea that an individual is shaped, in part, by her environments – that one's identity is an amalgam of race, class, sex, and so forth – is of eminent concern for Berlin, Faigley, and others in composition pedagogy. For these compositionists, the self is dynamic and constituted in response to a social milieu. Cultural studies assumes that the self is constructed, and though the belief is not without its detractors, this assumption provides an interesting and useful foundation for teaching creative writing as well.

Aligning Foucault's revision of the author's role in the performance of self, Kurt Spellmeyer (1989) argues that a static performance of the self is generally validated by composition, while those performances that display uncertainty and inconsistency are deemed weak. However, the student writer is really supposed to become involved in the tangle, and where there are questions of voice, there gives rise to a sort of rethinking of the universal 'I' in writing. Spellmeyer writes: 'While there is, of course, no transcendental subjectivity, every event of language reconstitutes a speaking self as the "I", present implicitly or explicitly, which cannot "slip imperceptibly" into the flow of words that precede it. Only this "I", this always "exterior" self with its ability to change, can furnish the inconsistency discourse requires' (1989 p. 721). Defining the self, then, is always a difficult task, especially when grappling the dichotomy between subjective and objective perspectives. In Spellmeyer's view, and as it occurs to me now, neither position serves the writer fully, but rather, a critical engagement with both in the writing process is key to the evolution of a malleable and complex identity. In recognizing that any representation is a version of the writer, students insinuate themselves into the study, work to undermine the power of dominant, fixed representations. Additionally, students can view their own artistic judgments as part of a larger, ongoing intellectual and creative practice.

The idea of social constructionism has been problematic for me. Even though I recognized that individuals respond to influence, I felt there was an injustice done to the subject, the agent, and the author. I grappled with the notion that I'd become a function of language and identity, constituted predominantly by environment. In this case, my resistance to the idea of social constructionism was rather an uninformed reluctance toward claims against my right to speak as an individual. And I shared this attitude with students who felt that all personal writing, even all professional or academic writing, is a manifestation of one unique voice. The word 'unique,' here, is particularly laden because claiming a unique voice means shunning the disparate other voices a writer must, perforce, assimilate. My attitude shifted, but the dispute between the singular voice and the unconscious collective of others always speaking has never quieted. I've come to acknowledge my own situation so much that I feel compelled to make this discussion a part of classroom practice. The divide between self and world, the 'unique voice' against the caucus of disparate voices, is not a wrangle that I can easily overcome.

According to Joseph Trimbur (1989), 'It can be misleading to tell students, as social constructionists do, that learning to write means learning to participate in the conversation and consensual practices of various discourse communities. Instead, we need to ask students to explore the rhetoric of dissensus that pervades writing situations' (p. 610). Though my students and I have not come to resolution over whether one's identity is entirely a product of one's culture, the quandary makes for interesting discussion. What's more, those theorists who still recognize the self, the individual, the unique voice, as it interacts with a larger system or discourse have only bridged my arrival at this point in my thinking. Moreover, when viewing artistic choices and values as part of a larger system, it becomes important, and even necessary to view oneself as a participant in an ongoing discussion. The social-epistemic rhetoric outlined by James Berlin, for instance, provides an adequate model for viewing my role as a writer in a larger system: an interplay, an interaction. Berlin's (1996) *Rhetorics, Poetics, and Cultures* details the individual writer as a matrix of subjectivities, an agent who constructs and is constructed by a culture. His cultural studies approach encourages students to analyze their own dialogue with issues of race, gender, class, and sexual orientation, and fosters an instrument for resistance through critical writing concerning these issues. He writes that, 'The individual is the location of a variety of significations, but is also an agent of change, not simply an unwitting product of external discursive and material forces' (p. 78). In short, students in workshops can and should be directed to interrogate their experiences and perspectives; in so doing, they place themselves within the wider social context, and this placement encourages active participation.

In fact, as my students' perspectives and experiences grow more diverse, it becomes integral that they situate themselves within those narratives. L. Gregory Jones (1993) suggests that each critical and/or rhetorical tradition is fused of particular traditions, specific – or sometimes hidden assumptions – inscribed within the narrative. Each 'narrative,' or rather, the voice that is the mouthpiece for this narrative, will belie a particular critical bias. 'Once we recognize that there are diverse and competing narratives, then we also need to recognize the interests and purposes people have for narrating their lives, social settings, and the world in one way rather than another' (p. 12). The challenge lies in unpacking these various assumptions, aligning their various politics, in order to 'see' how a text means. However, the knowledge of one's situated-ness, and the desire to interpret the political agenda of what we read, does not mean that voice is a stayed issue. Rather, the way that we write and even function in the world becomes a sort of posing, a performance of ideology that can and often does misrepresent all sorts of assumptions that an author may not wish to claim. To recognize this rhetorical posturing, then, is to see the self and the act of writing as a mutual engagement, an exchange of ideologies and practices between an individual and the community she inhabits.

What's needed – in this vast landscape of what teachers understand about their students' performance of self – is a topography of sorts; A roadmap, a compass, a plan of action, a clear destination. Creating such a map necessarily involves transcribing theory into practice. One study has translated theory into practice by combining theories associated with rhetoric, culture studies and creative writing in a first-year composition course. Alan Kennedy et al (1994) attempts to assimilate and complement the many preceding voices that constituted the writing curricula at Carnegie Mellon University. In so doing, they encourage the blending of numerous genres, and the recognition that the writer's position is ultimately formed from a matrix of influences. This thinking inevitably disrupts student 'notions of individualism', yet by implementing a methodology of argumentation, as instituted by Gerald Graff, these authors work (the authors quote Kathleen McCormick) to avoid students' 'new insistence on the "correct" version of reality to be learned' (Kennedy: 252). The combined classroom's formation, however, produces an instrument designed 'for students to experience a productive tension between individual cognition and social process, personal beliefs, and ideology' (Kennedy, 1994 252). Particularly, self and voice are key subjects to compositionists, whereas practitioners hold little discussion of these topics in creative writing pedagogy. Perhaps this is because issues of self and voice have, for a long time now, been regarded as a given in the creative writing workshop. In essence, one way we can approach the uneven terrain of self and voice is to suggest to students that these ideas, these formations, aren't yet fully formed.

The stance I hope students will take is one of determined uncertainty. In this, I mean that we can frame our systems of belief with the knowledge that our thinking will inevitably change, and so thought is never felt to be static and immovable. Frank Farmer (1998) voices these concerns in 'Bahktin and Cultural Studies', in which he defines a critical attitude toward what we think we know, what we think others know, and the chasm that lies between. His argument for a situated knowledge poses that 'cultural critique needs dialogue to restrain its tendencies for authoritarian pronouncements, for 'last word truisms and disabling certainties' (p. 204). This disembodied questioning of what's true about the self should lead students to examine how to speak and how to engage knowledge on every level. However, the theory does leave a sort of cul-de-sac for the teacher seeking pat answers: 'Willing neither to silence our own commitments nor to require that the same be espoused by our students . . . teachers who embrace both dialogue and cultural studies find themselves inhabiting the always precarious territory of the between' (Farmer, 1998: 205). What I ask of my workshop students is what I ask of myself: to remain engaged in culture, to question power structures, to assume that words and actions are not as fixed as they may seem.

Finally, I hope that students will call into question how they might act when shackled with the knowledge that even our freedom is situated, and that the fact of the will (to power) is held under scrutiny. In *The Mythology of Voice*, Darsie Bowden (1999) asserts that, 'if we relinquish the idea that we are the ultimate arbiters of our lives and language, that we are prone in a large respect to the controlling influences of environments, contexts, and other people, we should also call into question a fundamental component of the Western self-conception: free will' (p. 65). To my mind, students still play a significant role in defining and investigating their own disparate voices. Even though voice becomes merely one of any number of poses, and though writing from any one perspective belies the particular influence of environments and cultures, we nonetheless must recreate ourselves with each act of writing. Writing is one way to draw distinctions between who we are and how we're influenced, and then to think about the outcomes more critically. My interest, then, lies in how competing theoretical perspectives influence creative writing pedagogy, a field that holds very different conceptions of self and voice.

In the case of writing, we cannot hope to understand which influences cause the pen to move across paper, nor can we causally equate one line of reasoning with any definite sequence of events in the artist's life. The event called 'writing' is a particularly complex scene, where all sorts of influences converge at once and appear, with the help of the author, manifest as text. Also, writing is a peculiar labor only inasmuch as it is mysterious and transformative; since reasons for the text's newly minted existence are both arbitrary and indefinite, the act of writing inhabits a convincingly mystical aura. Certainly, authors have been persuaded that since we cannot fully explain its causes, and since we cannot decipher its meaning, writing may be divine. However, once convinced that the individual self is fragmented, we question whether creativity can be defined in Romantic terms that depend upon a limited view of creative imagination. Jacques Maritain's 'Creative Intuition in Art and Poetry' (as qtd in Rothenberg and Housman, 1976), for instance, furthers the claims made by St. Thomas Aquinas by suggesting that:

> because the human person is an ontologically perfect and fully equipped agent, master of his actions, the Illuminating Intellect cannot be separate, but must be an inherent part of each individual's soul and intellectual structure ... (p. 107)

Clearly, this is the language of autonomy that seems, to a large degree, suspect. That said, the idea of the individual becomes suspect, and so creative process narratives seem both limiting and disingenuous. Rather, 'selves' seems more apt when referring to the author, and 'processes' better names the author's diverse modes of creative functioning. But the nature of creativity seems to me to be a great deal more than a semantic squabble. By simply renaming Romantic notions of creativity and versions of inspiration, we gloss over the key issue: How artists define process is, in short, also how they define themselves.

Two competing identities seem to predominate the writer's condition. One identity is that of the mysterious and elusive self, the darker other behind the scrim – Maritain's 'illuminating intellect,' or Jung's 'rebel without a cause.' The poststructuralists' 'socially constituted agent' represents the other identity – or rather, the opposing quorum of identities. If we recognize the writer involved in such a dynamic interplay, we reaffirm the existence of discourse communities that affect process. Viewing any representation as one of many 'versions', students insinuate themselves into study, undermine representations, and seek ways of narrating themselves counter to prevailing tropes. Since familiar terms such as 'voice' and 'style' are largely dependent upon the 'autonomous self', this rethinking of the independent author is not an easy task. In fact the profession is perforated by arguments for and against creative writing, because something in the art seems to inherently privilege the individual over the social. Although workshop atmospheres are largely social in nature, literary production is still largely a solitary endeavor. Clearly, we see all the influences involved in the construction of text, though these influences are often discounted in the scene of the lone auteur. At once, we are being asked to resist the Romantic representation of the autonomous author, while maintaining an awareness of the crisis between subjective agency and a dynamic creative process. Creative writing, in short, is both social and individual, and both identities are held within the self. As an alternative to the romantic ideal of the independent genius, the writer composes in response to specific environments and ideologies. To this end, creative writers should examine deep-seated, romantic representations, and then investigate alternative ones.

In every writer there are two identities, and there's value in both these selves. For some, a Romantic identity provides a sort of security blanket. My students, for instance, are skeptical when the origin of creative work is called into question – some learners argue that poems originate in the heart, of course, or in the soul. Culture, then, is merely an abstract environment that leaves little impression upon the artist. Fine, I say. Fine. Especially since even professional authors are reluctant to deny the existence of self, or soul, or will, or that indefinite spiritual drive that allows each person to act. In a study of numerous remarkable artists throughout history, Benjamin Taylor (1995) asserts that, for all his Nietzschean tendencies, he cannot successfully unmask the notion of the Romantic self. 'We are nowadays inclined to speak of Romanticism not just as a literary and philosophical movement but as a perdurable environment of thought and feeling to which we ourselves belong' (p. 102). The total denial of a Romantic self acting in a meaningful world spells the death of freedom and will – two metanarratives which, for some at least, can never be entirely disrupted. Without freedom, without will, there seems to be no hope. Without hope only meaninglessness and despair. Modernism's lovely mystery, the autonomous identity is still a part of many writerly fictions.

Just as the Romantic identity is still ingrained in the writer's consciousness, so too the complicated multiplicity of self cannot be denied, and the social strata in which we are situated admittedly shape much of our identity. I want to explore these two poles because I feel the pull of numerous identities even now, and the presence of all these wishes for what I write goads me to believe that nearly all writers are bound by a state of ineluctable conflict. Simply put, there is conflict between what some call the self – which, in terms of artistic creation, is manifest as the 'autonomous author' – and the social situation in which the self is housed. Since the act of writing is, of its own accord, a way of figuring out what we know, and since the cause, the influence, the impetus, the call for writing is both diverse and mysterious, it appears to me now that writers, as a peculiar sort of inquisitive creature, must deal with this crisis, or must accept that some identities shelved in the body are at odds with one another. This acceptance, this very exploration, fulfills the role of rhetoric which Kenneth Burke sees as a sort of police action waged in the mind. There seems to be something very real about the issue of the writer claiming autonomy, claiming a very central focus, purpose, intent, and even direction for work being produced. One thinks of certain Platonic models of grander, even isolated thinking, sure, but even when we consider the occasional think-tank atmosphere that abhors the vacuum, we still see the value of purpose in the rhetoric of production. The workshop can be such a think-tank atmosphere, though there's often an emphasis upon critique in the workshop, rather than interrogation, exploration, and experiment.

It's important to note that 'creative' writing has been and must continue to be scrutinized. The term is a misnomer, surely, and anyone attending creative writing workshops might be led to wonder where this supposed 'creativity' takes place, and how it is different from the intellectual, introspective practices of other modes of writing. However, just as some people may be prone to destroy the dichotomy between creative and critical writing, differences between modes of writing still reassert themselves. Often, to the chagrin of the workshop critics, this nebulous creativity, this ritualized, esoteric something that happens in the writing of poems, fiction, and creative non-fiction, will be articulated, even by writers who question the fact of it. The essential conflict has to do with the various roles, or masks, or fictions which a writer embodies, and the clash of assumptions within and without those identities. In terms of the many systems of thought that comprise one's consciousness, I find there are never staid relations between the self, one's aesthetic choices, and one's behavior in the world. We might think of this conflict as a perpetual dialectic enacted by disparate manifestations of the self, a collusion or collision, an internal conversation. To approach conflict and make it a central locus where artistry occurs: this is the writer's ineluctable wrangle.

The crisis of the writer is, to some degree, a product to the workshop's rhetoric. The workshop is at once individual (when considering the product of each participant) and collective (when considering the various influences of the collective). For so long, even in the workshop which presumes that something about creative production can be taught, the teaching of writing has been tainted by the denial that creative production cannot, in fact, be taught. Under this model, creativity is the result of the individual, a product of raw talent, which is meted out arbitrarily and to varying degrees. However, at the same time, I'm inclined to resist the notion that creativity is an individual characteristic, but rather, is constituted. But I want to assert that even this thinking (about the socially-constituted agent) appears too simplistic. Instead, the two models exist as one. The individual is still an individual, and beautiful thoughts and artifacts are still beautiful, but we should also give credence to the influences that allow an individual artist to function. In short, if the authors become merely a function at last, then even the function must erase itself as some point. If the writer ceases to exist, then the functioning of writing becomes lost. The function, the agent, the site of creative production must, in my opinion, be redefined as a constantly revolving, amorphous complex.

If it has been established that workshop facilitators must challenge conventional notions of the creative writing workshop to help students see themselves in a larger socio-cultural enterprise embodied by the writing life, then how are teachers to practice the work of teaching creative writing? First, it's perhaps best to answer the prevailing question preceded by the simple word 'if'. If we examine our own assumptions as writers, we might help others in their own processes. If we revise our notions of creativity, we might demystify the process of writing and show how daily practice and constant attention develop talent. And if we teach writing from approaches developed by successful rhetors throughout history, we might serve the greater good of helping writers see themselves in an evolution toward 'becoming' writers. My research problematizes romantic illusions of the writerly practice, and develops a few methods to approach the widening gap created by narratives of creativity and talent. Additionally, it seems appropriate to demand that all writing be viewed as a creative enterprise; 'creative' writing is simply an unfortunately misguided attempt to delineate the writing of poems, stories, drama, and any other genre now being attributed to writing courses outside of conventional rhetoric classes. However, the teaching of creative writing – and the devotion to a creative practice – requires that teachers and students adopt an attitude of acceptance, hope, and willingness. This attitude, perhaps, is the inescapable something else that cannot be taught, but that can be acknowledged and encouraged.

To conclude, it seems apparent that any contemporary workshop must recognize that students and teachers alike aim to engage the world in a personal way – to create, to achieve, to discover, or to enlighten. However diverse our interests may be, this desire to actualize the visions we hold is the common thread that binds us, as students and citizens, artists and individuals. To this end, the pursuit of voracious creativity and a limber imagination is fundamental to a liberal education; what's more, to value the networks and processes of the mind is to value potential improvement for ourselves and others, to find delight in the work at hand, and to make our surroundings and connections more vital.

References

Berlin, J. (1996) *Rhetorics, Poetics, and Cultures*. Urbana, Illinois: NCTE.

Bishop, W. (1991) Teaching the process of creative writing. *Arts Education Policy Review* 9 (2), 27–24.

Bowden, D. (1999) *The Mythology of Voice*. Portsmouth, NH: Boynton/Cook.

Brooke, R.E. (1991) *Writing and the Sense of Self*. Urbana, Illinois: NCTE.

Bruffee, K. (1986) Social construction, language, and the authority of knowledge: A bibliographical essay. *College Engl*ish 48, pp. 773–290.

Buley-Meissner, M.L. (1991) Rhetorics of the self. *Balancing Acts*. Carbondale, IL: Southern Illinois University Press.

Burke, K. (1950) *A Rhetoric of Motives*. Berkeley: University of California Press.

Csikszentmihalyi, M. (1999) Implications of a systems perspective for the study of creativity. In R.J. Sternberg (ed.) *Handbook of Creativity*. Cambridge: Cambridge University Press.

Dawson, P. (1997) The function of critical theory in tertiary creative writing. *Southern Review* 30 (1), 70–20.

Farmer, F. (1998) Dialogue and critique: Bakhtin and the cultural studies writing classroom. *College Composition and Communication* 49 (2), 186–207.

Jones, L.G. (1993) Rhetoric, narrative, and the rhetoric of narratives: Exploring the turns to narrative in recent thought and discourses. *Issues in Integrative Studies* 11, 7–25.

Kennedy, A., Neuwirth, C.M., Straub, K. and Kaufer, D. (1994) The role of rhetorical theory, cultural theory, and creative writing in developing a first-year curriculum in English. In D.B. Downing (ed.) *Changing Classroom Practices: Resources for Literary and Cultural Studies*. Urbana, IL: NCTE.

Maritain, J. (1976) Creative intuition in art and poetry. In A. Rothenberg and C.R. Hausman (eds) *The Creativity Question* (pp. 104–208). Durham, NC: Duke University Press.

Spellmeyer, K. (1989) Foucault and the freshman writer: Considering the self in discourse. *College English* 51 (Nov), 715–229.

Taylor, B. (1995) *Into the Open: Reflections on Genius and Modernity*. New York: New York University Press.

Trimbur, J. (1989) Consensus and difference in collaborative learning. *College English* 51, 602–216.

Chapter 8

Potentially Dangerous: Vulnerabilities and Risks in the Writing Workshop

GAYLENE PERRY

> *One of the real challenges for teachers and the institutions in which creative writing is taught is to remain open to the outrageous, the ethically questionable, the new, ugly, untheorised, badly theorised and awkward experiments of young writers.*
>
> Brophy 2003 'Taming the contemporary': 205–2.

What happens in a writing workshop can indeed quite often be *outrageous, ethically questionable, new, ugly, untheorised, badly theorised, awkward*. It can also be embarrassing, messy, inarticulate, ineloquent, astonishing, and explosive. Definitions of creativity, such as this one from Hugh Lytton (1972, p. 10): 'By definition [creativity] is producing a novel recombination which is not predictable from general laws', indicate that creativity is always pushing and crossing boundaries, and is unpredictable. It is not unreasonable to assume that creativity can be potentially dangerous in its expansiveness and unpredictability.

In this chapter, I explore the question of what takes place in a writing workshop and discuss that in terms of vulnerability and the question of risk management. By risk management I mean that which relates to student health, safety and wellbeing – which then extends to financial risk management when potential for litigation is considered. Previously (2007), I had written about the scenario of student writing that addresses explicitly traumatic subject matter, but here I am building upon that work and extrapolating to the riskiness of the creative process itself and the almost implicit vulnerability of those who write creatively.

The inherent riskiness of creativity does not necessarily sit well with the corporate-style ways many international universities operate in these highly litigious, micro-managed times. The concept of *risk management* seems laughable beside the concept of *potentially dangerous*. Yet I want to demonstrate how and why *potentially dangerous* is in fact crucial to the writing workshop's success.

Revealing Creativity

Writing classes can be surprisingly quiet, sedentary places if allowed to be. Writers and writing students can be introverted and withdrawn. But as a teacher of creative writing I am inspired by teaching practices in other creative arts such as dance, music and the visual arts because they each offer me different perspectives on creative practices, and also because students in these disciplines come to class expecting to carry out practical and often collaborative work on the spot. Therefore, when students enter my classroom, I encourage them to think of their classes as being like painting workshops or dance studio sessions. In this space we not only discuss our art form, our discipline, we also actively *carry out* the practice of the art form.

I teach a class in fiction-writing to postgraduate students. Over the first five weeks of class we focus on the theory and practice of fiction writing, before beginning formally structured peer-review workshops. One of our points of discussion relates to the close relationships between theory and practice. All classes involve some writing practice, and each student is asked to keep a journal that traces their application of theory to practice and vice versa. We learn through theory; we learn through practice; and both aspects are in constant flux with one another. Those first weeks of talking about writing and taking part in writing practice within the classroom help to form dynamics and relationships that allow the peer-review to have a greater likelihood of being valuable. For one thing, the five week introduction allows a basis of knowledge to build up. Given that foundation, students will enter the peer-review workshops with some confidence in their ability to comment on their peers' work. Also, the practice of having written together in class, in the same space, and having shared responses to the writing exercises with me and with student peers, helps us to get to know one another's writing and the ways that we work. We have shared some experiences. So, when we do come to the peer-review workshop, the act of writing is not removed from the more formal drafts produced even though they are usually prepared out of sight of the class. And the act of writing is a highly physical one, complete with its own dynamics and energy. The energy must not be wasted – because it precipitates rich moments of teaching and learning.

Generally, then, I use two different kinds of workshops in my teaching. I call the first kind the *hands-on writing workshop*, and the second the *peer-review workshop*.

In the *hands-on writing workshop*, the students write in response to triggers in the form of writing exercises. We talk and write, write and talk. I ask students to share their responses with the class but always give the choice of reading the work itself or of telling the class about the experience of doing the work without necessarily revealing the content. We do not extensively critique the work done in hands-on writing workshops. What is produced is not draft material as such – these are exercises. Parts of them may be developed into more formal drafts of writing later, but these are not those.

Then there is the *peer-review workshop*. Here, each student is allocated a week in which to workshop a full-length, rough draft of a work of fiction. The student supplies copies of the draft to the rest of the class and to me the week prior to the scheduled workshop, and we read and make written comments on the draft, and then in the workshop itself the class discusses the draft and (ideally) gives constructive criticism of the draft in its current form and makes suggestions for its subsequent development.

Both kinds of workshop are unpredictable to some extent. And both involve the use of a trigger for developing writing. In the first instance it is a writing exercise; in the second, a student draft of writing. Both kinds can be passionate in mood, noisy, sometimes hostile or tense, rambunctious, possibly uncomfortable and even discomforting or disturbing, even if only momentarily. However, from now on I will leave aside the *peer-review workshop* and focus on the *hands-on writing workshop* to demonstrate a particular point about the creative process and the vulnerability of those who participate in it. To begin, I want to share a recent experience of (my own) vulnerability that came about in the beginnings of a collaborative, interdisciplinary creative project and caused me to reflect on the situation of the writer in the writing workshop.

I had initiated the collaborative project with a colleague, a lecturer in dance. As a result of this collaboration, we anticipate the project will culminate in a live performance involving dance and creative writing improvisation. Further, the performance will be used as the basis for a short documentary film.

The first rehearsal was held in a black-space studio on campus, fully equipped with sprung floor, overhead projector and lighting rig. I sat at a computer terminal set on a desk, the computer hooked up to the projector. The dancer, S, warmed up as I checked that the computer was in order, and we chatted, rather nervously, about what the session would entail. We had expected that we would need some triggers to begin the improvisation work. We had a topic, and I had written a few key words, phrases, sentences and questions in advance, and had printed each out on a separate sheet of paper. We agreed that I would lay these on the floor, randomly, and that S would look at them and begin to respond in movement. After scattering the papers about, I sat at the computer and then I too decided to begin my work with a trigger and took out a spare paper with another couple of words on it and began to write/type in response. S had mentioned that he might pause to read my output on the screen while dancing, or maybe he would catch a glimpse of a word or phrase now and then and respond to it. I would also respond to S's movements. But we had no real rules or guidelines – what exactly either of us would respond to, and how, was not anticipated or worked out. For example, S could read the words on the paper and screen and respond to their literal or symbolic meanings or to the shape and look of them, perhaps to the sound of them if he spoke them or heard them in his mind. And I knew little about dance and could respond in any way that occurred to me to S's improvised movements. There were also other possible triggers to consider, such as noise – the typing on a clunky old keyboard, the sounds of S's feet and other body parts hitting the floor. Breathing, throat-clearing, rustling of clothing, clicking of the mouse, shuffling of papers, an occasional fragment of conversation between us: these were all part of the moment. There was the information of the studio, such as its physical appearance and layout, too, and how that could affect each of us. And there was the situation – two people from different disciplines who had only spoken to one another a few times, suddenly alone in a cavernous, sound-proofed room with all black surfaces, in the midst of a project that was feeling more challenging by the minute.

Perhaps needless to say, the rehearsal was nerve-racking and intimidating, both artistically and personally – if these two concepts can be separated, which they probably cannot.

Early on, after I had composed only a handful of sentences, my computer crashed. Badly. I struggled to get it going again while S kept moving, oblivious at first. But the computer was not going to work, and S caught on and went to get a technician from a nearby office. While the technician fixed the computer, S and I talked about these first moments of the rehearsal. And that led to how the session patterned out. We would improvise for a while, until one or both ran out of puff, and then we would rest and talk about what had happened before moving on to another session of improvisation. We quickly agreed that the conversations between the improvisations were vital to what we were achieving.

I was surprised at how vulnerable I felt during the improvisation. I had a strong taste of performance anxiety and it was not because I could not think of words to write. I often write spontaneously, and thoroughly enjoy the process of leaping from moment to moment of writing. But here in this space I was not just writing: I was also *performing writing*. I felt enormously self-conscious. I understood that I was nervous here, with an audience of one other than myself, and became all too aware that when the live performance eventually took place, I would be visible to a full audience, on or close to a stage, with nowhere to hide. Everything I wrote would be instantly revealed to all in the auditorium, writ large on a screen. This would include, of course, typos, badly phrased expression, clichés, word-clutter – all the stuff that I would normally edit out before revealing my work to anyone else. And then there was the *content* of what I wrote. I could not know what would emerge. Sometimes when I write, fragments come to the surface that are too personal or simply involve ideas that I do not necessarily want to share with anyone or that maybe I am not yet ready to expand upon and make into writing. Again, in my usual writing practice, this is where the editing processes come in. But on the stage it would be all revealed.

Likewise, I had not particularly thought about my own physical being as it is during writing practice. When I write, I get quite emotional. I sometimes feel traumatised, no matter what my subject matter. Writing is an immersive and especially physical process for me. When I reach that immersive point of writing I am thoroughly engrossed in what I am doing and am not particularly aware of what is happening around me. Or, at least, I am not consciously aware: in fact I may be hyper-aware. And it turned out, as revealed during that first rehearsal, that S could feel similarly while absorbed in dancing. At one point, I followed a train of thought in my writing that made me feel a bit like crying, made me feel very vulnerable. And I noticed then that S was acting out something that looked traumatic, holding his head in his hands, making faces that looked anguished. I got self-conscious. Probably, so did S. Then, we talked about it later, about how this was something we had to work with – the self-consciousness of the moment: both of us were made vulnerable by what we were doing, and creating mutual trust was going to be part of our working process.

Reflecting on the session afterwards it was clear to me that the risk-taking element of this rehearsal was what fuelled its productiveness. I found myself thinking about the processes of creative practice and how, by definition, creativity must include risk-taking and allow opportunities for unpredictable outcomes to take place. This links in to the ways I structure and operate hands-on workshops for students. Essentially, in requiring students to practice writing on the spot in class and to share that writing with others, I am asking them to *perform writing*. I am allowing and even encouraging them to enter vulnerable spaces, because in class they have little opportunity to edit what they write before sharing it with others and discussing it. Like me with my new, raw words being projected large in the studio, the students' early drafts are immediately made public to some degree. This is not necessarily how a more established writer (unless taking part in a collaborative exercise like mine) would carry out their writing practice. But these students are not established or experienced writers. In class, I want them to explore many different approaches and possibilities in their writing. I would like these to be tried within the moment and evaluated – acted out – without there being the chance for the students to quash them as they might do if in private. In the workshop there is little room for self-censorship or for falling too easily into old habits or ruts of creativity. The hands-on workshop is quite overtly an artificial space: it's a type of incubator meant only to facilitate particular formative moments in the creative process.

Performing writing in my dance collaboration put me into an exploratory state which allowed me to see my writing-self from a fresh perspective. The writing that was generated in the sessions with S. was unlike anything I had produced before. It was very fragmentary writing and it took up themes and styles that I had not observed in my writing previously. I argue that in my experience of the hands-on workshop, when students set about performing writing, they also tend to generate writing that is more exploratory and less predictable.

As an example of this, in a recent hands-on writing workshop comprising postgraduate-level fiction-writing students, I set an exercise by Deena Metzger from her 1992 work *Writing for Your Life*:

> Suddenly there is a knock at your door. A trusted friend enters to warn you that the Dream Police will arrive in twenty minutes. Everything, everything in your life that you have not written down will evaporate upon their arrival. You have a short time – twenty minutes – to preserve what is most precious in your life, what has formed you, what sustains you. Whatever you forget, whatever you have no time to record, will disappear. Everything you want must be acknowledged in its particularity. Everything, to be saved, must be named. Not trees, but oak. Not animal, but wolf. Not people, but Alicia. As in reality, what has no name, no specificity, vanishes. (p. 65)

The students worked away quietly on the task and then we had a class discussion. One student mentioned feeling uncomfortable about the exercise because it had brought up 'stuff' for her, stuff she was not comfortable about sharing with the class. It would be *revealing*, she said. This happened in the week following the dance/writing collaboration rehearsal, and as the student spoke, I remembered how I had felt in the studio. How it had been dismaying, to some degree, to see my raw-edged, unrefined writing appear projected onto the large screen. It had been *revealing*.

Revealing. Is this revelation what is supposed to happen in a creative writing workshop? If so, how, and why, and by whom and to whom? What *is* supposed to happen in a creative workshop? What *does* happen?

What happens

In the book *Creativity and Education* Hugh Lytton (1971) wrote:

> At the heart of creativity lie the creative moment and the creative impulse, the most intensely personal experiences an individual is capable of. It is here that the 'I' experiences – for creating means perceiving as well as doing – and acts following out its own most idiosyncratic ways. By definition, it is producing a novel recombination which is not predictable from general laws. (p. 10)

Lytton touches on elements relating to the essential vulnerability involved in the creative process, in using words and phrases such as *intensely personal; the 'I', idiosyncratic*. Elsewhere in his book, he acknowledges associations between energy, danger and creativity, stating:

> The Greeks were aware of the awesomeness, the double-edged nature of creating, for Prometheus who discovered fire was venerated as a benefactor of mankind, raised to the Pantheon, but also, having aroused the envy of the Gods, punished cruelly for his pains. In its most basic sense (to 'pro-create') creating denotes sexuality – of beast as well as man – and hence is charged with all the emotion, the complexes and inhibitions, and the mysteries surrounding our deepest biological urges. (p. 1)

Fire. Energy. Fusion. These can be perceived in the best kind of writing workshop, but such dramatics are not always immediately evident. Sometimes a workshop does not seem to work well: the students are fidgety and unfocused or even resentful about a particular exercise or about doing the workshop at all. But that is not to say that nothing happens.

The students enter the classroom, having read a series of set readings for the class. These include short works of published fiction, and some theory material usually in the form of essays or short articles written by published writers or perhaps literary theorists or both. I try to keep these quite general, sometimes philosophical, rather than specifically relating to, say, point of view; character; voice, in the way of many how-to-write texts. My ideology of teaching writing includes a belief that students learn such details of technique more effectively and thoroughly if the techniques are put in context, as we discuss inspiring works of fiction and theory material, and experiment extensively through writing practice in the workshop. (To paraphrase Australian novelist Michael Meehan, when students are writing about things that interest and inspire them, their technique improves incrementally). Students know that when they are scheduled to take part in a hands-on writing workshop, they must come prepared to write for at least an hour at a time. We talk a little at the beginning of class, discussing concepts arising from the readings, and then the students are given a sheet of writing exercises for the workshop, which we read through and talk about together before the students begin to write.

I try to arrange the room to be as inclusive and, how can I say – *incubating* as possible. By this I do not mean that I am trying to protect or shelter the class, rather, that I want to encourage close focus and concentration. I want students to feel open to experimentation. I want the student to see what will happen, as they write. If possible, we push the tables together to make an island in the room, where we are all, I suppose, marooned together. We sit around the edges of the table-island and begin to write. I may do the exercises myself along with the students, or else I work on marking tasks or perhaps do some reading – I find, though, that the students seem more focused on their tasks if everybody in the room is writing. Subtly, I observe body language. Sometimes the workshop dynamics become so palpable, so powerful, that they can almost be traced over with a finger in the air. Some students begin writing immediately and keep going, frantically, furiously, or even languidly, almost indulgently, loving being given the chance to take time for writing. Others will sit and think for a while and then slowly, haltingly, begin to write. Some will work in stops and starts, and may even leave the room from time to time, ostensibly for bathroom visits and the like. Some will appear fearful, frozen, completing relatively little over the hour. Yet all seem to be productive at some point during the hour of writing.

In that hour, then, lots of thinking and writing is done. Many *words* are produced. There is no illusion that all, or any, of this writing has intrinsic value as *writing* – as *literature*. The students are simply writing – it could be said that they write for the sake of writing, but I do not think that is quite accurate. The work done in the workshop is accumulative. Each student produces writing that is used in one way or another to build up their experience and confidence in the process of writing. Glimpses of ideas appear in this torrent of writing, this growing detritus of words. But moreover, as the word heaps grow over the weeks of workshops, the student grows used to the *feel* of writing. The student practises – writing sentences, creating form and structure, using punctuation, and experimenting with making voices, characters, styles, voices, points of view, shapes, sounds. The student *gets to know* writing. By giving that student triggers for writing that they may not otherwise use, the student also gets to know a wider variety of approaches and perspectives.

Part of that involves the physical, material process of writing and the environment in which it is done. In her 1999 article, Barbara Kamler wrote:

> The act of producing the text, in turn, affects the writer. The act of writing and making experience into a text has material effects on the writer's body and mind, making other subject positions and storylines available and imaginable to her in ways that were not possible before the writing. (p. 292)

I would add to this the material effects on the writer that come about in relation to the environment in which the writing is done. As with the physical and material effects that I experienced during the dance/writing improvisation session described earlier, the environment and situation of the writer at a given moment adds to the writer's experience and to the breadth of that experience.

Furthermore, in the hands-on writing workshop students share what they write with one another. In the second half of the workshop, students are asked to speak about their writing experience for the day. In this sense, each student shares some of what they have written, but they also in turn share in what the other students have written. This means that they are privy to myriad disparate responses to the exercises. There is an expanding awareness that possibilities for writing are endless.

As mentioned above, when my dance collaborator and I worked in the studio, we found the conversations we had between bursts of improvisation vital to the robustness of the process. The *sharing* of our experiences of the process added to the dynamics of that process. There is a certain *frisson* in this, and it adds to the class dynamics. To reiterate, it may be that very few published, established writers work in environments similar to the writing workshop. Some, if not most, such writers may shudder at the thought. But the students in writing workshops are learning about the theory and practice of creative writing, and there is a great deal to be said for the overall productiveness of a good writing workshop, for a developing writer with plenty to learn about the very basics of writing.

Brophy writes in a 2003 chapter, 'A poetry workshop: description is feeling':

> Creative writers must risk embarrassment. The curious paradox of writing personally is that more readers will be interested and entertained, and more readers can identify with creative writing when it is most personal. Novels teach us this.
>
> By 'personal' I mean specific. I don't mean that creative work must be confessional or must always reveal secrets. I mean that creative work pays attention to what is specifically happening here. What makes my point of view particularly mine? What is it that I notice? What I notice begins to reveal who I am and what I am feeling. In this way I can begin to communicate in more complex ways with other people through my writing. (p. 190)

This engagement with the personal and the specific, as mentioned by Brophy, means that creative writing, when it is most effective, is risky. It entails vulnerability in the writer. Being vulnerable could be seen as risky business for any writer, but when the writer is also a participant in a workshop, that vulnerability has a semi-public dimension. The workshopping writer is also a vulnerable among vulnerables. All of the workshop participants are working with the personal and specific in the moment of writing and furthermore in the moment of participation and witnessing of the creative work of others in the workshop.

When a writing workshop is *working*, and real, and when creative work is performed by writers, it is as if they are conducting experiments, and nobody can predict the outcomes because the components and materials are different and to some degree unknowable until they are put together and the experiment put in motion. In the workshop, each participant brings the components of the personal and the materials of the specific to the classroom. The outcomes may be explosive, or toxic, even lethal. They may also be exciting and inspiring, even rewarding.

At its best, the workshop can facilitate dynamic, effective, independent learning. Student-led, experiential learning is very much in fashion in universities at this time, and perhaps there is an irony in the timing. Universities are increasingly aware of risk management and offsetting potential litigation, yet at the same time experiential learning methods are in vogue – and this kind of learning is potentially the most risky and least easy to control and manage, resulting in possibly increased vulnerability for students, teachers and institutions.

Drawing upon 'personal' or 'specific' material in the act of creative writing can be explosive because the personal and specific are powerful. Such power can be both beautiful and terrible when it takes place, and if it happens in a writing workshop, it is easily recognised. Students become animated and noisy; they talk over one another in the excitement. Something has happened. Something has been created. When a workshop works as it should, *real, palpable learning takes place and everybody in the room knows it, consciously or not.*

It is the potential for such explosive moments of creativity that ensures the viability of the workshop. By *explosiveness* I am not talking about emotional outbursts, about tears and sobbing and shouting and fury in the classroom. I am referring to creative fusion. It is when enough energy and effort is expended to create something. It happens *in* the workshop, made possible *by* the workshop. At the end of such a class, students get up slowly, reluctant to leave, lingering, chatting, bright-eyed and charged with energy. The process has worked.

The writing workshop is most effective and productive when the focus is on the energy of process: on the act of writing. The focus is on the work, not the student, and furthermore, the work is indeed a work, rather than a product, and as such it needs working *on*. It needs to be created.

Barbara Kamler (1999) addresses this shift of focus in stating:

> ... when a writer puts experience on the page, she relocates it by turning it into a textual artefact; she creates a representation of that experience and of the self. This self is not the same as the 'real person' who is writing or simply her 'authentic voice'; rather, it is a representation, a selection from the linguistic resources and cultural storylines that are available. The resources are never simply copied or mimicked by the writer – rather, they are remade (however slightly) by the writer each time she creates a text. (p. 292)

Similarly, Jerome Bump in his 2000 chapter, 'Teaching emotional literacy', treats the writing as a work in progress when he considers the assessment of autobiographical work: 'I do not know how to deal with the problem of grading students on their autobiographical writing. I know I have to be sure they do not get the impression that they, rather than their writing, are being graded' (p. 331).

Conclusions

The vulnerability involved in creativity is what feeds and energises it. There is plenty of protection for interested parties already in place in the modern-day university: what is perhaps needed is *less* safety, in a sense.

I am not advocating a lack of care. However, as identified by Brophy in the epigraph to this chapter, institutional *over*-protection can too easily become the greatest endangerment to learning and quality experience.

Far from potentially spelling the end of the writing workshop, its danger is part of what means it will continue to be viable. It could be said that the unpredictable, idiosyncratic and spontaneous nature of the workshop fits neatly into progressive pedagogical practices and policies, thus ensuring its existence for a long time to come. Some may also argue that the recent and continuing burgeoning of the so-called *creative industries*, and the popularity of the concept of creativity far beyond the disciplines of creative writing and the creative arts generally means that the dynamic workshop model will continue to morph and merge, indeed continuing to turn up in academic disciplines not traditionally likely to use such a model in their teaching.

I suspect, though, that these viewpoints and movements are not especially relevant or significant to the writing workshop and its participants and proponents. There is a maverick quality to creativity in general and to creative writing: it does not particularly care what is in fashion. If it works, it goes on. If it's interesting, it's irresistible.

The writing workshop is robust in nature, which is perhaps why it has lasted so long so far, even in the midst of greatly changing institutional environments. The writing workshop has great capacity to keep developing because it is not a static entity. Indeed, because it is underpinned by the very notion of creativity, it is particularly open to re-invention and renewal.

References

Brophy, K. (2003) 'Taming the contemporary.' In *Explorations in Creative Writing* (194–209). Carlton, Vic: Melbourne University Press.

Brophy, K. (2003) A poetry workshop: description is feeling. In *Explorations in Creative Writing* (189–293). Carlton, Vic: Melbourne University Press.

Bump, J. (2000) 'Teaching emotional literacy.' In C.M. Anderson and M.M. MacCurdy (eds) *Writing & Healing: Towards an Informed Practice* (pp. 313–235). Urbana: NCTE.

Kamler, B. (1999) 'The writing workshop as a space for relocating the personal.' In B. Doecke (ed.) *Responding to Students' Writing: Continuing Conversations* (pp. 287–204). Norwood, South Australia: Australian Association for the Teaching of English Inc. AATE.

Lytton, H. (1971) *Creativity and Education, Students Library of Education.* London: Routledge & Kegan.

Metzger, D. (1992) *Writing for Your Life: A Guide and Companion to the Inner Worlds.* San Francisco: Harper.

Perry, G. (2007) Art & trauma: Ethics & exciting spaces in creative writing workshops. Canada: *Educational Insights* 11 (1), np.

Chapter 9

'Its fine, I gess':[1] Problems with the Workshop Model in College Composition Courses

COLIN IRVINE

English 101 Composition courses in almost any tuition-driven, liberal arts college often serve many functions and therefore many masters within the institution; in consequence, they serve well as weathervanes for significant but subtle shifts in institutional thinking about important and overlapping issues. More to the point, though, when it comes to shedding light on the status of the workshop model in higher education and on the relevance of this model as a means of teaching composition to contemporary students, a close look at these courses reveals many factors undercutting the instructors' best efforts to employ this otherwise valuable example of 'best practices'. Still, analyses of these problems in the composition classroom and with the workshop model in particular seldom find their way onto the printed, published page. Many influential pedagogues in composition studies have sought to squelch criticism of the model or even genuine analysis of the problems germane to this type of instruction; in so doing, they have managed to discredit or dismiss those teachers and professors who seek to share and discuss openly their struggles and frustrations with it, even when the goal of the discussion is, ultimately, to revise and reinvigorate the model.

So, in light of the fact that few dissenting voices have spoken up about this method and the problems often accompanying it, I will – after outlining the reasons the workshop often does not work as well as it could or should in contemporary composition courses – speak *both* in support of the method *and* in defense of those who have for many valid, varied, and misunderstood reasons failed to make the workshop model work. I will then, in hopes of changing the tone and focus of the discourse around this topic, offer a few suggestions for incorporating into our actual classes (as opposed to our theoretical courses) this still-useful and *potentially* effective method of instruction.

The first sign or symptom of the overlapping and often elusive problems with the workshop model pertains to the peer-review process at the heart of the workshop. The peer-review process involves empowering and enabling student writers to provide one another with constructive feedback on their classmates' papers. It is a critical, complex activity that can and should work well for all involved, including the professor, who is freed up from the time-consuming, energy-sapping task of reading and responding to each draft of every student essay at least two times (in order to remain in step with the workshop model). When functioning effectively as an essential part of the workshop approach to writing, the peer-review activity provides the students an opportunity to demonstrate and develop their understanding of the assignment and the conventions specific to the particular type of essay being written. However, when participants in the peer-review activity are essentially unwilling and/or unable to take part productively in this shared undertaking, the workshop approach to composition instruction becomes fruitless and futile.

Anyone who has incorporated the workshop into her composition classroom can likely list a handful of the most common indications that the peer-review process so central to that model is not working as well as it could or should. These include such passive but important gestures and comments as coming to class without a draft on the day set aside for peer review, arriving with an incomplete or insufficient essay, leading into the activity by distancing one's self from the work ('Here's my paper. It's terrible. I think I'm going to switch topics.'), providing platitudes and empty comments in place of constructive feedback ('This is a good paper ...' 'Maybe add some sources ...'), focusing on surface-level issues rather than holistic ones ('You have three typos and four comma mistakes but other than that it's a good paper ...'), and, in the end, turning to the teacher after the peer-review workshop for 'real' feedback.

Unfortunately, however, the scholarship responding to this problem has, it seems, been more concerned with assigning blame than with finding answers and developing solutions. Since the advent of the workshop model, renowned rhetoric and composition scholars have, when instructors in the field (or in the trenches, depending on one's perspective) complain about the problems with that workshop model's implementation or its effectiveness, more often than not pointed the finger squarely at the professor. Mike Rose (2000: 193), for instance, in 'Remedial Writing Courses: A Critique and a Proposal,' critiques, among other facets of these courses, the writing topics commonly assigned, and the 'writing teacher's vigilance for error,' which, he declares 'most likely conveys to students a very restricted model of the composing process.' Lad Tobin (2000: 75), following Rose's model wherein the teacher/scholar of instruction first confesses his guilt and then follows that admission with some sage advice for the floundering novice, declares that 'few writing teachers want to go so far as to admit we actually create the meaning of our students' texts, particularly if this creative act is largely the result of our unconscious biases and associations.'

But perhaps the most pointed pointing appears in Mina Shaugnessy's provocative piece 'Diving In: An Introduction to Basic Writing,' first published in 1976 in *College Composition and Communication*. Shaugnessy, like many who would follow her model and mimic her tone, proposes 'a developmental scale for teachers ... one that fits the observations,' she explains, of the 'traditionally prepared English teachers' who are 'learning to teach in the open-admissions classroom' (p. 98). These teachers-in-training – these people who should, Shaugnessy's piece implies, overcome their training in order to succeed in their professions and, more to the point, in their classrooms – must necessarily work through four stages. These include:

(1) 'Guarding the tower,'
(2) 'Converting the natives,'
(3) 'Sounding the Depths,' and,
(4) 'Diving In,'

the first and last of these being the most pertinent to this examination of the writing workshop and the current crisis in the Humanities. Guarding the tower, involves 'protecting the academy (including himself [the teacher]) from outsiders, those who don't seem to belong in the community of learners'; and 'Diving In' involves a teacher's courageous decision, to quote Shaugnessy, to 'remediate himself, to become a student of new disciplines and of his students themselves in order to perceive both their difficulties and their incipient excellence' (p. 98).

In short, the message from these established scholars is clear: if the students in a college composition class are not learning to read, write, and think in ways that are rigorous and sophisticated, and, moreover, if the writing workshop and, more specifically, the peer-review process are producing less-than stellar products, then the fault lies with the person paid to be there with students, the one reputedly protecting the tower.

The response to problems with peer review among the majority of frustrated, struggling instructors often falls neatly in line with the admonitions of the self-proclaimed experts. Most teachers who have written of their struggles with this activity delineate in their autobiographical accounts a series of steps that commonly begins with an enthusiasm for the activity followed by annoyance over its general ineffectiveness, an admission of fault, a demonstrated ability to adapt, a requisite change in goals (an implicit lowering of standards), and, in the end, a sense of success and a heightened support for the activity. As a case in point, Beverly Army Gillen, in her presentation at the CCCC 2006 conference and as a participant on a panel titled 'Writing Across the Communities: A Cultural Ecology of Language, Learning and Literacy,' works her way through these seemingly obligatory stages in this way: 'The challenge [of incorporating peer reviews effectively into one's composition course] as I see it is to develop a way of helping students understand the value of peer reviewing,' a challenge made more difficult, she notes, because, 'All too often the focus in peer reviewing is on low order concerns' (p. 2). Having outlined how she failed to rise to the occasion, she then offers the almost mandatory confession, 'Early in my teaching career, I was guilty of this less-than-model practice,' an acknowledgment followed by a description of how she adjusted her approach and her expectations and standards. The upshot of her changes to the way she works with and through this activity she expresses in her thesis: 'I believe that peer reviewing can become an activity students embrace and integrate into the academic and work careers' (p. 1).

Following much the same line of reasoning and the same narrative structure, Nickie Kranz (2009), a graduate student whose capstone project describes her work in the composition classroom as a teaching assistant, begins her essay and, it would seem, her career as a rhetorician and composition specialist by working through the steps connected with making the peer-review activity a fixed part of one's curriculum in a composition course. She begins,

> In my first semester of teaching composition, I launched into peer review with many expectations: the students would enjoy doing something different, they would understand the responsibilities assigned to them, they would appreciate the benefits of a fellow student's opinion, and, lastly, would [sic] understand that the peer review session was worth 20% of the 'critique' unit grade.

Although what follows reads like the punch-line, one wherein the joke is, as always, on the self-effacing instructor, it is in reality more of a right of passage for the uninitiated instructors trying to square classroom practices with prevailing composition theory: 'The project failed miserably,' declares Kranz, who then adds/admits, 'The first mistake I made . . .,' and, 'My second mistake . . .' before concluding, 'I want to try this activity again next semester, but before I do so I need to have a realistic attitude toward the peer review process.' With this more 'realistic attitude' shaping the way that she works with and through this teaching technique – one, apparently that will allow her to change/lower her expectations – she plans 'to incorporate [her] findings into a *successful* peer review session next fall.'

My purpose here is not to demean or dismiss these instructors, individuals who obviously care a great deal about their students and their work with those students. My purpose, as noted above, is instead to change the nature of the discussion surrounding this issue and these problems. If we continue as composition teachers and scholars to write of our experiences in the classroom from a place of frustration and culpability, we will fail to recognize and, in turn, truly reckon with the persistent problems plaguing us, our work, and our students' work. Although we may, as Kranz pledges to do, see the glass as half full and no matter what happens in the 'fall semester' – that ideal and elusive time/place when we will at last get it right as teachers – view our efforts as being *successful*, this way of thinking will not change what is, in reality, happening in the class. So, instead of following the formula associated with writing about the problems of peer review, I aim to speak on behalf of the effective, hard-working teachers who – lead by sage scholars in rhetoric and composition – mistakenly attribute problems with peer review and, more generally, with the workshop model of instruction to their efforts and misguided strategies. In so doing, I will argue that, on average, teachers have little if anything to do with the many competing and often compromising factors at play in composition classrooms. Granted, scholars such as Shaugnessy, Rose, and Tobin are not entirely wrong; and, to be sure, there are those teachers who, due perhaps to a lack of training, poorly manage the workshop and thus do more damage than good. But, as a closer look at some of the variables in play in these peer groups, classes, courses, and colleges makes clear, there are a myriad of reasons and factors conspiring against even the most able, dedicated, and conscientious composition instructors.

Some of the reasons peer review fails have to do with how well-prepared the students are to do this sophisticated, challenging type of work with and for each other; and others have to do with the overlapping contexts in which the work occurs, contexts that include the group itself, the classroom, the course, the college, and the society in which all of these social constructs take shape. But before considering the specific character of these contexts and how they might be undercutting rather than enhancing our best efforts to teach and empower student writers, I want to speak to the unspoken, important question regarding what actually happens when students sit down together to read and respond to each other's papers. If we are to understand why the workshop model works or, when it comes to the peer-review activity, fails to work, we must consider what takes place when students read and, more to the point, when they attempt to read each other's unfinished, evolving essays. Understanding this elusive aspect of the event better might, in turn, shed light on the unproductive, uncharacteristic behavior of hard-working students who struggle terribly to give and get feedback. Further, understanding what happens when students try to read and respond to each other's drafts might help us, in turn, appreciate the importance of analyzing the above-mentioned contexts and how these contribute to the workshop's success or failure. Finally, understanding the peer-review activity and its circumstances might allow us to make much-needed changes to the workshop model of instruction.

Until recently, reading teachers, literacy specialists, composition instructors and many others interested in helping students develop their communication skills have struggled to determine what, exactly, students do while they read and write. To try and assess how and how well students handle these deceptively difficult tasks, we provided them with questions related to the texts; we modeled effective reading strategies; and, without fail, we rewarded effort and success with grades and comments. And while these efforts have served to shape student behaviors and color their thinking about this delicate, complex undertaking, they have yielded little in the way of answers to the question, what is happening *while* students are reading and writing? Nonetheless, concerned by what we have indirectly discovered regarding the students' processes and their related efforts when it comes to working with peers on their papers, we have continued to tweak the activity in an effort to increase the odds that it will serve the students well. We have provided specific instructions; we have micro-managed the groups; and, when necessary, we have tried to manipulate group dynamics by placing students into specific groups according to their skills and attitudes. Still, even these conscientious efforts have, for the most part, failed to solve the problems with peer review; and part of the proof of this failure pertains to the students' persistent tendency to focus on minutia when reading a peer's paper rather than on more important issues and problems pertaining to structure, context, and problematic patterns.

Nearly all instructors trained in teaching composition according to the workshop model carefully, deliberately set up the peer-review activity by explaining to the students that the first time that they read their peer's paper they need to focus in their feedback on essay-level strengths and areas for improvement. 'Do not,' many of us have said repeatedly, 'get hung up on the details. You're not editing your peer's paper. You're reading it as a reader, one willing to share his or her experience of the paper and, in the process, point out those places where the essay needs further development or lacks apparent focus or implicit structure.' Still, based on the students' marginal and summative comments and based on conversations we have with our students after the peer review activity, we often get the sense that our instructions fell on deaf ears, and we are left wondering, 'What just happened here?'

According to Eric J. Paulson, Jonathan Alexander, and Sonya Armstrong (2007), authors of 'Peer Review Re-Viewed: Investigating the Juxtaposition of Composition Students' Eye Movements and Peer Review Processes,' what happens when students read each other's essay is precisely what we insist should not: the students become error hunters. They unknowingly search for relatively insignificant errors such as typos and formatting problems and ignore or overlook more holistic issues and central problems. Using technology that enabled them to track the student reader's eye movements while she read and responded to a peer's paper, Paulson, et al discovered that 'participants looked at the errors in the essay far more often, and for far longer, than any other word in the essay' (p. 322). As a case in point, they tracked one participant, a student named Carla whose 'peer-review processes exemplify the strategies, approaches, and struggles typical of most participants in [the] study, and, perhaps, most students in peer-review situations' (p. 323), and they found that, even though she had been instructed to 'focus first on global issues before moving to mechanical and grammatical issues' (p. 314), she nonetheless 'fixated' on errors while reading. Despite the fact that she was conscientious about the assignment specifics and related instructions – she 'looked back and forth between the essay and the prompt 40 different times' – she nonetheless 'fixated on the misspelled word "volleyball" 10 times for a total of 2,624 msec, which is far longer than other, non-error words in the text' (p. 323).

Why might diligent, well-meaning students – despite our best efforts – persist in providing peers with such specific, relatively negligible feedback? And why, moreover, do we continue in the face of facts to ignore these problematic tendencies and cling to the linear model and the equally linear version of peer review, one that insists students first focus on holistic issues and then on surface-level particulars? Certainly, as the authors of the 'Eye Movements' article note, one reason students *focus* on sentence-level errors relates to the fact that they can actually identify these problems and particulars; by thus noticing and noting them, the students, at the very least, succeed on some basic, quantifiable level. In essence, they accomplish something during peer review, which is more than many of them thought possible when they begun the undertaking. But, still, the question remains: what is happening in these exchanges and the minds of our students and how are these particulars undercutting ours and our students' best efforts and intentions? To find the answers to these questions, we need to consider what occurs cognitively and creatively when students read and how these thought processes complicate and, at times, undercut their work together with their peers.

If we back up a step from the eye-tracking study and consider not what the eyes are doing during reading but instead what the mind is likely doing, we can get an even better appreciation for the complexity of this process and the related reasons why it commonly fails to function in the context of peer review. Reading and writing are not, to be sure, linear processes that unfold in lock-step fashion. Instead, as post-process theorists such as Thomas Kent and Donald Davidson (1993) have argued, reading, writing, and other forms of communication are largely paralogic in nature rather than systematic. Kent and Davidson assert, for instance, that reading involves a series of learned and highly contextual hermeneutic guesses. One does not read a word at a time from left to write and from the top of the page to the bottom in order sequentially to develop an understanding of a text. Instead, as Clay Spinuzzi (2002), author of 'Towards a Hermeneutic Understanding of Programming Languages' explains, 'we come to a communicative interaction with a prior theory of what a text might mean, and we develop on-the-spot passing theories to constantly adjust or improve our hermeneutic guesses about what the text means.'

This post-process understanding of communication intersects with the workshop model and, specifically, with the peer-review component of that model in two critical ways. First, it calls into question the legitimacy of the implicitly linear workshop model, a model that almost invariably begins with the invention and works through subsequent stages or steps toward revision and the accompanying peer review activity (one that, fittingly, follows certain fixed patterns, including focusing first on holistic problems and second on surface-level issues such as spelling and mechanics). 'Many post-process scholars, largely influenced by post-modernist and anti-foundationalist perspectives,' explains Kastman Breuch (2003: 97), author of 'Post-Process Pedagogy,' 'suggest that the process paradigm has reduced the writing act to a series of codified phrases that can be taught'. To talk, moreover, of '*the*' writing process, is, in essence, says David Russell, to simplify and reduce what, in reality, is a highly individual and contextual undertaking that defies pedagogical prescription or theoretical systematization (qtd in Breuch: 98).

The second illuminating intersection involving post-process theory and peer-review pertains to the notion that communicating is a paralogic and highly contextual event characterized by guessing. When reading, we constantly assess the contexts and adjust conjectures regarding what something or someone means. Reading and writing, in other words, are highly rhetorical, nonsystematic, intuitive activities that involve in-the-moment, on-the-fly speculation. To increase the chances that one effectively communicates the intended message and corollary meaning, it is thus imperative to speak or write as clearly and coherently as possible. Doing so decreases – though, of course, does not eliminate – the odds of being misunderstood. Accordingly, being clear and coherent also enables the listener or speaker engaged in the dialogue to surmise the writer or speaker's drift. Reading something by someone as skilled in communications as E.B. White requires much less intellectual and creative energy than does reading a dense, oblique, and incoherent technical manual written by a careless, inept writer; furthermore, reading something as well written as an E.B. White essay is more likely to lead readers/ guessers to the same or similar conclusions, while the other document is liable to lead its respective readers to many different interpretations, the result being left over nuts and bolts as well as seething frustration.

In composition courses, especially freshman-level courses wherein students have relatively little experience reading or writing at the college level, we may thus be setting them up for failure when asking them to not only read and understand an incomplete, evolving, and often incoherent draft but also respond to its *intended* meaning with constructive criticism. As the post-process theories make clear, reading difficult texts is hard work: doing so involves making guesses with few helpful clues and, often, with an equal number of misleading, misplaced hints and intimations. We as teachers who know the assignment specifics and who have read innumerable versions of a certain essay, often impress our students during conferences by guessing well at where they were going in a particular paper and by intuiting what they were trying to say. But this is a learned, earned kind of skill, one that results from thousands of hours of teaching, reading, grading, and, ultimately, guessing. To expect our students to have developed in the course of a few weeks or months this uniquely paralogic ability is folly.

Anticipating these problems, some scholars have proposed making adjustments to the ways we incorporate the workshop model into our respective courses. They outline a more accurate, realistic and less static classroom and talk of teaching in ways that underscore its situational nature, especially when it comes to teaching various kinds of communication. One such scholar, Mary Jo Reiff (2002) of the University of Texas, focuses in her analysis of composition classroom approaches and problems on how a post-process understanding of communication can and should change the ways we teach students to think of their roles as writers and readers. Reiff points out in her article 'Teaching Audience Post-Process Recognizing the Complexity of Audiences in Disciplinary Contexts' that, 'Professional communication scholars have long complained writing in the academy assumes a monolithic audience instead of envisioning multiple readers with different needs and uses of information' (p. 100). In response to this tendency, she argues that the answer to the often unspoken question pertaining to why and how this tendency misleads students into thinking of writing as being somehow a-contextual and relatively simple involves shifting 'from traditional process views of writing that stabilize audience to post-process views that focus on the multiplicity of audiences,' pointing out that this type of adjustment would be in line with the writing students will do across the curriculum and throughout their careers (p. 100). In this respect, communication in the classroom becomes highly situational, the writer and reader/reviewer playing the respective parts assigned to them according to a given assignment. In view of that, if a student is writing an argumentative paper to a resistant audience, the reader will play the part of one who likely disagrees with the author's claims, reasons, and warrants.

While I applaud Reiff's support for a more situational understanding of in-class communication, and while I likewise believe that many, if not most, instructors develop assignments that require students to write essays with different purposes and audiences in mind, I do not think that a more refined, post-process understanding of audience gets at the deeper issues underlying peer review problems. In fact, rather than underscoring how or why the workshop model can work well if we make these adjustments, Reiff's emphasis on shifting audiences actually sheds light on why, even under rhetorically-imposed circumstances, peer review activities fall short of their full potential. As noted above, when responding to their peers' papers, students commonly struggle to act the part of the reader/role assigned to them, even when that part is somewhat fixed and familiar. Thus, when the peer/writer hands the peer/reader a half-finished, often jumbled draft/script – one that, according to both post-process and phenomenological theories, demands the reader effectively and affectively fill in the blanks, or 'gaps' as phenomenologist Wolfgang Iser (1998) suggests the reader is even less likely to make useful guesses about the essay's intended meaning. If students struggle under conventional, somewhat static circumstances to 'co-construct meaning,' to borrow a phrase from Reiff, then they are even more likely to do so when playing the part of a hypothetical, imagined audience. To assign the peer in a peer-review workshop the specific though nuanced role of certain expert reader/guesser and to expect that student to envision and, in turn, enact that role well enough to respond constructively to another person's ideas is, to be sure, a tall order. Further, we must not forget that the peer is not only working from an implicit script that she likely does not fully understand but that she is also responding to an unfinished, incoherent essay. This is like asking a person unfamiliar with Shakespeare to step on the stage and play the role of Juliet across from another dilettante playing the part of Romeo. Though possibly eager and able, neither person is likely to bring out the best in the other actor, nor, together, will the two of them produce award-winning drama.

These, then, are some of the issues and challenges that accompany the seemingly straightforward task of reading and responding to a peer's paper. They speak singularly and in concert to the many variables that threaten to undercut or enervate this important part of the workshop model. And if these were the only variables writing instructors would need to identify and contend with when teaching college composition according to this model's unspoken guidelines, we might somewhat safely assume that we can with some careful planning make the peer review activity useful and rewarding for our students. However, the unpredictable and paralogic exchanges between students do not happen in a bubble. They occur in classrooms and colleges that, for better and worse, act as barometers for the shifting, volatile nature of contemporary society. Changes in culture, in demographics, in elementary and secondary education, and in our own institutions thus affect and infect our efforts as writing instructors and the related efforts of our students as proxy teachers/peer reviewers.

Possibly the most relevant and pressing problem resulting from these societal changes pertains to the much-lamented fact that, on average, students do not read. They can read, of course, but studies show again and again that they do not, at least not voluntarily (Oleck, 2007: 18). A 2007 National Endowment for the Arts' study titled 'To Read or Not to Read: A Question of National Consequence,' notes that although there has been measurable progress in recent years in reading ability at the elementary school level, all progress appears to halt as children enter their teenage years (p. 3). Not surprisingly, this trend coincides with reading habits among adults; but what is most alarming, explains NFA Chairman Dana Gioia, is the fact that 'both reading ability and the habit of regular reading have greatly declined among college graduates' (p. 3). The NEA report points out that since 1982, '65% of college freshman read for pleasure for less than an hour per week or not at all,' and that the 'percentage among these students has nearly doubled – climbing 18 points since they graduated from high school' (p. 7). The study adds that, 'By the time they become seniors, one in three students read nothing at all for pleasure in a given week' (p. 7), a disconcerting statistic when we recall the demands that accompany reading and responding to unfinished, evolving essays written by peers.

Further complicating the issues and challenges that accompany teaching composition is the fact that, ironically, teachers at the elementary and secondary levels have in recent years been reducing and simplifying the writing process to a series of discrete steps. Out of a sense of urgency and in response to 'changing demographics and a growing demand to meet the needs of learners from diverse linguistic cultural backgrounds' (many teachers unknowingly converted the process of writing into a series of approachable, tacitly connected, and verifiable steps (Sherff & Piazza, 2005: 273). In this way, explain the authors of 'The More Things Change, the More They Stay the Same: A Survey of High School Students' Writing Experiences,' the view of writing as a profound, intellectual, and imaginative undertaking 'began to give way to test-driven writing, a trend ... that often replaced instructional priorities with legislative accountability,' and one wherein 'the five-paragraph theme soon became synonymous with learning to write' (Sherff and Piazza, 2005: 273).

The combination of these trends regarding reading habits and writing instruction suggests that the likelihood that we can, as college instructors, successfully assemble small groups for the purposes of designing a situation wherein each student writer offers the others instructive feedback is remarkably slim. And, under certain circumstances and in particular courses, the odds become slimmer still when we consider that many institutions use writing-placement exams and standardized tests to place students into courses such as Developmental Writing, Effective Writing, and Advanced Writing. As the authors of one recent investigation into the implications of tracking student writers state in their essay titled 'Exploring the Impact of a High-Stake Direct Writing Assessment in Two High School Classrooms,' these writing classes and the activities central to them illumine problems that precede and accompany the work the students do together (Ketter & Pool, 2001: 344). If one finds herself as an instructor working with those students labeled either implicitly or explicitly 'developmental' or even 'effective' (as opposed to 'advanced'), odds are she will soon discover that she must reconsider and more than likely rework such otherwise reliable methods and techniques as the workshop model and the peer review activity.

Because 'writing is historically determined and situationally constrained' (Sherff & Piazza, 2005: 274), because it often occurs in diverse discourse communities with representatives of many educational and cultural backgrounds, and because it is – despite educational trends that might suggest otherwise – paralogic and nonlinear, it should come as no surprise that the peer review activity so central to the workshop model often proves less than productive. It is not, to return to the claims made by the likes of Shaugnessy and Rose, in most cases the fault of the teacher; nor is it the fault of the students, their previous teachers, or the institutions. It is instead, as I hope this essay makes clear, the result of many interconnected, complex issues and problems.

In sum, when one is teaching a typical composition course at a typical college – one that is tuition-driven and access-oriented as opposed to endowment-rich and exclusive – there is likely to be a relatively high-percentage of non-readers in the makeup; additionally, there is likely to be in that same classroom mix many students coming from diverse cultural backgrounds, and many more coming from high school and elementary classes and courses that have ingrained in the student writer a deceptively simple, fixed and formulaic understanding of the writing process; and, finally, there is likely to be a relatively high percentage of students with learning disabilities, students who until fairly recently would not likely have been admitted to college because most colleges lacked the support services needed to help them succeed. Given these variables, we cannot and should not naïvely assume that the workshop model of instruction will, in fact, work and that the students will be able and/or inclined to offer each instructive feedback on their papers. Instead, we should be realistic and we should be honest about what we can expect of our student writers in composition courses and about how we as individuals and institutions should proceed. To this end, I offer these considerations for moving forward and making the workshop worthwhile and relevant.

First, we need to be honest with ourselves, our students, and our colleagues about what is working, when, why, and how well. Failure, ultimately, may not be an option, but admitting to it might be, if, in the end, we are going to succeed not as individuals but as a group of professionals invested in the success of our student writers.

Second, early in the term, we might need to consider having our students focus primarily on lower-level issues and concerns when providing feedback. Allowing them in this way to feel and be successful before insisting that they offer more substantive feedback could, by the end of the term, help them to help each other later with the more holistic issues and essay-level problems.

Third, we may need to stop tracking student writers – placing some in advanced writing courses and others in developmental – or start doing so in ways that are more diplomatic and discrete. Along these lines, we might explore new ways of bringing together writers of different inclinations and abilities so that all involved in the undertaking will benefit. According to the article 'Teaching English in Untracked Classrooms,' 'Those who have examined the effects of tracking have found that the practice depresses the academic achievement of students placed in the lower tracks and does not provide special benefit to those in the higher tracks, with gaps in achievement widening across the school years' (Freedman, 2005: 63). To place 22 students in a college composition course, title it 'Developmental Writing,' and assume the students will not perceive of themselves when giving each other feedback as unqualified is at best naïve and at worst misleading.

Fourth, we need to mix it up. The workshop model initially represented a break from the long-standing routine that preceded it, one wherein the development of the paper happened before and outside the class/course and the response to it by the teacher/reader happened outside of the class and after the deadline; in this regard, when first introduced, the workshop marked a shift in the teacher's thinking toward the course, the class, and the individual student writers, a change likely detected by all involved. The result was, in many cases, a dynamic and participatory event/activity, one wherein the students as well as the teacher felt present and empowered: the students, moreover, were in the moment and participating with each other and their teacher in something new, novel, and constructive. Now, however, when students know only this model/method, the routine has become, well, routine. The result is equally predictable: students, as noted above, mindlessly go through the motions as writers and as readers. To counter these tendencies, we need to introduce into our composition courses other models of instruction if we are to save this important one from itself.

Fifth, and finally, at the risk of preaching to the choir, I offer this outrageous response to the problems with workshop model in general and the peer-review activity in particular: reduce composition class sizes by half and/or offer professors who teach writing-intensive loads an FTE that will allow them sufficient time to respond to papers as well-trained, hypothetical peers (rather than as professors/graders) and to conference with student writers throughout the writing process.

Note

1. 'Its fine, I gess,' was written by a student in my fall 2007 Developmental Writing composition course in response to another classmate's writing.

References

Breuch, L.M.K. (2003) Post-process 'pedagogy': A philosophical exercise. In V. Villanueva (ed.) *Cross-Talk in Comp Theory: A Reader* (2nd edn) (pp. 97–224). Urbana: NCTE.

Crisis at the core: Preparing all students for college and work: Executive summary. *Information for Policy Makers*, 2004. Retrieved March 10, 2007. <http://www.act.org/path/policy/pdf/crisis–report.pdf>.

Freedman, S.W., Delp, V. and Crawford, S.M. (2005) Teaching English in untracked classrooms. *Research in the Teaching of English* 40 (1) Aug. 62–226.

Gillen, B.A. (2006) Writing across communities: Peer reviewing among diverse students. *CCCC 2006 panel: Writing Across Communities: A Cultural Ecology of Language, Learning, and Literacy*. March 24.

Gioia, D. (2007) 'Preface.' *To Read or Not to Read: A Question of National Consequence*. Research Report #47: Executive Summary (pp. 3–2). Washington, DC: National Endowment for the Arts.

Iser, W. (1998) The reading process: A phenomenological approach. In D. Richter (ed.) *Critical Tradition: Classic Texts and Contemporary Trends* (2nd edn) (pp. 956–968). Boston: Bedford Books.

Kent, T. (1989) Paralogic hermeneutics and the possibilities of rhetoric. *Rhetoric Review* 8 (1), 24–42.

Kent, T. (1993) *Paralogic Rhetoric: A Theory of Communicative Interaction*. Lewisburg: Bucknell University Press.

Ketter, J. and Pool, J. (2001) Exploring the impact of a high-stakes direct writing assessment in two high school classrooms. *Research in the Teaching of English* 35 (3), 344–294.

Kirszner, L.G. and Mandell, S.R. (2008) *Focus on Writing: Paragraphs and Essays. Instructor's Annotated Edition*. Boston, MA: Bedford/St. Martin's.

Kranz, N. Peer-review – Worth a second try. CETL Capstone Project. Minnesota State University Mankato. 14 March 2009. Web. 15 May 2009. <https://www.mnsu.edu/cetl/teachingcertprogs/pdfs/PDF2007/NickieKranz-ENG101.pdf>.

Oleck, J. (2007) Poor literacy skills threaten our future. *School Library Journal* 53 (3) March, 18.

Paulson, E.J., Alexander, J. and Armstrong, S. (2007). Peer review re-viewed: Investigating the juxtaposition of composition students' eye movements and peer-review processes. *Research in the Teaching of English* 41 (3) Feb. 304–239.

Reiff, M.J. (2002) Teaching audience post-process: Recognizing the complexity of audiences in disciplinary contexts. *The WAC Journal* 13 June 100–211.

Rose, M. (2000) Remedial writing courses: A critique and a proposal. In E.P.J. Corbett, N. Meyers and G. Tate (eds) *The Writing Teacher's Sourcebook* (4th edn) (pp. 193–211). Oxford University Press.

Shaughnessy, M.P. (2000) Diving in: An introduction to basic writing. In E.P.J. Corbett, N. Meyers and G. Tate (eds) *The Writing Teacher's Sourcebook* (4th edn) (pp. 94–29). Oxford University Press.

Sherff, L. and Piazza, C. (2005) The more things change, the more they stay the same: A survey of high school students' writing experiences. *Research in the Teaching of English* 39 (3) Feb., 271–295.

Spinuzzi, C. (2002) Towards a hermeneutic understanding of programming languages. *Currents in Electronic Literacy* spring (6). December 12, 2007 <http://www.cwrl.utexas.edu/currents/spring02/spinuzzi.html>.

Tobin, Lad (2000) Reading students, reading ourselves: Revising the teacher's role in the writing class. In E.P.J. Corbett, N. Meyers and G. Tate (eds) *The Writing Teacher's Sourcebook* (4th edn) (pp. 72–26). Oxford University Press.

SECTION THREE

THE NON-NORMATIVE WORKSHOP

Chapter 10

The Creative Writing Workshop in the Two-Year College: Who Cares?

DAVID STARKEY

1. Inevitably . . .

Inevitably, as instructors of creative writing, our opinions about writing workshops are influenced less by the theories we read or the pedagogies we embrace than by our own experiences in the classroom. Until I came to Santa Barbara City College nine years ago, my participation in workshops – as both a student and teacher – was, though not without its problems, generally positive. On any given day at the end of the last millennium, if you happened to walk into one of my creative writing classes in the four-year college where I taught, chances are a workshop would be in progress. *Most* of the students would be *mostly* prepared. The goals I had set for the class period – group discussion of *x* number of manuscripts by *x* number of students – would usually be accomplished. And I knew that students were themselves usually satisfied with the results: class evaluations often named the workshop as the most effective method of classroom instruction.

The fact that I was able to lead a successful writing workshop shouldn't have been surprising, of course, since I had been part of so many of them for so many years. Despite my involvement in the emerging field of creative writing pedagogy, the workshop seemed an ingrained and inevitable aspect of creative writing instruction, the only really legitimate way for one writer to teach another. Like all effective ideologies, its 'naturalness' was practically invisible.

While I, like most academic writers of my generation, had participated in undergraduate workshops, it was in graduate school where the model truly exerted its monolithic control on classroom pedagogy. My professors in the MFA program at Louisiana State University in the late 1980s relied on the workshop extensively, if not exclusively.

In fact, I often had the sense that Vance Bourjaily, the director of the program at the time, was making his first reading of student stories *while* the workshop was underway. As we went around the big table, each student making her or his comment, Vance kept one ear on our conversation, and one eye on the manuscript under discussion. However he accomplished the task, I had to admit that he nearly always offered useful revision strategies before the workshop was over.

Andrei Codrescu seemed to have read our manuscripts beforehand, but his comments were often as gnomic as his poetry and as acerbic as his commentaries on National Public Radio. In his class, the workshop seemed more like a play built around a movie star. Or was it performance art? Sometimes we just sat in the seminar room in Allen Hall and smoked cigarettes while Andrei opened his mail and read us the good bits aloud.

Rodger Kamenetz initially tried to teach us a little prosody via literature – Yeats's 'The Wild Swans at Coole' was a passion – but ultimately he succumbed to *student* pressure to spend most of our class time workshopping our poems.

The advantages of the writing workshop for my graduate-level instructors were clear: they only had to be partial participants in their own classes, and their preparation time was limited to reading a handful of manuscripts each week. The rest of the time they could do what we all wanted to be doing: writing.

For us students, the payoff was less certain. Sure, we were able to show our writing to people who were willing to read it – that was why we were there in the first place. And a word of praise from someone famous like Andrei was a genuine ego-boost. I also found workshopping an effective winnowing process; it helped me suss out the students who, like me, were bent on literary success. We ambitious ones gravitated toward one another to share our work privately, and we tended to avoid those students who had joined the still relatively nascent program simply because they couldn't think of anything better to do.

However, after my first year at LSU, I began to feel as though I wasn't learning anything I didn't already know. Instead, my own beliefs and prejudices were merely deepened and confirmed. By the end of any semester, it was fairly easy to predict how the teacher would respond to a certain type of story and what the other students would say before they even opened their mouths. While I nearly always came away with something useful when my own work was being critiqued, at my most cynical I felt the workshop encouraged risk-aversion and intellectual laziness in all of us.

But, really, what difference did it make? Like most American graduate students in creative writing, I believed that the workshop – or anything having to do with teaching – was clearly secondary to my own writing. No one was hiring good *teachers*; colleges and universities wanted well-published *writers*. If the workshop gave us all more time to write, who could complain about that?

When I managed to secure one of those much sought-after creative writing jobs, I did what most everyone I knew was doing: I reproduced the only fully operational model I knew. Mostly, the old standby held up well enough. Although my first two full-time jobs were at two very different types of institutions, my workshopping experiences were remarkable similar at both.

My first position was at a rural state university in South Carolina with an essentially open admissions policy. It was far from the urban bohemia I'd once imagined as my academic home: a swamp snaked along one edge of campus; across the highway was a tobacco field. The student population was approximately 30% African American and 65% white. The students were typically underprepared and often the first in their families to attend college. The general attitude among both students and faculty was that this was a place where you went when you couldn't get in or afford to go anywhere else.

In sharp contrast, my second job was at an upwardly mobile, Methodist-affiliated private college in the booming 'technoburbs' west of Chicago. The first year I taught there, the school was 93% white. Recently, the college had begun getting listed in *US News and World Report*'s Top Ten Regional Colleges, and there was a sense that someday soon we would be 'the new Drake' or 'the next Carleton'. Few students were the first in their families to attend college, and most had actually *chosen* to attend this particular institution.

And yet in both South Carolina and Illinois – in these two places so unlike one another – students enrolling in the introductory creative writing class had to have already passed a sophomore-level literature or writing course. Most of the young men and women in my workshops were majoring in English; many were minoring in creative writing. I could count on my students to copy and circulate their work the class meeting before it was to be discussed, and – with the assistance of frequent quizzes and paper checks – I could usually find ways to ensure that they had read and commented on the work before the day it was being discussed. The students who were enrolled in the class at the beginning of the term were usually all still there when the time for final grading came around.

Then I moved to California and began teaching in a community college, and everything changed.

2. The Creative Writing Workshop in the Two-Year College

Wendy Bishop and I noted a number of recurring complaints about the workshop in our survey of the state of the discipline, *Keywords in Creative Writing*. Opponents of the workshop argued that it tended to punish risk-taking and experimentation and reward uniformity (Donald's Hall's McPoems and McStories); it sometimes provided students with a bewildering array of wildly contradictory advice; by silencing the author during the discussion of her own work, it destabilized the necessarily dialogic nature of the writing process; it undercut its own *raison d'être* by ultimately privileging the voice of the instructor over her students; it could be a harrowing emotional experience for the writer whose work was under discussion; and it gave short shrift to the invention exercises beginning creative writing students often need to generate writing in the first place.

That said; we found that the workshop remained the dominant method of instruction throughout the country. In the minds of the majority of creative writing instructors, its strengths outweighed its weaknesses. Proponents touted the workshop's emphasis on craft and revision. They noted that it offered the writer a plurality of critical voices, helped create consensus regarding revision strategies, and demonstrated that the teacher's opinion was not the only one that mattered.

However one feels about the pedagogical pros and cons faced by students and professors in graduate programs and four-year colleges and universities, the workshop takes on an entirely different cast in the two-year college. This book asks the question, 'Is the writing workshop model still working?' Based on my own experience, and on conversations with two-year college colleagues, I doubt if the workshop has ever truly thrived in the 'pure' fashion described above, where it is the sole or primary method of instruction. For the reasons outlined below, I believe that for a workshop to succeed in a community college setting it must be only one component of a multifaceted approach to teaching creative writing.

Eric Melbye's experience of the graduate creative writing workshop mirrored my own: 'What needed fixing usually seemed to revolve around the respondents' personal literary tastes ... When the students were finished, the instructor took his turn, usually using the student author's work as a springboard to a mini-lecture on how to employ a specific craft element.' Not surprisingly, Melbye finds several significant flaws in this model for his own students at the two-year Middletown campus of Ohio's Miami University:

> It assumes students already know how to read and respond to work in progress, and it separates student writers from their work in unproductive ways. Most importantly, it doesn't focus at all on the writing process, which is something all writers, especially beginning writers, are wise to consider. Instead, this workshop conceives of the student as a producer and the creative work as a product with design flaws that need to be corrected according to the personal standards of those in the workshop.

Granted, certain conjunctions of students may – magically, it sometimes seems – work well together in a workshop setting. Nevertheless, I remain convinced that for *most* community college creative writing instructors *most* of the time, extensive or sole reliance on the writing workshop is a mistake. The personal and academic lives of most two-year college students are simply ill-suited to the workshop's demands. More effective methods of instruction for my students include individual conferences, small peer groups, in-class invention exercises, and, above all, in-depth discussion and analysis of professional writing with an emphasis on the vocabulary writers use to talk about their own work.

I couldn't help but be astonished at last year's graduation ceremony when I saw that among the more than 1000 students listed in the elegantly printed program, only *one* had declared herself an English major. That may be an anomaly, even for Santa Barbara City College, but it does point to a significant difference between two- and four-year college creative writing students: the former are far less likely to have read, discussed and written about other writers than their four-year counterparts.

Admittedly, students in an Intro to Creative Writing class at a private college or state university may come from a variety of disciplines. However, in the junior and senior-level advanced courses in specific genres – the poetry and fiction writing classes – most students are likely to be not only English majors, but also to have a writing emphasis in the major. That's simply not the case in the two-year college, where there are, of course, no junior- or senior-level classes. And our records at SBCC show that there are nearly as many non-English majors in the single-genre classes (fiction, poetry, creative nonfiction and playwriting) as there are in our multi-genre introductory courses.

I noted earlier that at my previous two institutions students were required to have successfully completed one sophomore-level literature or writing class before enrolling in the introductory creative writing course. At SBCC, as in many other two-year colleges, the only requirement for enrolling in *any* creative writing class – whether it is single-genre or the multi-genre introduction – is successful completion of English 110, our first-semester composition course. This is a practical decision on our part: by the time most students completed a sophomore-level literature class, they would be ready to transfer, and we would be unable to populate our courses.

Community college students shouldn't, therefore, be blamed if they are inadequately prepared to become successful workshop participants. Unlike four-year college English majors – who are immersed in literature, and possibly critical theory – students here are still struggling to develop an adequate vocabulary to discuss the work of their fellow students. Their own creative writing has probably never received any meaningful feedback in an academic setting, and their range of literary reference is extremely limited.

It goes almost without saying that perceptions of failure and success play an integral role in the learning process. Most graduate students in creative writing are motivated to succeed as creative writers. Most four-year college creative writing students, especially if they are juniors or seniors, are similarly determined. My colleague and former two-year college Association Chair Jody Millward likes to say that no one comes to college to fail, but failure at a community college doesn't, unfortunately, come as a shock to many of our students.

It is a statistic both closely guarded and hotly disputed, but individuals at my institution with access to such information tell me that only 10–25% of the students who enroll at Santa Barbara City College with the goal of receiving a Bachelor's degree ever actually achieve that objective. SBCC boasts that it has one of the highest transfer rates in the country, and currently claims to have the number one rate of students transferring to the University of California. However, you won't find the actual percentages without a little digging. According to a small paragraph tucked deep in the 2006–2007 catalog, the percentage of students from the Fall 2002 cohort who had completed their Associates degree four years later was 37%. The transfer rate was 34.9%. These numbers turn out to be comparable to statewide completion rates (36%) and transfer rates (29.6%).

A completion rate of 37% at a four-year school would be cause for grave concern. At the community college, we brag about it.

I note this fact not to belittle my students' abilities, or the hard work of my colleagues, but simply to provide concrete evidence of the radically different expectations for academic success between *entering* two- and four-year college students. Community college students who end up transferring to four-year schools usually perform comparable to native four-year students in terms of GPA and graduation rate (see Solomon, Tatiana and Dowd). Nevertheless, it has been my experience that entering community college students are generally underprepared than entering four-year college students. They have often had less success in high school and therefore have less academic self-esteem in college. As two-year college instructors know, this combination may result in fear of failure and self-sabotage. Unfortunately, the student besieged by self-doubt is not an ideal workshop participant. As Steve Abbott notes, ultimately, 'it's less what two-year schools have to offer than who they offer it to' (interviewed in Waggoner 60).

One of the California Community College system's chief assets – its low cost – is, ironically, another reason I would argue that writing workshops don't work as well here. As I write, during the spring semester of 2008, one unit of community college credit costs $20. Even with the small student activity fee tacked on, enrolling in my class for a semester is less than many students' monthly cell phone bills. Compared to the student who has taken out huge loans to attend a four-year college, or whose parents are paying tens of thousands of dollars a year for tuition, the community college student has considerably less motivation to complete the class than a student in a four-year college.

And this is not just in laidback Southern California. Jim Sullivan of Illinois Central College notes, 'Tuition is low and commitment to getting a degree is often equally low among many students, so dropping or just no longer coming to a class incurs no great cost either financially or psychically.'

Again, an unmotivated student, one who cannot be counted on to show up and be prepared for every class, is – as every instructor knows – a serious impediment to a successful workshop. The workshop is a collective, a shared endeavor in which all students must be responsible to one another. If a quarter of the class may go missing on any given day, that sense of communal accountability collapses.

Of course, there is a potential benefit. As Sullivan points out, 'sometimes the group attrits down to the really committed and we can have some really good conversations.' When all the students present in a workshop are serious, interested and prepared, a two-year college workshop can function on as high a level as most any university workshop. Unfortunately, those occasions are infrequent. More often, though, the intellectual energy and acumen is insufficient to sustain a thorough and extended discussion of the student work. 'Sometimes,' as Sullivan acknowledges, 'to be honest, it means the size of the group drops below critical mass of serious writers, so the discussions are a bit strained.'

While tuition is relatively low, many students attend community college precisely because they are financially stressed and otherwise over-committed in their personal lives. Therefore, even the most motivated students may face difficulties when it comes to workshop basics such photocopying or emailing work ahead of their scheduled workshop date. Our students, in short, often work and live on a thin financial margin. They may not have the money to repair broken computer equipment, or they may be sharing a single computer with a number of family members, or relying on the limited time they can access a terminal at school. Social and economic class, in short, affects the workshop, just as it shapes every other aspect of higher education.

After many disappointments, here are a few things I've learned that an instructor can*not* count on when conducting a writing workshop in a community college class:

- the work will be efficiently distributed to other students;
- students will read the work before the workshop;
- all, or even most, of the students will show up to critique the work;
- the student author will be present during class.

When those are the terms of the workshop, can it even be called a workshop anymore?

Finally, it's worth noting that even students who can be relied upon to do their work on time often enter the two-year college through a nontraditional path, one that does not prepare them to thrive in a workshop setting. I'm thinking now of several recent students with significant potential as creative writers: a white male octogenarian whose comic gift touched even 18-year olds; a Latina in her late forties with an MBA in Healthcare Administration; an African-American man in his late fifties who had just finished serving 18 years for armed robbery. These were all bright, highly motivated people, but they did not possess even the rudimentary literary and critical background of the average English major at a state university.

This is not to say that the workshop cannot be effectively incorporated into a successful community college creative writing course. While I may only use the workshop several times a semester – and I do so in part simply to prepare my transfer-oriented students for what they are likely to encounter in a four-year setting – some of my colleagues employ the workshop more actively.

Kris Bigalk of Normandale Community College in Minnesota emphasizes directed writing activities on the part of student respondents. Bigalk insists that her students use worksheets to evaluate the writing of workshop participants:

> These worksheets direct [respondents] through the habits and steps that an experienced workshop participant knows by instinct, such as reading aloud, analyzing work for craft elements, and pointing out potential problem areas without feeling obligated to 'solve the problem' for the writer. I also usually base these workshop worksheets on reading that was due that day. For example, if the students just completed a reading assignment about writing effective dialogue, and brought in a short story for workshop, the workshop worksheet would reference page numbers from the assigned reading and ask students to mark all instances of a specific element of dialogue – for instance, indirect dialogue – and then write three or four complete sentences analyzing how that element contributes to the piece as a whole. This approach not only teaches students to workshop, but it also teaches them to synthesize information from the text into actual practice.

Eric Melbye has devised a number of practices to help his students focus on the overall writing process and therefore see themselves as 'meaning-makers'. Melbye asks students to investigate literature as a genre 'similar to and different from other genres of writing' and to practice 'reading the world as a text', with a focus on journal-keeping. These activities lead to a scaffolded series of four workshops that move from 'brainstorming the possibilities' in a student's early draft – 'our job is to nurture the work and provide it with opportunities to grow on its own' – to small group 'interviews' with the writer, to the distribution of a revised draft for full-class discussion. 'The fourth workshop … focuses even more tightly on developing the work rather than brainstorming new directions, though brainstorming possibilities is still a strong component.'

Significantly, while Melbye grades the workshops, he does not grade the quality of the work itself: 'Instead, I determine the grade based on evidence I see that the students understand how we've discussed literary craft, that they're educating themselves on how it can and does work, and that they're developing a strong sense of the writing process and how it can work for them.' He believes that this focus on reaching the student's own individual goals is a deterrent to apathy and attrition:

> Since the students' writing comes out of their own lives, they're almost automatically engaged in it and want to develop it. Since the creative work is never graded or fully completed, the pressure is off to do it 'correctly' – they're free to pursue interesting tangents, take risks, make mistakes (which are as educational as anything), and productively engage in the writing process.

And Jim Sullivan finds that though 'the first half of the semester, the students are usually more tentative in their comments on one another's work,' the passage of time and the students' gradual understanding and accommodation of one another and their instructor results in increased confidence on their part and more adroit workshop commentary.

3. Who Cares?

I went to some effort in the first part of this chapter to detail my own experiences as a workshop participant and leader not only to emphasize the stark contrast between my past and present encounters with the workshop, but also – because I am the only contributor to this volume who teaches at a two-year college – to highlight my common background with my readers, most of whom probably do not teach at community colleges. Indeed, these readers may well be asking themselves: 'What difference does it make what happens in community college creative writing courses?'

After all, if professors at four-year institutions and in graduate programs would seem to have little investment in the issue, doesn't the absence of any sustained scholarship by two-year college creative writers indicate that community college faculty themselves aren't particularly interested in the subject?

Who, in short, cares?

Whether or not anyone actually does care, I think all of us who teach creative writing ought to. I suspect the attitude of most current graduate students is not unlike my own 20 years ago. They want to write, above all, and if they have to take a teaching gig, it had better be a sweet one with lots of perks. Unfortunately, the creative writing job market appears as though it will remain dauntingly competitive for the foreseeable future. As a result, many new MFAs and PhDs in creative writing will turn to teaching at community colleges. Forward-looking graduate programs will embrace this opportunity, and look to prepare these new teachers for what is still a largely uncharted exploration.

Moreover, as the cost of four-year colleges continues to increase, more and more students will elect to attend community colleges as freshmen and sophomores. Consequently, an increasing number of students who end up in four-year college creative writing programs will have completed at least one such class at a community college.

Community college transfer students do not enter four-year colleges with badges around their necks. Indeed, they may actively hide their matriculation history, particularly if they are surprised by the level of dedication and craft of their fellow creative writers, native four-year students who have come to think of the workshop as a second home. Clearly, then, one of the most important obligations four-year college instructors have toward these students is identifying (without embarrassing) them, and discovering what they know and what they don't.

Having come from classes where most of their fellow students were non-majors, some transfer students will feel less comfortable sharing their work with a class composed mostly of those who are specializing in English. Transfer students may also assume that any writing shared in the workshop will be anonymous. (My students frequently request workshop anonymity, which has evidently been routinely granted them in high school.) Four-year college instructors will need to reassure their new students that a workshop in which everyone knows the author's name is not normally fatal.

However, for instructors looking to break out of a workshop-only classroom, these transfer students will be a boon. Rather than viewing the workshop as the inevitable model of instruction, they will be more open and adaptable to new pedagogical approaches. They will bring a diversity of lived experiences that are far different from many of the students and teachers, in their new institutional settings. Indeed, Kris Bigalk reports hearing 'from [her] four-year colleagues that community college transfer students often are better than their peers in workshop, because they have had the advantage of being taught by tenured, degreed professors (vs TA's) who have taught them how to analyze both their own work and their peers' work.'

Bigalk adds that 'community college students, in my opinion, should not be portrayed as lacking anything because they chose to attend a community college.' If there's a note of defensiveness in her tone, it's because there's still occasionally a stigma attached to two-year colleges – even though my state's current Governor, Arnold Schwarzenegger, is a proud graduate of Santa Monica College and a staunch defender of the system. Not everyone, however, shares Arnold's enthusiasm, and we community college instructors can grow very protective of our students who are about to transfer to four-year settings. They are the real answers to the question, 'Who cares?'

I think of the single mother of mixed race in her early thirties, formerly addicted to crack cocaine, who has just moved into her own apartment after three and a half years living in a shelter. She will need to be eased in gently to the competitive, sometimes self-serving nature of the workshop. She may have to miss class if her daughter is ill and she has no one else to care for her. She will flourish, though, if matched with an instructor willing to spend individual time with her.

I think of the veteran returned home from the war in Iraq, desperate to write about his experiences, but hampered by his lack of training as a writer, occasionally crippled by the pain of his memories. He, too, will need more than a mere workshop to elicit what he has to say.

And I think of the Latina student in her early twenties whose first language is Spanish. Though she writes fluently in English, she needs extra praise and close personal attention to her stories and poems. Building up her self-esteem took me all semester, and I felt it could crumble at an unkind word.

Naturally, I was pleased when she asked me for a letter of recommendation in support of her application to a four-year university. She has much to recommend her: she reads voluminously; she's kept a journal since she could scratch letters onto paper. She tells me she's been writing all her life.

References

Bigalk, K. Emails to David Starkey. 24 Apr. 2009 and 4 May 2009.

Bishop, W. and Starkey, D. (2006) *Keywords in Creative Writing*. Logan, UT: Utah State University Press.

Melbye, E. Email to David Starkey. 30 Apr. 2009.

Melquizo, T. and Dowd, A.C. (2009) Baccalaureate success of transfers and rising 4-year college juniors. *Teachers College Record* 111 (1), 55–29.

Santa Barbara City College 2006–2007 Catalog. 8 Mar. 2008 <http://www.sbcc.edu/2006–2007–catalog/index.php?sec=7>.

Solomon, I.E. (2001) Articulation, college transfer, and academic success: Northern Virginia Community College transfer students and post-transfer success at George Mason University. Diss. George Mason Univ.

Sullivan, J. Email to David Starkey. 27 Apr. 2009.

Waggoner, T. (2001) Our corner of the sky: Two-year college creative writing. *Teaching English in the Two-Year College* 29 (1) Sept 57–28.

Chapter 11
Workshopping Lives

MARY ELLEN BERTOLINI

My tongue will tell the anger of my heart,
Or else my heart, concealing it, will break;
And rather than it shall, I will be free
Even to the uttermost, as I please, in words.

Katherina, *The Taming of the Shrew*,
William Shakespeare

An automobile accident, in April 2000, resulted in the deaths of four promising first-year female students on our campus. The deep grief that descended on Middlebury College led me to design a course in 'Writing to Heal'. The roots of this course began in the '4 Divas Writing Project,' a series of writing workshops that students and I organized to help cope with campus shock and grief. The project culminated in the publication of a commemorative booklet honoring the four students who had died and other losses our group had suffered. We presented our booklet to the families and to the college community at the one-year anniversary of the girls' death. Students who helped create the booklet thought it not only a wonderful tribute to the young women we had lost but a rewarding endeavor on its own. Students who participated in the Divas Project experienced relief both from writing their own narratives and in reading those of others. Reading others' narratives helped students locate their own experience in a larger pattern of grief and recovery. Writing their own narratives helped participants heal the pain of losing friends and lessened, as one student told me, 'the hole in my heart'.

Seeing the benefits of connection, closure and solace to students who participated in the '4 Divas Project,' I envisioned teaching a 'Writing to Heal' course with a writing workshop component. Before I could design and teach such a course, I faced the dilemma of how I might conduct a writing workshop when the subject matter of the writing would be the raw material of students' lives. Although the workshop experience had become central to my writing pedagogy, I knew that even the best student writers could feel threatened by insecurity and rejection when sharing their writing in a conventional workshop model. How would students endure criticism of their writing when its content was their own sorrow and grief? How would students respond to other students' criticism of papers describing *their* sister's anorexia, *their* mother's breast cancer, *their* father's abandonment of the family, *their* own sexual abuse?

My greatest challenge in integrating the writing workshop in the 'Writing to Heal' course was not to violate students in any manner – not in their words, their losses, or their lives. I needed to find a way to protect my students and still find a place for the workshop, a primary pedagogy in all my writing classes. Instead of abandoning the workshop in the 'Writing to Heal' course, I rethought the entire course structure and the part the workshop played within it. The workable solution to my dilemma came from this insight: students needed time to trust one another, and they needed a familiar discourse for discussing loss; therefore, as part of my course design, I intentionally postponed the writing and the subsequent workshopping of the personal essay that addressed students' losses until the second half of the course. Instead, I created a tiered approach to writing and reading through shared in-class writing prompts, selected readings that dealt with loss in literary works and memoirs, and readings of theorists such as Gabrielle Rico and James Pennebaker. Finally, I added sequenced writing assignments and strategically-placed writing workshops. The combined elements of this pedagogical scaffolding created the trust and discourse that enabled participants of the writing workshop to respond to each other with intelligence, grace, and compassion.

Shared Writing

Pennebaker (1995: 9) describes the harmful physical and psychological effects of inhibiting 'thoughts and feelings' associated with traumatic events, and he points out the positive value of 'talk[ing] a great deal in a group'. Following Pennebaker's theory, we read our informal writing aloud or talk through our feelings about our writing to the class. Students write for 15 minutes to a prompt that often stems from a passage we have read. Prompts move students from safe topics, such as 'describe a metaphor for healing,' to riskier ones, such as, 'I fear ...' After writing, students choose one of three options: read what they had written, describe what they had written, or tell a joke. In this way, students have to risk something, but choose their own degree of risk. The joke option works as a compromise between opposing values of risk and trust. If I allow students to 'pass' after the prompt, they might never open themselves to the class, but students still have an 'out' if their writing feels too close to the bone. Some may question whether telling a joke in this setting takes a certain degree of risk, but some students find it more threatening to tell a joke than to discuss their personal lives; furthermore, jokes can provide a welcomed release when student writing exposes painful memories and revelations.

As we share our writing responses, we open ourselves and learn about each other: whose father has died, whose friend is bipolar, whose brother is on drugs, who is in remission, who has been rejected by a lover, whose sister has run away, who dreads moving out of a childhood home. During class, I write and share my own response to the writing prompts with my students. Sharing our stories binds us to each other in empathy and experience and prepares us for the more intense workshop moments. Students begin to face demons, some more slowly than others. My student Paul, for one, was so traumatized by an event that he came into my class unable to talk about what he referred to as 'It'. His in-class writings described the way he walked down the stairs the day 'It' happened, but he could not (or would not) name his trauma. When Paul and I discussed a topic for his memoir, I reassured him that he did not have to write about 'It'. I advised him to write about a different loss – a lacrosse game, a room key, anything. But he said, 'Nothing else bothers me.' Paul was caught in the paradox that Gabriele Rico (1991: 110) describes as '[T]he more you try to avoid painful feelings, the more signals you send to your brain that they are important; because they have the power to scare you, the pain becomes worse'. Paul finally found something to write about and writing that paper opened him up a crack more.

Pennebaker (1995: 102) suggests that repeated writing benefits people like Paul because when they understand events that have weighed upon them, 'they no longer need to inhibit their talking.' Repeated writing propelled Paul forward to face his trauma. Rico (1991: 167) sees potential for recovery from writing about trauma because 'naming' pain can create 'a private key' that '*un*lock[s] a door to new options'. Paul's pain over 'It' did not completely disappear, but framing, or contextualizing his trauma, helped him change. By the end of the semester, Paul not only named 'It,' but could write and speak about healthy ways of coping with the pain of his parents' divorce. Rico suggests using techniques such as 'naming' and 'framing' a trauma to transform painful, chaotic feelings into ones 'formed, framed, thus, manageable' (p. 9). Paul's initial inability to refer to his parents' divorce as anything but 'It,' may seem anti-climatic to an outsider, but the framing of his trauma through repeated written and oral work allowed Paul to change, so that his whole identity no longer centered on feelings of abandonment.

Shared Intellectual Dialogue

Although many creative workshop models discourage the writer from speaking, I encourage student writers to participate in their own workshops – first by reading their papers aloud, second by engaging in a discussion of the paper, and third, by requesting specific help and advice from the workshop participants. Vu, one of my international students, workshopped an essay about his girlfriend in Cambodia whose parents convinced her to marry an older, richer man. When Vu finished reading, he looked up and saw tears on my face.

'I'm sorry I made you cry', he said.

'Don't be', I told him. 'You succeeded. You moved your readers.'

The students in the workshop nodded, and Vu smiled. We had listened, and his misery was lightened. In his paper, Vu transferred the experience of his loss to his readers. He succeeded because his readers keenly felt that loss in their own hearts. In the workshop, we talked for a while about his ex-girlfriend, and then we discussed the structure of his paper. One student noted her confusion about when a particular event had taken place. 'Did this happen this past summer or when you first went away?' she asked. 'Oh, I can fix that.' Vu said, and he made a note to clarify the times for his second draft. Not only had Vu succeeded in his writing, but readers of his paper succeeded as workshop partners when they helped him craft a memoir that was clearer and more technically sound. Vu used the suggestions from the workshop when he wrote a revised draft of his memoir.

Preparing Vu and his classmates to successfully workshop their personal essays takes a full seven weeks and involves both emotional and intellectual trust. Before the workshop can take place, Vu and the other students needed to share intellectual dialogue. While repeated, shared writing provides the first layer in my scaffolding pedagogy, our texts create the second important step: shared intellectual dialogue. Readings move students through a balance of risk and comfort, so trust and critical thinking (such that is in line with Pennebaker's theories) follow. Online and in class discussions of texts allow the class to develop a shared language to examine loss. Stanley Fish (1980: 318) describes this familiar discourse as a 'structure of assumptions.' In the first group of texts the class reads, the literature of loss establishes themes and problems in a safe zone. We read and examine loss in Susan Minot's (1986) *Monkeys*, Jane Austen's (1818) *Persuasion*, Arthur Miller's (1947) *All My Sons*, and in the poetry of Auden, Bishop, Dickinson, and Wordsworth. The texts explore illness, death, alcoholism, parental neglect, depression, infidelity, loss of status, criminal culpability, and poverty, among other issues of loss. At first, the class discusses how these losses affect characters in the texts. However, as we continue to discuss the literature, students gradually begin to share similar situations from their own lives. Young men, in particular, respond to the father and son dynamic in *All My Sons*. For example, two young men in class vigorously debated the importance of family loyalty versus obligation to society. The debate could occur because these students felt comfortable by first talking about the assigned texts in the class. The young man who argued that society was more important than family eventually wrote a personal essay honoring sacrifices his own father had made for their family. Subsequently, students *become* the texts we read by the end of the semester.

In an effort to ground students in writing to heal theory, we read Pennebaker's (1995) *Opening Up* and Rico's (1991) *Pain and Possibility*. These texts introduce students to some of the best research in the field. Memoirs such as Frank McCourts's (1996) *Angela's Ashes*, C.S. Lewis's (1961) *On Grief* and Joan Didion's (2005) *The Year of Magical Thinking* offer models that help beginning memoir writers better use creative non-fiction techniques when they write and workshop their personal essays.

Hybrid Assignments Leading to the Memoir

Leading to the memoir workshop, the third pedagogical scaffold involves writing assignments that ready students for the personal essay. Hybrid assignments that fuse genres encourage students to integrate personal narrative with discussions of texts. For example, students might compare the coping methods of characters in Susan Minot's *Monkeys* to their own ways of coping with loss. Students often respond to the alcoholism alluded to in Susan Minot's *Monkeys* by exploring a family member's alcohol abuse. Once students have made these comparisons, they become more comfortable sharing personal problems with addiction.

When students thread personal experiences into literary analyses of texts, they become more confident workshopping papers and more comfortable sharing sensitive material. Sarah explored the role of letters in Jane Austen's *Persuasion* and in her own life. When Sarah's mother was diagnosed with breast cancer, Sarah received a letter from her then third grade teacher. As Sarah wrote and workshopped her paper, she realized the hope that letter had brought her. Literature opened a well of feelings that made Sarah remember the fear of losing her mother and the comfort of her teacher's letter. Writing about this letter made Sarah aware of the impact her teacher had had on her life. Sarah concluded she 'must have been a whole different person back then' before she had identified the source of her courage. Hybrid papers such as these ease students into writing about their personal lives in a small, safe way. Moreover, sound strategies in early workshops build the trust needed to workshop personal essays later in the semester.

When students finally receive the memoir assignment, they long to write their own stories. Students write a three to five page essay in which they react to a loss or a difficulty in their own lives. This may be the loss of a person, a relationship, an opportunity, a competition, a job, a health issue, an object, a place, a memory, a dream, anything real or imagined that they miss or mourn. The loss may be large and vitally important or small and passing. They have waited weeks to write not just a slice, but a whole story. My student Sachini liked this delay because it took that long for students in the class to 'open' to each other. She believed her peers 'were all in a state of being ready,' as 'everything was more personal,' just not on 'a scary level'. I warn students not to overextend themselves if writing this essay becomes painful, and they learn all the campus resources (counselor, deans, chaplains) available to them if writing brings up issues that bother them deeply. Even though writing about these traumas can be painful, Pennebaker suggests several benefits. First, the work of inhibiting ourselves from discussing or writing about traumatic events is exhausting, depleting, and harmful to our health. Second, if we do not resolve the 'upsetting experience[s]', we continue to live with them (p. 103). For Sachini, writing her personal essay was the first step toward analysis. It was for her a venue to situate 'thoughts in another place and allow [these thoughts] to sit and be analyzed rather than brewing up in an already jumbled-up mind.' This statement is in line with Pennebaker's theory of writing about the trauma. Once the students have written their personal narratives, the workshop will allow them to start the process of resolution.

Resolution in the Workshop

Where writing relieves, analysis resolves, and analysis begins in the writing workshop. The workshop helped my student, Pat, confront aspects of his loss that he had not faced in writing. He said the workshop process helped him 'to not only read but thoroughly discuss the traumatic event.' Workshopping also positioned him 'to face the event for what it was, while [understanding] it better.' Pat's workshop allowed him to start the process of resolution. Through earlier workshops of their literature papers, students had seen the benefits of the workshop process. Initially, some questioned whether or not their peers knew enough about writing to provide helpful feedback. This concern was legitimate. Some students may be perceptive readers, and some may have experience as writers, but all must learn how to become effective, knowledgeable, and courteous workshop partners.

To help my students reap the full benefit of each specific writing workshop, I teach them how to be perceptive readers by focusing on the craft each genre requires. For the personal essay, we concentrate on techniques students have discussed in fiction, poetry, and drama. For example, we discuss how the writer orients the reader in time and space, in what ways the beginning of the piece grabs our interest, and if and how the writer use concrete details effectively. All the staging for the 'Writing to Heal' course has led us to this workshop, and still the workshop sharing is difficult. One student, Will, told me that after workshopping his essay he 'almost came to tears' because his writing had affected him, and still did 'so deeply'. In the workshop, students see how their stories affect readers sitting right in front of them (as Vu's story did). Writers need to have confidence emotionally and intellectually in the workshop process and in their workshop partners. When they do, workshop participants can help writers mold their stories into forms that honor the losses described.

In any writing course, but most especially in 'Writing to Heal' self-awareness, reflection, and intentionality prove key both to improvement in writing and, in this case, in recovery from trauma. For Sarah, the entire workshop and draft process allowed her time between each draft 'to let it sit'. She was then able to re-envision the piece. Her experience of slowing down and reflecting coincides with Pennebaker's observations that repeated writings help us organize our thoughts by slowing down our thinking. When all process occurs in the head, writers jump from thought to thought without following one idea through to its conclusion. Pennebaker suggests that as 'emotional responses become less extreme' the ability to think clearly may improve (p. 95). Situated within a three-draft writing process (review, revise, revisit), the writing workshop begins the slowing down of thought that contributes to higher-level analytical thinking and, in the case of personal essays, a quicker recovery from grief.

Even with careful preparation for the workshop, many students become nervous workshopping their personal essays. Jessie certainly found it 'difficult'. In class, she would agonize over letting others read her work. However, the newly-acquired skill of her workshop partners and their 'compassion' helped, she said, in 'building me up'. Just as in Vu's case, once Jessie felt that her group valued the narrative of her trauma, she could accept the group's suggestions about improving her paper. The writing workshop works best when it functions as part of an orchestrated continuum to improve writing. After reading her paper a second time, Jessie could emotionally detach from the subject and revisit the topic with less pain. This emotional detachment, as part of the continuum to improve writing, has its basis in Pennebaker's theory of repeated writing (p. 95). Very occasionally, a student has material so raw that he or she is reluctant to bring that work to workshop. In that case, I offer to let the student hand-pick the other students in the group, or, I offer to have the student workshop an incomplete piece that leaves out the most difficult parts of the story. A more drastic option is for a student to workshop one piece and share a different piece with me privately. Only one student to date has exercised this option.

The human impulse drives us to narrative, compels us to tell our stories, like Coleridge's (1919) 'Ancient Mariner,' who holds the wedding guest 'with his glittering eye' (line 3). We create narrative because we want to understand. Pennebaker suggests, 'the mind torments itself thinking about unresolved and confusing issues,' and repeated writing can act as 'a powerful tool to discover meaning' (p. 93). In my 'Writing to Heal' course, I prepare for and situate the writing workshop to provide a safe, disciplined space in which students can seek meaning and tell the stories that must be heard. In doing so, the writing workshop lives, flourishes, and plays a vital role in the learning and healing that students experience by the end of the course.

As I completed this article, my campus lived in a suspended state of anticipatory grief. One of our students had been missing for three months. As we walked the campus that winter, we scanned the snow banks in dread. Experts searched nearby rivers. We were not ready to write this story. It was too close, too raw, too unresolved, and all semester we felt the weight of this unfinished story pressing upon us all. Someday, it will be a story that some among us will need to write and share.

References

Coleridge, S.T. (1919) The rime of the ancient mariner. In A.T. Quiller-Couch (ed.) *The Oxford Book of English Verse, 1250–1900*. Oxford: Clarendon.

Fish, S. (1980) *Is There a Text in this Class?* Cambridge: Harvard University Press.
Jessie. Personal email interview. 4/20/2008.
Patrick. Personal email interview. 4/24/2008.
Pennebaker, J.W. (1995) *Opening Up: The Healing Power of Emotions*. New York: The Guilford Press.
Rico, G. (1991) *Pain and Possibility*. New York: St. Martin's Press.
Sachini. Personal email interview. 3/11/07.
Sarah. Personal email interview. 3/11/07.
Will. Personal email interview. 4/20/2008.

Chapter 12

The Things I Used To Do: Workshops Old and New

KEITH KUMASEN ABBOTT

When I transferred to the University of Washington in 1963, literature was on fire for me. New discoveries, such as Pynchon's novel *V*, Celine's *Death on the Installment Plan* and Lorca's *Poet in New York*, were exciting and contagious. I had spare money from a summer construction job and the University District bookstores to prowl, not to mention the superb literature library in Parrington Hall. My plan was to study with Theodore Roethke and to take fall classes in the Russian 19th Century Novel (Nikolai Gogol was a favorite author, via Nabokov) and Chinese Philosophy. Unfortunately, Roethke died late that summer, but even that didn't dampen my optimism.

I assumed that Roethke's presence attracted other English department writing writers/writing instructors of high quality. However, a hip senior assured me that the Philosophy department held vibrant upcoming young professors. Due to my interest in logic, I registered as a Philosophy major. His advice turned out to be right, and my Philosophy courses kept me at the U of W for two years more. With one exception I'll discuss later, it turned out that my workshops were the first step in a long undistinguished slog on my way to a graduate degree.

My first fiction workshop involved a professor of a certain age who kept lit cigarettes in her left and right hand ashtrays, essentially smoking two or more at a time. Of course strictly forbidden, but she sat near an open window. Due to rising fumes, this was more séance than a workshop. Keeping in that spirit her remarks on Jamesian mysteries of point of view floated out and evanesced in those vapors, too. As our mentor she confined herself to coughing chuckles over our fictions. She wasn't mean-spirited; our ignorance merely appalled or amused her. But as a disciple of James, she never stooped to basic concepts. And once, when a red-haired cherubic farm boy innocently turned in some science fiction, her eruption of richly fruity laughter so overwhelmed her lungs, all she could do was dismiss class with a wave of her arm: 'That wuh-wuh-won't *do*, young man.'

Our class short story anthology sported two columns per page, in small black dense type – ending in questions about content in dim grey italic. This rivaled my sociology text for its soporific powers. In the morning I often woke up *face en face* with this anthology's fiction. For this beginning workshop our smoker's lectures were far too erudite. Our assigned readings were seldom discussed in any depth, and osmosis by proximity to great works seemed the implied method of absorption. Granted, anthologies designed only for creative writing students were in their infancy, as were departments solely in the discipline. English departments ruled.

At three subsequent colleges my workshops were always taken with hope, though, that my continuing love affair with writing would be fed. But the truth was they mainly functioned as credit fodder for my degree requirements. Three issues were really constant. Well-meaning English department professors with second careers as writers, literary historical anthologies rather than writer's craft anthologies and no patterns of sequenced training for editorial competence regarding class critiques.

In my first workshop in California, one or two writers or particular texts were set up for our competitive imitation, and the first student to produce a facsimile received benediction. For all the students brought in their work, sometimes read it aloud, and then students applied their critiques with little, if any, training. Technical terms as basic as indirect versus direct dialogue were never mentioned. Imitation works, but only if analysis of artistic effects accompanies it.

For critiques, typically structural changes were the norm. I often imagined what would happen if famous authors underwent this workshop process: point of view changes ('How about having Oedipus' mother tell this story?'), pleas for more back-story ('How did Gregor's family treat him before he went buggy?') and wholesale changes in relationships ('Why "doncha" make Jay Gatsby a fake doctor, instead?'). All these are, in screenplay lingo, called heavy lifting. Because such suggestions imply an editorial arrogance, I soon learned that they are best used sparingly.

Different species of competition structured other workshops. An anthology of recognized masterpieces was our text. The instructors were published writers who picked the anthology writers that we were required to read. Understandably the instructors used their favorites, and if a student were ambitious and/or prudent, those favorites became the student's favorites. Those same students searched out the instructors' books and usually found evidence how favorite anthology authors had influenced our instructors' works. So, for some, this was how the workshop's orders of value and process were set: serial versions of Thirteen Ways of Looking At Our Instructor Looking at Wallace Stevens' Blackbird.

There was little or no line editing, the close reading for revelations via removal or adjustment. That is the hardest way to work, as an instructor, but ultimately the kindest to the writer's original structures and intentions. In this matter I was fortunate, as I found mentors during my journalism career, notably Tom Bates at the *Los Angeles Sunday Times* magazine. I still have that first 7500 word manuscript of mine that Tom shrank by 2500 words, and the information and intentions remained exactly the same, only much clearer.

Upon earning my graduate degree in English Literature, I vowed never to be a writing professor. A vow I kept until age 45, busy with fiction, journalism, editorial work and the rare book trade. The magazine market dried up and/or list journalism became the norm ('10 Foolproof Ways to Find Your Spa This Summer'). Due to my wife's chronic problems from cancer chemotherapy leading to job loss and disability, I entered the workshop ranks for a steady salary and benefits. So after 30 years in California we left for Colorado.

Some anomalies need acknowledgement. My employer, Naropa, was the only accredited Buddhist University in North America. This posed no personal problems as I was a student of Buddhism from age 19 and, while working at Naropa, became an ordained lay Soto Zen monk. Secondly, Naropa's writing program was 15 years old and well established as a poetry program. There was no English Department.

Part of my job was to fashion a prose concentration curriculum with my colleague Bobbie Louise Hawkins. We agreed on the principle of writers teaching writers and took that option for our texts whenever possible. We created sequenced workshops for first draft students onward past their second drafts, leading to the production of their final manuscript for both BA and MFA students. She supplied the benefit of her workshop and theatrical experiences – especially how she used films in her Monologue class – and we reviewed her supply of anthologies.

The newer creative writing anthologies and assignments had changed for the better, because literary history was not the dominant approach. Novelty assignments seemed the vogue, arising out of Kenneth Koch's approaches for children. While fun, some seemed remote for instilling skill-sets. Our basic formula remained the same: students submitted their work, but each class started with assignments designed to engage students in editorial training so workshop members critiqued manuscripts with shared vocabularies.

Hawkins used David Madden's (1988) *Revising Fiction a Handbook for Writers.* For MFA courses it had advantages, but for undergraduates Madden presumed far too wide a background in literature. Ann Charters' (1990) excellent *The Story and Its Writer*, featuring writers' essays on other writers' fiction, became a basic anthology for selected uses in beginning BA workshops.

However, I created my own fiction manual, with examples used from the texts and films taught during my courses. The techniques generating our critical vocabulary were grounded in the students' workshop experiences.

Luckily, several alumni received agents, publications, awards and honors, such as Sean Murphy's (1999) Naropa MFA manuscript *The Hope Valley Hubcap King* that won the Hemingway First Novel award. Rising quality of our prose applicants brought more motivated writers. These trends allowed Hawkins and I experimentation with advanced teaching techniques.

Reality Check 1: Allow Me To Introduce Yourself

Fiction technique is a vast ocean, and few writers know all of its currents. I'm not one of those writers. So my first job was to create ways to introduce and reapply basic principles of character-based fiction throughout the workshop's duration.

Not every student starts with the same skill-sets. I needed some means to name and demonstrate principles repeatedly so those were used in student creative works and applied to their critiques of our readings and fellow students. My first day survey served as an introduction not only for me – but also for the students to map out their artistic, writing and reading habits and vocabularies.

The survey begins with general questions about past experiences, such as:

> *What is your first, earliest, strongest, experience with 'Art' i.e. when you recognized that someone made X or Y or Z for your pleasure, transformation or edification?*

And then to make sure the students know that the workshop will be conducted with humor about the many uses of art:

> *Langston Hughes wanted 'Do Nothing Til You Hear From Me' played at his funeral. What music would you have played at your funeral?*

One valuable gauge for student levels of skill-set recognition was:

What authors do you RE-READ?

If Jane Austen is rubbing shoulders with Tom Robbins, or Jeanette Winterson is sandwiched between Jonathan Safran Foer and Gabriel Garcia Marquez, then that gives me a quick scan of their reading skills and habits. Plus I connect their face and name to an author, to aid my diminishing capacities to recall such vital matters.

Questions on what genres were previously written and what genre they want to write, mixed with more plebian ones, such as:

Has your work been edited for publication?
Have you ever edited someone else's work for publication?
Has an audience's reaction at a reading made you change your work?
What length of writing workshops have you taken? How many taken?
1 day — Weekend — Week — 3–5 Weeks — 14 weeks — One-year —

The last question reveals some very important details for future interactions. Shorter workshops are usually taught by adjunct faculty or visiting artists. Because of money considerations, most want to return, and therefore humor and/or inspire their students. So serious revisions or critiques seldom are given because of the instructor's need for positive evaluations. I know this because I have taught in those situations. Many veterans of multiple workshops turned out to have no idea that, before publication, work often undergoes structural, style and proof edits.

After I read the first day surveys, usually on the break, I selected replies from each student for further discussion, thereby getting to know that student better. But this allows the students to know each other and to hear their cohorts talk about their experiences and skills.

Some survey questions I answer for myself, and discuss why I chose particular ones, and why I stress those principles and concepts, such as point of view.

One student's first experience with art was a fabulously engaging reply, involving caging money from a reluctant grandmother, a strange circus act and inept clowns. Then she confessed that she was a liar and this was a fantasy, earning her an instant A on the first day of the workshop. She turned out to be a superb student of fiction.

Reality Check 2: Men and Women

The percentage breakdown of gender needs to be incorporated into the workshop curriculum. (Currently 60 % female and 40 % male this year at

Naropa.) My own inclinations to study women authors created a 50/50 split of men and women authors for my courses. That includes various nonfiction texts on gender issues. With our dialogue studies, for example, among other sources I use excerpts from Deborah Tannen's (1990) study, *You Just Don't Understand* (which contains an ace discussion of Lorrie Moore's 'And You're Ugly, Too'). Somehow it seems important to study how each half of our world talks and just how different expectations, patterns and signals in dialogue are for men and women.

Some technical courses, such as my Building Blocks workshop for beginning writers, uses mostly male writers, usually in very short excerpts, for certain standard principles such as characterization, scene, etc. simply because I teach those the best. To offset that bias, I employed as parallel outside reading, stories by Alice Munro and Amy Hempel for examples of how some standard principles may be morphed. Munro's stories 'Vandals' and 'Fits' are used to demonstrate how subtle diverse effects may be created with adroit and innovative POV management.

My inclination is to show students how some principle works, rather than talk about it, so I use short scenes from various films (and their screenplays). The opening scenes for *To Die For* (1995) are ideal, where separate monologues by different characters mutate into intersecting dialogues, sometimes across discontinuous time and space due to expert cutting, and then revert to straight monologues again.

I never show an entire movie. When movies are over, most students habitually want to go get a latte and/or get friendly. Most have little interest in discussion, usually because there's so much to cover.

Sequences of scenes are screened, but interrupted to ask: What did you see? What new info did you learn? Scenes are always repeated, but no script read until after the second or third showings. For instance, Stephan Frears' (1988) *Dangerous Liaisons*, which was built out of Christopher Hampton's play, has remarkable stage-tested dialogue. I often rerun its opening scenes focusing on each character's comments, asking how each works for that character, that scene and the film's main objective. Then we view the script. Usually I employ films that are 10 years old or older, to avoid celebrity dialogue between students. *Double Indemnity* (1944) is a fossil to current students, but noir always works, as it involves the writer's best friends, the Seven Deadly Sins.

Reality Check 3: Beyond Genre

For me workshops need a specific subject or subjects outside genre. And throughout a course each subject needs to be experienced in a variety of genres. The issues of diversity (and my own inclinations to study social class in American fiction, non-fiction and cinema) created my first workshop. I now teach three workshops dedicated to social class at the BA and MFA levels: *Happy Days, American Beauty* and *Fade to Black: Tragedy*. Workshops may create hothouses behavior; I was appreciative when Bobbie Louise Hawkins showed me how outside assignments, like her eavesdropping in town for dialogue, disperses ingrown hothouse effects.

Social class distinctions are unavoidable, actually, because they structure a classroom. Where the students sit, whom they sit by, and what they habitually wear, eat and say function as class signals that we all monitor.

For those who resist this notion, claiming America is a classless society, in our first two classes I screen a documentary titled *Presumed Guilty* (2002) about the Public Defender's office in San Francisco. The PD lawyers and their clients come from just about every race and social class in San Francisco, and who wins and who loses is directly related to their standing in the social mix. Judges are Lace Curtain Irish; Cops are Shanty Irish, Low to Middle Class African Americans or Hispanics; the citizens are a Laotian Boat political refugee, a Mexican immigrant, a Swedish alcoholic teacher, an African American street person, a transvestite hooker, etc. At the end the head honcho Public Defender, Japanese-American Jeff Adachi, who is extremely competent, is fired from his job of many years. The Mayor's best friend's daughter (fresh out of law school) is appointed new director partially because the Mayor and his best friend (a State Senator) shared a law school that Adachi lacked the foresight to attend. And besides, the daughter – a Japanese American herself – needed a job. The casual treachery at the Mayor's press conference is breathtaking. So far none of my students have yet to predict this twist, as I ask them at the end of our first class which person in our documentary is a candidate for the biggest shafting. Most pick one of the accused citizens on trial.

Because of its crosscuts between cases, I interrupt this documentary constantly to discuss what we witness, usually to identify class status of a member. Half the film is shown the first week, the next half the next week, and a flow chart of scenes and characters for a crib sheet is provided with questions.

Before *Presumed Guilty* is screened, in my survey I ask particular questions about events that occur in or are fundamental to this film.

> *Is social class is determined by money/education or how you spend your money?*
>
> *Have you ever been discriminated against because of your social class? When and how?*

What signals for you an upper class house, person or education?

What signals for you a middle-class house, person or education?

Do you believe that people may be killed because of their class? Their accent? Know of anyone?

Do you believe that people may lose their freedom, legal rights, or jobs via class discrimination? Know of anyone?

Our fiction writers include Raymond Carver, Bobbie Ann Mason, Jamaica Kincaid, Tobias Wolf, Alice Munro, Dagoberto Gilb, and A.M. Homes among others. Paul Fussell's iconoclastic study *Class* and essays from Paula S. Rothenberg's *Race, Class, and Gender in the United States* (2004, 6th Edition) provide insights. I use the novel, screenplay and film of Jim Thompson's (1985) *The Grifters*, where the criminals display fine distinctions about what specific crooks matter and which types of crook are déclassé. This segment takes at least four classes, one for the novel, screenplay and two for the screening so we can cover each metamorphosis of its plot and characters in each genre.

Reality Check 4: Apprenticeships

Harkening back to my nicotine infused James scholar and her Quaalude anthology, it seems to me a disservice to teach *only* Quality Lit to neophyte writers. After all, they lack training for those levels of technical perception; they are apprentices, in the best sense of the word. The texts used are a mix of masterpieces, mid-range works, mediocre works and failed works. Undergraduate students are prone to feel inferior or defeated by Greatest Works anthologies; an awkward pulp novel like *The Grifters* (1963) can be instructive and approachable, especially as a very good movie was made from it. Usually juicy discussions arise, because the screenplay alters the novel plot, and the film reworks the screenplay significantly. In their critical response essays the students must discuss two of the three, and those prove very useful for designing further editorial tactics for teaching.

My basic approach is every fiction writer has the same simple issues, such as the visual and/or psychological logic of portraying scenes or characters. An apprentice gains hope to see that imperfect work does get published or filmed and even rewarded with vast sums of money.

My favorite exercise gives the students anonymous paragraphs from various authors that introduce a new character (this I keep in a file labeled Bad Prose). For one plucky and fashionable Judith Krantz heroine, I ask a student to read the paragraph while I draw on the chalkboard exactly how Krantz describes her; this drawing shows a 1930sesque Picassoid one-eyed woman accessorized in Canadian Mountie leather.

Reality Check 5: Endless Strife Contemplative Life

Competition between workshop students seems inevitable. And writers often are hard on themselves, too. However, because Naropa is a Buddhist University and because I am bound under the Four Precepts of my ordination to use skillful means to reduce suffering, aggression and ignorance, a contemplative approach offers many solutions. One tested method expands the students' vistas and severs the delusion of personal ownership. Like from picayune to cosmic: the old Buddha mojo train.

For class etiquette I use a boilerplate insert in my syllabus and read it aloud.

> Editorial and Critical Reactions as Positive Reading
>
> Solutions: When discussing another student's work, if you have a comment about the need for improvement, *please give a solution after you locate and discuss the passage.*
>
> Feelings: If there is a part in the student's writing which you feel is going awry, but you do *not* have a solution: then clearly state this is only *a feeling* you have. The writer then may use such comments or *not use them*.
>
> However if others share those feelings and in discussion solutions or experiments are suggested, then the writer may use such solutions or not use them.
>
> Technical terms for writing situations should be used, such as arcs, through-line, plot, POV, beat, Ping-Pong dialogue, visual logic, pathetic fallacies, mis-matched similes and illogical metafurs.[1] These terms help revision of your text and facilitate discussion among your peers. Please remember there are many technical terms for common issues in writing and the more you know, the better you can talk about your own work.

I keep compilations of past students' responses to such particular issues as gender, social class, specific authors and especially fiction techniques. These are distributed *after* each assignment is done. Students then connect to current or alumni peers (and disconnect from their current reactions and group gestalt). This also may reduce competition between workshop members by dissolving this workshop's particular pecking order and introducing an outside perspective.

Also on the first day displaying the books of Naropa alumni who passed through our workshops never fails to expand their sense of possibilities available to them in this particular workshop and from its instructor. Some of those alumni books I teach, such as Will Christopher Baer's novels, *Kiss Me, Judas* (1998) and *Hell's Half Acre* (2004); this outside affirmation builds confidence in our process.

I often stress that every writer writes badly. There is no way to avoid doing so. Habits that have supported us and led us to write competently may not suffice for our new job, the creation of our new characters and scenes. This is painful, but often true.

For my technical exercises I make it clear that I do not expect everyone or each assignment to succeed, and I don't grade them.

I only want students to try them out and see what happens to them and report back. My syllabus quotes one of my fellow Zen calligraphers, Kaz Tanahashi (1990), from his book *Brush Mind*: 'Failure now may be more interesting than success later.'

Sometimes I discuss my apprenticeship as a brush calligrapher. For a long time I was not allowed to use ink. I used water on newspaper. In the high dry air of Colorado those beautiful or gnarly strokes evaporated, leaving only rumpled paper. Hard to take pride in invisible art. And I was also restricted to one stroke, a single horizontal line: the Chinese number one – which reflects back, of course, on my own personal sense of my place in the universe. But until one can make that stroke correctly, the rest of the calligraphic strokes are off-limits, because this movement is essential for some part of all characters.

So, in the spirit of that practice, I ask students to write four types of dialogue: Sympathetic, Controlling, Intimate and Grammar Specific (where the syntax, diction and grammar of the two characters differ from each other, and then have one character adopt the other's patterns.) Usually this tests them in ways they appreciate. They recognize that to write fiction, their characters will probably need to express these states of mind.

Guided contemplative visualization exercises are also useful, drawn from various Buddhist traditions. For this short article, these oral instructions are too site and time specific to present in detail. Each is unique and they are not written down for the students, but rather lead students to a point where the instructions disappear in their becoming and their job is to write what happens next. These exercises deflate aggression, for how can one disparage what each imagination creates from the same words that everyone has heard. Because these image trails are so momentary, this often creates a kinder sense toward one's self.

Another method *starts* the workshop with exercises that promote collaboration. One I employ is the Habits List, under the notion that habitual actions define character. And anyone can write a list. It is difficult, but not impossible, to manufacture overweening pride for a list, and some do manage it. Without resorting to a relative, the student lists what a friend or someone else habitually says, eats, wears and enjoys. We read these lists aloud in class and then each student is assigned to write a monologue about or by the person found in another student's list of habits. Your list is off-limits. To combine a second student's list is fine, too. I recommend blending characteristics from multiple sources as a hedge against personal assaults and libel suits.

Then the next workshop those monologues are read aloud. And their next assignment is to write a dialogue between another student's monologue character and a new character of the writer's choice in a setting.

So, by class four we are three steps away from personal ownership of anyone's characters, basically. By writing the list, monologue and dialogue, they are using their editorial skills to chose and create new points of view, characters, scenes, descriptions and dialogue. These are the five skills that I use to judge their writing and use for picking our texts. This becomes a pre-emptive strike because they receive a form at mid-term with my editorial comments on their progress in those five skills.

And toward the end of class I ask them to fill out a particular evaluation sheet on the workshop, separate from the University's evaluations, about what they found useful as writers. So, from the earliest classes, by witnessing those skills in our readings and in their workshop examples, and by sharing our editorial perceptions of their own prose and their perceptions of the workshop's elements, we all share equally these basic issues and vocabularies for writing.

Reality Check 6: Common Goals, Common Roles

In our lives apprenticeship is a common role. Starting over or starting anew usually involves a need for change. And for change people need guides to share their expertise. Instructors do well when they recall that each workshop requires some changes for them and that their apprenticeship is to the students. The instructors find out what the students know and how they know it. Then the goal is to discover where the students use those skills in their lives – not necessarily in the classroom – and to create an environment for them to employ those same skills in their writing.

These remarks attempted to sketch three workshop goals. One to write work based on everyday human relationships and habits. Another to find ways to use our mind's habitual motions to create emotionally engaging works. Apprenticeship forms a third goal: that the students apprentice themselves to acquire writing skills; in turn the instructor becomes an apprentice in the students and in the means for helping students utilize those skills. It's useful for writers and instructors to recall that no one is an apprentice human being. All of us come with a wealth of human resources.

Note

1. My colleague, linguist and poet Anselm Hollo, uses this phonetic version of 'metaphors' to deflate theoretical gravitas with this image of a metaphysical hair shirt and to introduce word play into unlikely contexts, such as a syllabus; I follow suit.

SECTION FOUR

NEW MODELS FOR RELOCATING THE WORKSHOP

Chapter 13

Re-envisioning the Workshop: Hybrid Classrooms, Hybrid Texts

KATHARINE HAAKE

Some years ago I attended a showing of an award-winning video, the first work in film by photographer Judy Fiskin, in which she remarks, 'After 20 years, I find I am no longer interested in making photographs.' Nearly wordless, the film continues to explore landscapes devoid of people and marked by subtle movement. Toward the end of the film, she describes a dream, which presents itself to her as a blank screen. When she awakes, she thinks, 'Yes, but how can I represent that.'

What follows is a little bit about that blank screen.

For as I'm fond of telling students, the story you should most want to write is the one you don't yet know how to write, and that goes for the classroom too. In creative writing, this usually means the workshop, which despite my own long held ambivalence about it – at least in its publication-centered, mentor-driven, ideal text/flawed student writing fix-it model incarnation – has remained as close to a home as we are ever going to come in the academy. And yet the one thing we can say with any certainty about it remains, 'that's not it, that's still not it'. Of course at least part of what we can't get right about it grows out of the more general challenge of what a sustainable literary practice – for both writing and teaching – might look like in a century where literacy itself is sometimes said to be at risk. Even putting aside the question of whether or not people 'still read', how might we begin to imagine a language-based art that remains both central and vital to a time and culture already saturated with narrative and image, and characterized by the free and immediate circulation of personal expression of all kinds.

But first, a disclaimer: I use the term 'creative writing' because that's what the discipline comes with, but in my view the qualifier is unfortunate – 'creative' being one of those terms that marks the parsimoniousness with which the culture marks and constructs who gets to be it. As we entertain new possibilities for our own writing workshops, it's worth at least acknowledging that every occasion for writing is an occasion for writing, that it is all 'creative', and that this particular discussion should be part of the larger project of re-configuring English studies itself as an intra-disciplinary site where, valued for difference as well as for sameness, all the strands of scholarship and creativity intersect and commingle to enrich one another without losing their discrete autonomy. But yet, in our departments and the various associations that define us, and even the arguments we frame for ourselves, the disciplines too often remain at odds. David Richter's (1999) book *Falling into Theory* is organized into three questions – how we read, what we read, why we read – and it's always seemed to me our real job is to integrate these questions – all three of them together – into any English studies teaching practice, though as the late Wendy Bishop would say, in our case, the subject is writing.

In general, we do the best we can, playing out the complex juggling acts of our professions, our writing, and our lives, and over the years, if we're persistent and lucky, learn somehow to balance the competing demands of too many classes and students with all the rest of it, including what some of us in creative writing still like to call our 'real' work. For this, we – all of us – need to be inventive, maybe play the bricoleur, use bits of this and that from here and there to assemble classroom strategies that, like Barthes' tissue of quotations, work – at least for us, and for the time being.

Mary Louise Pratt's (1991) essay, 'Arts in the Contact Zone', offers some provocative insight that may help us conceive a new kind of workshop that responds to the challenge of writing in the twenty-first century by celebrating student work even as it complicates some naive assumptions about what it is they think they're doing when they are doing it. In her own gorgeous hybrid text, Pratt takes us from the pedagogic richness of her young son's collection of baseball cards, to a 17th century Quechuan text that lay unread for 350 years, to once standard notions of speech communities and the seamlessness with which they were perceived to operate, to the uneasy contours of our own classrooms where heterogeneity can no longer be unproblematically subsumed by the monologic ethos of the teacher or the singular standards and traditions of the literary discourse she purports to represent and, in the case of creative writing, reproduce.

Pratt describes the space of such a classroom as a 'contact zone', 'which brings together voices from multiple, diverse worlds to intersect in ways that contradict what we once hopefully embraced as a kind of celebratory multiculturalism. Characterized by the presence of students not just from different cultural backgrounds but with long histories shaped – both positively and negatively – by prior interactions with others from cultural backgrounds that are not their own, such classrooms are not so likely as we once thought to be straightforward and harmonious but are, instead, deeply uneasy, fraught with potential misunderstanding and conflict. A century beyond the anachronistic concept of the US as a 'happy melting pot' (if it ever was), Pratt advocates the construction of what she calls 'safe houses', where students who share common backgrounds are free to experience and express cultural affinities that may have eluded them as they made their way through an educational system largely deaf to the autonomous expressions of those the dominant group loosely defines as 'other'.

Using Guaman Poma's Quechuan text as a model, Pratt describes her 'autoethnography', as a genre in which 'people undertake to describe themselves in ways that engage with representations other have made of them.' Poma's text, titled *The First New Chronicle and Good Government* (2006) and written as a letter from Cuzco to King Phillip of Spain in 1613, is significant in many ways, not the least of which is that it is 1200 pages long and written in a mixture of 'ungrammatical, expressive Spanish', representational line drawings, and phonetic Quechuan, despite the fact it's been widely believed no such written language existed, nor any literate culture for it to write about. That it took some 350 years for methods of transcultural reading to develop strategies that were at all capable of engaging this text is also worth noting.

For Pratt, autoethnographic texts are to be distinguished from conventional ethnographies – which attempt to represent the self of the dominant group, either to others like themselves or to those whose presence they may have muted – by the manner in which they are constructed of 'representations that the so defined others construct *in response to* or in dialogue with texts' from the dominant group. As such, they involve 'selective collaboration with and appropriation of idioms [and/or conventions] of the metropolis or the conqueror' to merge with, infiltrate, and intervene with the understandings the dominant group has constructed of this 'other'. Thus, Pratt argues:

> Autoethnography, transculturation, critique, collaboration, bilingualism, mediation, parody, denunciation, imaginary dialogue, vernacular expression – these are some of the literate arts of the contact zone. Miscomprehension, incomprehension, dead letters, unread masterpieces, absolute heterogeneity of meaning – these are some of the perils of writing in the contact zone. They all live among us today

> in the transnationalized metropolis of the United States and are becoming more widely visible, more pressing, and, like Guaman Poma's text, more decipherable to those who once would have ignored them in defense of a stable, centered sense of knowledge and reality.

It is easy to see how Pratt's argument can be adapted to today's undergraduate creative writing classrooms, which are nothing if not raucous contact zones. It is even possible to argue that in the context of such classrooms, each student represents an 'otherness' that the conventional workshop effectively suppresses in its idealization of certain approved, if not always explicitly acknowledged, texts. Here it seems useful to invoke Roland Barthes' old distinction between the 'readerly' and the 'writerly', and to note that while the creative writing workshop typically proceeds as if its proper outcome were the production of the literary artifact in a readerly mode, a powerful alternative exists when it is framed instead as a space where students are encouraged to define for themselves precisely what might count as writerly, for whom, and in what contexts.

Here 'autoethnography' finds important parallels between what student-as-other-as-writer may bring to the workshop text. Perhaps it is self-evident to suggest that the worst thing writers do to their writing, novices and experts alike, is to try make it sound the way they think it is supposed to sound, though of course we all do this – it's how we start out, how we learn, how we learn by our failures. Because of course we know how unnatural, how tortured the page is when, despite our best efforts to master it, it ends up sounding, instead, like nothing at all. Learning this, and then unlearning the bad habits of a lifetime, has taken me, well, a lifetime. Today's students may find this challenge especially daunting, for in Pratt's terms, they've already long been muted by the ways they have adapted to the expectations and conventions of, at the very least, the academic system (and creative writing inside it) they have come through, never mind the larger cultural constraints produced by differences in nationality, race, class, gender, religion, sexual orientation, and the rest – all of which now also have their dominant and muted groups, their arguments and conflicts, their contact zones. In the midst of all this noise, how can students possibly begin to imagine what they might sound like if they were to sound like themselves?

Imagine, instead, a student writing artifact that adopts the logic of the autoethnographic text and constructs itself '*in response to* or in dialogue with' dominant literary conventions, selectively engaging them even as it retains the vitality and imperative of the student's own vernacular? How this intersection differs from the conventional creative writing clichés to 'write what you know' or 'find your own voice' is that it proceeds from systematic strategies of reading that work to produce a critical engagement with text, history, culture, and the life of the student herself, and can be used across discourses and institutions in the world as the student moves on. In the short term, of course, it raises the bar and presents students with not just a challenge but also an obligation to claim and make writing that matters *to them*.

And this matters to the rest of us – it matters a lot – because there is another 'zone of contact' that is critical to this space, and that is Mikhail Bahktin's (1988: 48) description of the novel as the only 'ever developing genre that takes place in a zone of contact with the present in all its open-endedness.' This is the zone of contact that charges, with new meaning, art critic Linda Nochlin's observation that 'nothing is more interesting, more poignant, or more difficult to seize than the intersection between self and history' (qtd in Roth, 1994: 18), even as it enables what Trinh Minh-Ha might call the 'coming into being of the structure of the moment.' At least one potential learning outcome of the contemporary writing workshop is to make all four concepts an explicit opportunity for student writers, and then to create a 'safe house' where they might explore them.

Naturally, this is a lot of work. And naturally, the work we have to do in any workshop already extends well beyond the limits of the time we have available to us, and I've struggled for years to balance the competing demands of writing, literature, and theory, doing the best I can to make this effort seem seamless and failing most of the time. As student Sean Macintrye writes:

> ... too often it seems creative writing teachers are trying to cram too much into a single semester, but this isn't a fault of theirs: there is simply not enough time in a day, in a semester to teach students about reading, about workshopping, about craft, about theory and tropes and conventions, about analysis and discussion of other people's manuscripts, have assignments and constraints and assigned reading, and then try to have workshops for two to three stories and possibly a revision when there are upwards of 20 people in a class. (email)

The creative writing workshop that attempts even a cursory engagement with literature or theory is confronted with two essential problems from the start: how amorphous the idea of 'contemporary literary writing' really is, and how relentlessly the institutions that govern the distribution of such writing in the United States have worked in the last thirty years to reduce what it might be and do. In such a workshop, the instructor assembles a careful reading list that introduces students to a range of 'good work', and then proceeds to try and fit it in along with workshops of the students' own writing. These discussions are necessarily rushed and reductive, and students finish classes – even whole degrees – with limited exposure to a small selection of writers whose work reflects the interests and tastes of a small group of teachers. As well, the workshop itself, is soon norm to a vaguely internalized sense of an 'ideal' text modeled after these readings, the work of the 'best' writers in class, student perceptions of teacher expectations, and a weird assortment of the students' own private reading and, of course, viewing, determined largely by the standing curriculum and that season's blockbuster TV and films. Once graduated, students of such workshops perpetuate these self same reading habits, with few skills to expand or complicate them. They may write very well in a particular mode – they may even be said to have found 'a voice'. But they have not been well served because they lack the skills to frame the next problem or take either their writing or, as importantly, their reading into and beyond what they don't know how to do yet.

But I'm nothing if not paradoxical, and as I've struggled in recent years to overcome my own ambivalence about the workshop, I've decided that since creative writing classes were already overloaded, one possible response would be to add another layer, do more. If students were so ill prepared both as readers and writers, I began to wonder what might happen if I were to introduce, in addition, an ambitious reading program and all its corollary critical inquiries, not as a supplement to the writing class, but as a fully integrated strand. What has evolved out of this deliberate overloading is a series of 'hybrid' classes, based on topics that arise from a focused exploration of work that challenges student ideas about what literature is and can do. By hybrid, I mean that the class is more or less evenly split between its reading and its writing expectations, but that the reading all proceeds from a writerly perspective and that the 'critical' work we do is always 'creative'.

This model is not altogether new for me, as some of the most exciting teaching I have done has always been in hybrid courses at the graduate level, along with, at the undergraduate level, a powerful creative writing course I taught in the nineties that proceeded from intensive work in both feminist theory and women's writing. What *is* new about these courses is that they're offered as a part of the regular curricular cycle under the aegis of Selected Topics in Creative Writing and available for credit in the major, just the same as any other workshop. These classes offer not just students but faculty as well important opportunities for exploration and new learning.

Topics offered since the course was established include the Long Poem, Writing and the Everyday, and the Contemporary Lyric. For myself, I have taught and will again be teaching a course on recent literatures in translation with the explicit objective of broadening the terms of our literary conversations and introducing students to global perspectives that consider not just how the role of the writer differs in differing cultures and political systems, but also how these differences affect possibilities for writing beyond borders in the world today. I've taught courses on speculative writing organized around the problem of reconciling a post-modern consciousness with plain, old-fashioned storytelling. Currently, I'm teaching classes on narrative hybridity in which we read 'strange' texts (at least in student views) and try to determine not just what might makes them 'hybrid', but also why, and the ways in which they may be distinguished from other 'experimental' texts, while linking these discussions to our own contact zone and foregrounding questions of student identity to strategies they bring to their writing.

Here, perhaps even more than in any conventional workshop, students want me to perform as the authority – to tell them what and how to think. But though I have written plenty of hybrid texts myself, I am no hybridity theorist, and so I must figure things out as we go along, the same as the students and right along with them. The results have surprised me and, I am told, my students, though each semester has been different, and the second time I offered the class was less gratifying, at least for me. I want to acknowledge this because it directly reflects on what I've written elsewhere about the pleasure of teaching what you don't know. The tentative, stumbling efforts I made last spring with my students toward defining what we might mean, in writerly terms, by narrative hybridity were replaced, this spring, by more certain expectations on my part. And the more certain I was, the less confident the students were.

One day, toward the end of this term's class, in a workshop where someone said one too many times, 'is this a hybrid element?' I found myself being uncharacteristically direct. 'Let's get this straight,' I said, pulling the words as if from some inchoate memory of my own, 'a hybrid text is one that brings together elements from disparate discourses, traditions, or conventions that would not ordinarily be found together to create either a new form or a kind of stitched together text so as to express something that cannot be expressed in other ways.'

The definitive sound of my own voice surprised even me.

And then, one of the more advanced students in the class ventured, 'Next time it might be helpful for you to say so at the start.'

It was only on later reflection that I realized I had. In fact, I'd said as much many times throughout the term – the students just couldn't hear it before they had worked it out on their own. We're happier, I think, taking a similar journey and arriving together, though this sometimes makes for more arduous teaching. A lesson for me is that every hybrid class – maybe every class, in general – should, like writing itself, proceed with all new material, making discovery part of the practice of learning.

Here is something that happened when we did:

In one of the texts for the class, Dubravka Ugresic's (1996: 162) *The Museum of Unconditional Surrender*, Ugresic describes the motivation for the placement of a friend's art installation on the ceiling like this:

> ... because through that act he wished:
>
> (a) to increase the level of desire (people would walk round the exhibit craning their necks, staring at the ceiling; the mere physical effort of their bodies and their altered perception would alert them to the existence of other 'worlds');
> (b) to raise the degree of pleasure (one had to do something silly and out of the ordinary for people to experience pleasure);
> (c) to break through the walls of the 'prison of dimensions' (we are all shut up in a prison, by the mere fact of dwelling in our bodies, accustomed to certain forms and their dimensions);
> (d) to use his favorite 'verticals' again (verticals imply stretching, breaking through, striving...). (162)

Then Ugresic repeats the words she likes: 'delight', 'pleasure', 'extension', 'reaching' ...

By George, I want to say, I understand that feeling, for it speaks, in important ways, to exactly the same writerly perspective on reading I try to encourage in all of my classes – that is, to read as if to discover not just what the text might mean but also what it must *desire*. And then we try to write in response, working more from a logic of nuanced resonance than of explicit imitation, though that too can sometimes be useful.

In last spring's hybrid class something unusually generative transpired. Our next book, W.G. Sebald's (1995) *The Rings of Saturn*, provided an almost uncanny (and wholly unpremeditated) synchronicity, as we found the text recursively circling, again and again, the preoccupations of that book's 'verticals' – its labyrinths and dreams, its relentless narratives of erosion and decay, its defaced and wounded planet, its silkworms and their trade routes, and its century after century of horrific human actions and their course of genocides – only nominally held together by the syntagmatic axis of Sebald's walking tour. Perhaps it was serendipitous that the two books would dovetail so nicely, the one introducing students, in concept, to the *idea* of the pleasure of the vertical, and the other enacting them.

What happened, for just one example, was that students learned to recognize their own preoccupations with the horizontals of their texts as an unproductive outcome of their misguided dread of 'boring' readers. For a larger than customary number of students certain transformations were effected in their reading habits – first by explicit instruction on how to read vertically, and second by exposure to a vertically oriented text. And this changed, as well, their sense of what was possible in writing, and I saw student writing, almost as if for the first time, that had stopped its mad dash for the finish line in order to examine each moment of the text as it unfolded. Something else Sebald and Ugresic share in common – the steady, unrelenting gaze that fixes their own 'personal' experience in the precise cultural and historical moment of its production – also served powerfully to give students permission to write themselves more fully into their own open-ended present.

Those of us who struggled to find form for our own mutedness in the latter part of the twentieth century will recognize the concept of exclusion as clearly, in this moment, as we did when we first started out and found the writing world strangely incompatible to us. Naturally, we embraced Foucault's logic of an author function, because we saw it, as it was intended, as profoundly liberatory. We, too, would have liked to have disappeared into the 'slender gap of language ...' (Foucault, 1972: 215). And we lived there, in the space of struggle to articulate a way of being on the page that somehow reflected not just our sense of our material, but also, importantly, of our own emerging aesthetics for so long it became, this space, second nature to us, so familiar as to seem almost natural and as if we had not chosen it, as in some sense we had. Along the way, we came to understand that at least one corollary of 'exhaustion' is 'exclusion'.

Students, of course, have a hard time seeing any literature as exhausted, but they have no trouble understanding it as exclusive. And they are surprisingly at home with hybrid constructs of both identity and writing, almost relieved they do not have to be just one thing, but are, instead like all of us, multiple and contradictory – both/and. Theorizing auto-ethnography as one model for writing that both aspires to significant engagement with dominant literary conventions, even as it works to disrupt and dismantle those conventions by integrating narrative and language from the students' own world provides a powerful alternative to writing the way 'you're supposed to write' (which always ends up badly anyway) that can help guide students toward a poetics of self and writing that is both informed and meaningful to them.

That's a lot to attempt in any given class, but despite the difficulties I encountered this spring, just last week something happened to surprise me. A tall and lanky boy of Chinese origin on the verge of graduation who'd written an unfortunate farce (birds pooping on servants and Monty Pythonesque dialogue) about spoiled young WWII era British aristocrats and a father who'd abandoned them to move to the country and spend time in a tree, had rewritten the story as 'radical revision' that relocated the father to revolutionary China and the narrating agent to a young man aimlessly driving Los Angeles freeways. The father, in China, also sat in a tree, scanning the countryside for movements of troops. The writing was stunning; the story, though unfinished, poignant, haunting, and full of promise. When I saw the writer at his graduation, he was thrilled by the experience, if somewhat mystified that it had taken him so long – until the final weeks of his undergraduate career – to break through in his work and so discover writing.

In their own ways and on their own time, students do rise to the level of our expectations, and exposing them to the hardest, most complex writing problems of our age is the single surest way I know for them to experience the primacy and imperative of writing, as writers do. Introducing them to the idea of contact zones as permeable spaces where they can find not just expression but form for work that grows out of their actual lives is one way of ensuring that their writing continues. Because we teach writing, we know how counter-intuitive this all is, for we know, above all, that students must learn to think small, to focus, to get down and dirty with their own texts. But between the micro and macro approach, some uneasy balance must be possible, and surely at least part of the time we should aspire to frame impossibly large expectations that challenge and reshape student expectations not just of themselves but of the page. The use of hybrid classes helps do this, even as it works to provide 'safe houses' for students to explore what they don't know how to do yet. But the same general principles apply to all creative writing classes, as the variety of ways we might construct them remains as rich and full of promise as any open-ended present moment.

Reflecting on my experience in these hybrid classes, I've been struck by how strongly reminiscent they are of their prototype, the feminist theory and literature based creative writing classes I taught in the nineties, especially in the way they seem to have the power to radically alter student writing. As I described it long ago, it was like the tops of their heads coming off. Looking back, I can't quite place the year, but by the time one millennium rolled around to another I'd stopped teaching that class at all. One reason for this is that, as an 'experimental' course, it could only be offered four times (a curricular obstacle this new selected topics course circumvents), but there were other reasons too. I'd begun to integrate some of its fundamental principles and logics into all my classes, yes, but also, to students, the class had somehow begun to seem 'dated'. What it turns out is not dated, what is never dated, are ideas of identities, along with those of power, how it works, who the student is in relation to it, how it may be negotiated and renegotiated, and what all this means for writing.

Students think – they always think this because it's what they've learned from their own beginnings – that writing is some artificial and painful activity where they have some idea in their heads that mysteriously exists outside of language and that they have to work very hard – 'sweat blood' – to find the right words for. And we all know how bad this can be for writing. Sometimes I think back on my older son – who, like Pratt's son, was a collector of sports cards – and his first grade book-making curriculum. How worried I was at the time that all the other children seemed happy to make books about visiting grandma or having a sleepover, while my son was so stingy with his words, refusing to write anything he considered frivolous. In that whole long year, he wrote only four books (the average being something like 20): one on golf courses, one on whales, one on black holes, and one I can't remember for the life of me. Then he refused to write anything at all for four long years until he could write like the books he read – like what he thought he was supposed to sound like. Always an impeccable writer, my son always held back and never held forth, and I can't help but wonder what we both missed out on.

For a long time now, it has been my goal to teach writing as a primary experience – what I call burrowing, or writing in the suture – which is as close as I can get to what writing really is and the only way I know to ensure it may continue in the lives of my students when they're no longer students with someone telling them what to do and when to do it and imposing their beloved/hated deadlines. In addition, I aim to leave students with the unambiguous challenge of imagining a language-based narrative art that will respond to the tedious problem of exhaustion and remake itself in the zone of contact of their very own present moment.

If the present is always open-ended, at least until it's not the present anymore, then so is the work that rises to meet it. Maybe that seems like overreaching in a creative writing workshop where the product is just writing and talk about writing. But the creative writing workshop has nothing less to offer than a lens through which to refract the world, and the skills that such a lens requires are skills that cross disciplines, genres, cultural milieus, and tasks, and enable students to become autonomous and self-aware producers and consumers of literature in a world where literacy itself is at risk. The space of the workshop in which this can happen, like the space of Pratt's contact zone, remains vexed, uneasy, and full of challenges. I don't think it is hyperbole to suggest that the creative writing class has an important role to play in sustaining literary culture in general. As writers and academics alike lament the fact that students no longer read, it's past time to assume some responsibility for that, beginning with transforming our own classrooms into 'safe houses', where all things in writing seem not just possible but necessary.

References

Bahktin, M.M. (1988) Epic and novel. In M.J. Hoffman and P. Murphy (eds) *Essentials of the Theory of Education* (pp. 48–29). Durham: Duke University Press.

Pratt, Mary Louise 'Arts of the Contact Zone.' In D. Bartholomae and A. Petroksky (eds) *Ways of Reading*, 5th Edition. 24 Mar 2008 <http://www.nwe.ufl.edu/~stripp/2504/pratt.html>.

Richter, D. (1999) *Falling into Theory*. New York: Bedford/St. Martin's Second Edition

Roth, M. (2000) Of self and history: Exchanges with Linda Nochlin. *Art Journal* 59 (3), 18–23.

Sebald, W.G. (1995) *The Rings of Saturn*. New York: New Directions Publishing Corporation.

Trihn, T.M. (1989) *Woman, Native, Other: Writing, Postcoloniality, and Feminism*. Bloomington: Indiana.

Ugresic, D. (1996) *The Museum of Unconditional Surrender*. Trans Celia Hawkesworth. New York: New Directions Publishing Corporation.

Chapter 14
Introducing Masterclasses

SUE ROE

> *Perhaps the quickest way to understand the elements of what a novelist is doing is not to read, but to write; to make your own experiment with the dangers and difficulties of words. Recall, then, some event that has left a distinct impression on you – how at the corner of the street, perhaps, you passed two people talking. A tree shook; an electric light danced; ... a whole vision, an entire conception, seemed contained in that moment.*
>
> *But when you attempt to reconstruct it in words, you will find that it breaks into a thousand conflicting impressions ... you will lose, probably, all grasp upon the emotion itself. Then turn from your blurred and littered pages to the opening pages of some great novelist – foe, Jane Austen, Hardy. Now you will be better able to appreciate their mastery.*
>
> Virginia Woolf (1993: 60)

I. Introduction

Workshops are the beating heart of creative writing teaching. They are popular, encouraging, they facilitate discussion, they encourage active class participation and they are an effective solution to the problem that even though students are presenting individual material, progressing at different speeds and in different ways and in an ideal world require individual ongoing tutorial supervision they need, for obvious logistical reasons, to be taught in groups.

Traditionally, creative writing workshops were the only way creative writing was taught and opportunities for teaching creative writing in universities grew up out of the success of creative writing workshops, when illustrious writers cut their teeth at the University of Iowa. But we are in a very different world now.

Today in universities increased numbers of students elect to study creative writing, usually but not invariably as a module within a

Literature degree. The average group size has jumped from about six to as many as 26. All are highly motivated. All have 'a story to tell'. But let us be blunt – not all are talented. No-one would expect a student who couldn't sing in tune to be learning musical composition; no-one would expect a student with no natural coordination to become a professional dancer. Students begin creative courses with no technique, no repertoire of reading and complete ignorance of the professional business of publishing. That applies at MA as well as BA levels. No-one can blame the student. Those things are what they expect to learn. But their expectations of *how* they expect to learn can set interesting challenges which in educational institutions must be met, along with the management of expectations regarding publication. When I interview students I ask them, what is their key ambition for their writing? They deliver the response, 'I just want to finish a novel and publish it' as if that were not a tall order and the realization of it exceptional. Students do expect to be published and institutions increasingly expect to produce published writers. But the difference between the responsibility of teachers (including, as we often are, successfully published writers) and that of editors and literary agents is fundamental. Editors and agents do not work with people with no immediately obvious talent or potential. Educators have to. That is the real challenge we face all the time, and it is why the complexities of teaching the subject, and the difficulties of determining clear vocational pathways, make us vulnerable to criticism from those teaching more obviously scholarly subjects (which normally encompass far fewer nuanced and subtle challenges of teaching and learning).

The workshop model of teaching creative writing is the oldest model for teaching a subject which necessarily requires the establishment of a particular, inter-related rhythm of practice and theory. Like studying music, art or dance, the study of writing primarily concerns the development of the student's own practice *in the context of* the study of works by successfully established practitioners. However the business of studying those works alongside the student's own practice is also complicated. Comparison might again be usefully made with the teaching and learning of other art forms. No reasonably accomplished player would get past grade five without understanding tonal relations, harmony and counterpointing; the names and values of musical notation. Any reasonably competent painter would be expected to recognize a Picasso painting and to distinguish it from a painting by Caravaggio or Renoir. No competent painter would get very far without an understanding of line and form, balance and rhythm and colour tones. Any dancer would be expected to learn steps, to know of the existence of Nijinsky, Martha Graham or Pina Bausch.

Because we understand all this, and because we know that there is an important sense in which writing is a performance, informed, ideally, by a rich interplay of knowledge and experience, by observation, memory, dream, desire and reading, all of which inform the development of the imagination, because we know that an imaginative piece of writing might be informed as richly by painting, music, dance or theatre as by an in-depth knowledge of literature we have always been reluctant to hook the study of creative writing in any rigid or inflexible way to the study of English literature. It may even be that the study of a range of modules across artistic media might more deeply inform the development of a student's creative writing. Equally, a revision of *how* literature should be studied (*as exemplary samples of successfully creative writing*) might be what we should really be turning our attention to at this point.

We are vulnerable as teachers of creative writing because, actually, no-one has ever been able to prove what makes a gifted and successful writer. A potentially gifted literary critic, a gifted pianist, a gifted scientist or a gifted plumber may all be easier to identify. As teachers our own creativity has to come into play and our selection of areas of study and activities to encourage practice may need to be as imaginative as our students' learning experience. All this makes learning strategies, let alone 'outcomes', difficult to predict. What skills do we want to develop? Who do we want our students to become? Novelists? Poets? Writers for screen, video or website production? Literary journalists? Advertising copy-writers? Catalogue copywriters? Website text writers? Can learning the rudiments of creative writing help them towards those goals? I would suggest it can.

Is it easy to spot, within the first year undergraduate creative writing group, who will become the next Poet Laureate, the next Booker Prize winner? I suggest that that would be less straightforward. Can we establish that good creative writing teaching will iron out flaws and teach the rudiments of creative writing? Certainly. Shall we agree that workshops constitute the best way of delivering that teaching? In my judgement, yes, probably ... with some caveats.

II. Workshops – The Advantages

The workshop is a try-out room, a rehearsal room; things emerge, in the presentation of work that might not emerge in solitude. Response is useful, provocative; can be enlightening. Comparison with the work of others is illuminating. But the emphasis needs to be on identifying problems and finding solutions.

Creative writing workshops offer companionship, the sharing of creative work, the germination, in connection with others, of new ideas, and encouragement in developing them. At best they should also offer a sharing of prior knowledge, enthusiasms about established writers and a platform to try out imaginative ideas. But the fundamental point and purpose of them is that they should provide an opportunity for students to acquire and practice fundamental technical skills.

The greatest fault in students' work is ignorance of technique – that is, of how to create atmospheric effects and dramatic impact, how to effect modulations of texture and pace; how to establish and maintain authorial authority, present a story to a reader and sustain technical elements across work of significant length.

Workshops should also be expected to provide a safe space in which students can learn to accept and incorporate criticism. Students need to gain a critical carapace because the key pedagogic principle is surely that their work is being presented for improvement, not (primarily) endorsement. The workshop setting should of course be about giving encouragement, but the teaching of creative writing must primarily be about refining and finessing the work. While offering support, encouragement and enthusiasm, student peers providing critical responses should perhaps be made aware that as unskilled writers they are acting primarily as readers rather than writers. Tutorial direction should be based on the objective of each student's developing his or her work so that eventually it is technically sound. How, actually, can we best achieve that? In workshops? Exclusively in workshops? Does the writing workshop actually constitute the best teaching and learning model?

III. Workshops – The Disadvantages

At the BA level we are still teaching the rudiments. Students commonly bring to workshops work displaying technical errors, flaws and misconceptions – a student may be convinced that every chapter should be the same length, that dialogue must be 'realistic' (at the expense of forward momentum or any kind of enlightenment) or that a character who appears only once is compelling and vital despite his or her disconnection from narrated events. Sandra Newman and Howard Mittelmark (2009): *How Not to Write a Novel* is packed with exactly the kinds of flaws to be found in the work of an aspiring undergraduate writer. Every creative writing tutor should read this book. Should every creative writing student?

The aspiring student writer beginning an undergraduate course has not yet been given an opportunity to ply new skills, let alone to learn to identify and understand the fundamental errors that typically do follow as the student develops his or her work. Perhaps errors need to be committed before being identified and understood; perhaps the freedom to run up against flaws is fundamental to the imaginative freedom required to think creatively. Should we decide to recommend this excellent book only to fellow tutors rather than to students? Or would that be over-cautious ... The teaching of creative writing is rife with such decisions. Here are some of the typical flaws cited by Newman and Mittelmark – to cite but a few:

(i) 'since great modern authors like Joyce and Faulkner are difficult to understand, writing that is difficult to understand is therefore great writing' (p. 126).
(ii) '... "that's how real people speak." True, but those very same people will not sit still to read it' (p. 142).
(iii) 'Having no interest in describing the setting in which she has placed her character, the author goes into a fantasy about something she finds more interesting. "She imagined this ballroom as it must once have been."' (186).
(iv) 'One of the simpler tasks the author faces is saying *what Joe looks like*. In the hands of the dedicated unpublished author, even this becomes a chance to flounder. Passages jam-packed with words remain impressively description free' (55).
(v) 'Many writers kill their plots in infancy with an ill-conceived premise or an unreadable opening' (p. 5).
(vi) Or 'the writer churns out endless scenes establishing background information with no main story in sight' (p. 8).
(vii) And, on research: 'Confine the fruits of your research to passages in which specialized knowledge is necessary and appropriate. While we do not want your astronomer to look at the night sky and see "pretty lights", we also do not want him to be reminded of the mathematics governing the formation of galaxies every time he stirs his coffee' (p. 210).

Acquiring technique involves understanding the skills of *artifice* – as Elizabeth Bowen (1975) puts it so beautifully, in 'Notes on Writing a Novel,' (N.B. The unanswerability of the question, from an outsider: '"Are the characters in your novel invented, or are they from real life?" Obviously, neither is true. The outsider's notion of "real life" and the novelist's are hopelessly apart)' (p. 173).

In a workshop space in which peer support and encouragement have been stressed as primary, students may be convinced that their own opinions carry as much weight as, or more weight than, the tutor's, privileging an emotional response over technical knowledge. Students may be prepared to let genre act as an excuse for slipshod technique (of course the character is relatively incoherent; he or she is a drunk/misfit/angry young man/vampire). Students in first year degree courses may yet to have established any significant frame of reference. They can seldom be expected to make referenced comparisons – something like this has been done before, but more effectively – go and have a look at 'The Ballad of the Sad Cafe' or 'The Doll's House', *Far From the Madding Crowd* or *Dr Faustus*. For an aspiring student, full of new ideas but as yet unversed in the need to learn technique, there may be a temptation to see peer discussion and feedback as fundamental, the rest (learning technique, reading comparable works; pursuing related research) as the academic padding.

In an environment in which student default mode is encouragement, students may express determination to privilege their imaginative development of their own work over the difficulty of hooking into academic subjects; they may find it difficult to accept tutorial guidance; they may express refusal to accept that they are, so far, qualified only as readers rather than as writers. The disadvantages of privileging creative writing workshops as central to the teaching and learning of the craft emerge when the workshop fails to achieve any of the objectives outlined at the head of this article, when it fails to provide an opportunity for listening and mimicking, learning from predecessors or acquiring technique. This may happen for a number of reasons, like when (again, to name but a few):

- Students are over confident, over opinionated.
- Students support and give misguided encouragement to a weak peer.
- Students have no editorial experience or judgement (with all due respect – if they were experienced editors they would not be studying on the Programme).
- Students hook into a character but can't see the potential limitations of that character over a complete structure or sustained length.
- Students approve and applaud a moment within a composition which on its own terms has appeal but potentially distorts or undermines the continuation of what went before, or of the main thrust or theme of the work.
- Students ignore/are unaware of technical hitches.

Addressing problems of over-writing or cliché, establishing modulations and points of change within the story, character development, using the senses, establishing motifs, having an eye on the whole structure of which each piece written as an assignment or presentation will constitute a part – all of this constitutes the development of the interaction of craftsmanship and instinct. Ideally, workshops should provide this full gamut of opportunity.

In my experience students tend to embark on the study of creative writing, even at Masters' level, with alarmingly rigid expectations of workshops. Typically they expect to present a brief example of their work for peer comment and to comment on the work of their peers. Positive 'feedback' on their characters, their plots, the emotions conveyed makes them satisfied they are doing the right thing and can move the story on. I have sometimes been concerned by their giving the impression that receiving suggestions to explore the work of other novelists, poets, painters, might positively hold them back rather than encouraging the kind of open-mindedness that was always surely supposed to be the point of education.

Writers don't *know* their outcomes. They write to discover them. We have got to understand that *before* and *in connection with* – not instead of – the rigours and technicalities of writing, enabling student writers to push back the boundaries of what they are doing and admit new influences, wider frames of reference; fresh air. The world is brimming with potential material and students need to learn to cultivate a process of reaching outwards, not just of looking inwards.

To make this possible the tutor needs to facilitate while assuming authority, since in the process of developing imaginative ideas skills need to be introduced and flaws ironed out. It has long been recognised that the best way of teaching technical skills is by identifying them within the student's own developing work, but that does not mean that established writers have nothing to teach them – exemplary work also needs to be brought into the ring.

IV. Solutions/Introducing Masterclasses

Within the context of a university education we are ideally placed to encourage student writers to see writing and reading as a two-way process and to view literary and other artistic works *as* creative practice (an approach which creates a pathway from 'A level' through to a Master's degree). One way of opening up creative writing workshops to a wider arena of technical knowledge is to introduce not only examples of established writing but the writings (notebooks, diary entries) of writers on writing – that is, on the practice of their craft. If students are introduced to what Ezra Pound (1913) was thinking when he looked for and 'found' the imagery of *In a Station of the Metro*, to the diagram Virginia Woolf (1983: 48) drew (in the shape of 'two blocks joined by a corridor') when planning *To the Lighthouse*, to Elizabeth Bowen's (1975: 173) train of thought as she planned her final (unfinished) novel ('dialogue ... must express character. It must advance plot ... Speech is what the characters *do to each other*'), discussion may be extended from 'what do you think of Anthea's story?' to '*why* do you think that section works/in relation to what/with the purpose of effecting what?'

The observation of artists across media may also provide illumination. For some reason artists have always tended to take a more active interest than writers in openly discussing the works of their predecessors. Students keen to acquaint themselves of the inspiring spectacle of contemporary artists discussing art need look no further than the internet where they will find fascinating examples of artists in dialogue. Here, for example, is David Bowie (1993: 5) in conversation with Tracey Emin:

> Bowie: She says her work has been compared to Joseph Beuys and Andy Warhol. I don't buy into this at all. If anyone springs to mind it's William Blake as a woman, written by Mike Leigh. There is little sarcasm, cynicism or even intended irony in her work ... It has more of the construct of the self. The dawning of late 18th century self-consciousness, that first realization of self you find in early 19th-century self-portraits. Or maybe, even, a Mary Shelley of Margate.

Here, the solidity of the frame of reference provides the context for the original insight. An intellectual climate in which practitioners are simultaneously studying the work of established artists in their medium (writing, painting, dance) surely provides the best opportunity not only for extending knowledge but also for encouraging originality – the two going, actually, hand in hand. Thus related academic study (and if Bowie's remarks about genre, style, self-reflexiveness, precedents and the rest are not academic I don't know what is), far from being a series of add-ons, becomes intrinsic to discussion as students learn, as a matter of course, to make cross-references across works and even media.

There is a strong argument for believing that tutors need to be on the ground. They need to be au fait with the examinations procedure, the principles and philosophies of the institution as a whole, the teaching and learning criteria of the institution. But there is also a strong argument for introducing into the academy a contribution to learning by literary agents and publishers. Agents and publishers – increasingly, in our culture – are not only the best judges of what will work in current markets, they are also well placed, and usually willing, to point out to a student what works, what doesn't and what might be developed. Their appearance as guests – annually, say, at a seminar or other event – injects a breath of fresh air, a feeling of new energy and enlightens students as to the difficulties and constraints of turning their work into a marketable product, a dream into a reality. However the main distinction between agents and editors is their understandable lack of concern with students who do not display the necessary credentials or skills to become published writers. Agents and editors would not be doing their job were they to expend time and energy on projects they know will not succeed in the market place. Tutors would not be doing theirs were they to ignore the authors of such projects, privileging the most obviously able.

Agents and publishers should be in universities, talent-spotting and keeping students and staff up to date with market forces and commercial issues. But the teacher's responsibility is the painstaking job of teaching the rudiments, setting reading and exercises tailored to each individual student's progress; gradually improving the quality of each and every student's work.

Should published novelists be brought in to lead workshops? Again, students need ongoing contact with tutors rather than simply exposure, on a one-off basis, to a starry name who might quite reasonably expect to be paid half a term's salary for a single appearance. In today's culture, the reality is that successful professional writers still normally need to supplement their income from writing and the hope is that doing so by teaching others, based on the fruits of their experience, will benefit all and introduce students to the rigours of preparing work for publication. Published writers of fiction and imaginative non-fiction understand how to tell a story, to establish material for each chapter and sew connective tissue linking chapters. They understand how to foreground a story and to main connective back-stories and sub-plots. They understand how to make a reader see, hear and touch the world they are describing, and they understand all those things with the endorsement of agents and publishers who have successfully brought their work before thousands of readers. By virtue of the fact that they are published by reputable publishers, their books work. Students can trust them – though that is not always apparent in workshop situations.

Developing workshops into masterclasses incorporating the range of issues I have described above is a way of introducing into the basic workshop model stronger than usual tutorial direction and some pearls of wisdom about craftsmanship, through the auspices of established authors introduced both in person and on the page. In my own teaching I have selected as 'masters' those whose work made an impact when I first read them and whose words continue to resonate – Elizabeth Bowen, Henry James, Ezra Pound, R.L. Stevenson, Virginia Woolf ... Unlike a doctor's or a scientist's, a novelist's new work does not supersede the 'findings' of previous work. *Bleak House* does not update or replace *David Copperfield*; *The Golden Bowl* does not replace *A Portrait of a Lady*. The publication of *Orlando* did not render *To the Lighthouse* invalid or in some essential way no longer representative of literary currency. The notes Elizabeth Bowen wrote for her own reference at the end of her life on the composition of her new novel apply just as pertinently to a student beginning a first novel as they did to her, the author of nine novels, as she embarked on her last. Picasso's 'Blue' period is not negated or superseded by his Cubist works; Beethoven's late quartets do not invalidate *The Moonlight Sonata* (which, *inter alia*, is why for creative artists an exercise such as the RAE, with its bossy dates and deadlines, is clearly unhelpful.

V. Conclusions

The effective teaching of creative writing in workshops needs to insist on

(i) the acquisition of technical rigour,
(ii) the recognition of students in peer feedback primarily as *readers* rather than writers,
(iii) strong tutor-led direction,
(iv) importance of reading,
(v) the recognition that reflexivity must not be allowed to lapse into solipsism (remembering, as Virginia Woolf (1928: 79) put it, 'to use writing as an art, not as method of self-expression'),
(vi) the introduction of knowledge of the rigours demanded by publishers and agents. (Recognising that the commercial world involves luck and serendipity is not, surely, really the business of educators).

Ideally, student writers elect to take creative writing courses to discover new sources of energy and vitality, to become acquainted with a wealth of sources, and the job of a tutor is to introduce new directions and to send students away at the end of a workshop in a new spirit of curiosity.

It is hard work deducing the fundamental mood or stance of each individual student's work, hearing its distant voices, scenting its particular fragrance, perceiving a part-skeleton, a glimpse of bones, and beginning to see how it might be given musculature and flesh, a blood supply, skin and then clothes. Many students work only with the clothes.

As tutors we need to dig deep, to feel the pulse of a fledgling work and to discern where to send the student to discover his or her own particular natural sources. Then we have to multiply that task by however many students there are in the class. Students tend in workshops to comment on what's there. The tutor's main task, with a support team of established writers, artists, composers of every kind in mind, is to see what *could* be there and to send the student to places – in the world, books, the imagination – where they might find it. Bringing those supplementary influences into workshops, adapting workshops so that they become masterclasses, is one way of doing this work.

The tutor's two main tasks comprise, firstly, refining, amending, editing and polishing and secondly, opening up the student's mind to new creative influences – in as wide, as varied, as multi-faceted and as multi-layered ways as we possibly can. The 'masters' (of writing, painting, music) have done that before us. Bringing their thoughts about work in progress into creative writing workshops should open new doors. They should establish new ways to ensure that the workshop model goes on working into the future, especially for students entering higher education from schools, who are sufficiently porous and impressionable to see writing as having as many sources as there are art forms. They should discover fresh ways to make creative learning as rich, rigorous, imaginative and textured as possible before sending our writers out into the world, where they will be subject to further rigours most of them will barely have dreamed of. Workshops have always been and will always be fundamental, but they are launch pads rather than flights, providing contexts for working rather than the announcement of the work itself, rehearsal strategies rather than the exigencies of polished and finessed performance. As such we should go on testing out and flexing their elasticity, with a view to expanding them to bring students' work into relation with as many influences, in as many media, as possible. Finally, if workshops in the future are going to be not just the realization of students' preconceptions it will be because they effectively develop a comprehension that the links with imagery, emotion and visualization may be fruitfully explored, not only in terms of the written word but also in connection with other creative practices.

References

Bowen, E. (1975) Notes on writing a novel. In E. Bowen *Pictures and Conversations: Chapters of an Autobiography* (pp. 173, 180–281). London: Allen Lane.

Bowie, D. (1993) It's art, Jim, but as we know it. Interview with T. Emin, in D. Bowie *Wonderworld: In His Own Words, the Buddha of Suburbia* (p. 5). (Sept 5) <http://www.bowiewonderworld.com/ownword.htm#Emin>.

Newman, S. and Mittelmark, H. (2009) *How Not to Write a Novel* (pp. 126, 142, 186, 55, 8, 210). London: Collins.

Woolf, V. (1945) *A Room of One's Own* (p. 79). London: Penguin.

Woolf, V. (1993) How should one read a book? In V. Wolf *The Crowded Dance of Modern Life* (p. 60), edited by R. Bowlby. London: Penguin.

Woolf, V. (1973) *To the Lighthouse: The Original Holograph Draft* (Appendix A., p. 48). Transcribed and edited by S. Dick. London: Hogarth.

Chapter 15
Wrestling Bartleby: Another Workshop Model for the Creative Writing Classroom

LESLIE KREINER WILSON

Confronted with change, many of us sink into a stubborn resistance not unlike that of our most famous scrivener and find ourselves muttering those immortal words, 'I would prefer not to'. We follow prescribed patterns of behavior, wearing paths in our carpeting and staring out the window at the same gray wall across the street. We eat bad food, fail to exercise, and watch too much television.

As Gretchen E. Henderson (2006: 146) reminds us in 'Through the Eyes of a Scrivener', the 'hermit copyist initially works industriously' then narrows his movements more and more until he refuses to leave the office 'with its view of a "dead brick wall"'. This 'dead wall' metonymically represents the dead within us, the torpidity, that which refuses to evolve, to move, to grow. Like us, 'The scrivener is pronounced unreachable and incurable' (Garland-Thomson, 2004: 795). He is immobile, fairly moored. This 'strange inertness', as Naomi C. Reed (2004: 250) phrases it in 'The Specter of Wall Street,' prohibits the scrivener, and all of us, from altering our behavior and therefore altering the trajectory of our experience.

But our creative writing students need creative teaching in order to achieve their maximum potential – whether that potential involves becoming a professional writer, getting into or graduating from an MFA program, or merely adhering to the liberal arts mandate of personal knowledge and growth. As D.W. Fenza (2000) reminds us in 'Creative Writing and Its Discontents', the work we do has a 'huge embrace'. If we do it well, it can represent the 'best of our republic.' This is a high flying call, indeed, and it is this challenge, this ethical obligation, that encourages me, as a teacher of some of the core, required creative writing classes at Pepperdine University, to overcome the resistance within and seek the most effective pedagogical tools for my students – which brings me to the point of this essay – I am issuing a clarion call for all of us to consider *letting go* and thereby allowing our students to take charge of their *own* workshop experience.

But allow me to take a few steps backward before I move on.

For some time, I had conducted my workshops in Introduction to Creative Writing like so many other instructors. Undergraduate students filed in on workshop day, copies of poetry, prose, or drama in hand. They sat in groups of four, read one another's work, offered compliments and criticism. For these introductory classes, I supplied guidance, forms to fill out, specific elements of craft to consider – controlling mechanisms. During the workshops, however, I sensed a certain malaise. Students often radiated dissatisfaction, frustration, and sometimes even downright disgust as they sat in their groups. Granted, some of this exasperation was due to facing negative reactions to their writing, in some cases for the first time, or from the wall of silence meek responders erected, but I felt there were deeper issues as well. I also understood that students who were unhappy would not do their best work; furthermore, they were signaling that they did not believe their material could evolve as much as it might unless it could escape this system. They instinctively felt there was a better way – a way that would help them change and grow at a faster pace.

Of course, we have had heard of – and some of us have even tried – creative writing workshops conducted in the manner described by T.C. Boyle (1999) in 'This Monkey, My Back':

> Workshops in those days were still evolving and the conduct of [Krishna Vaid's] class was fairly elementary. He would ask a few students to write something for the following week, at which time they would read the result aloud while the rest of us sat in mortified and uncomprehending silence, preparatory to saying absolutely nothing about it. (p. 4)

While the idea of working together as a class appeals to some of us, obviously the result of mortification, non-comprehension, and preparation-to-say-nothing doesn't sound appealing at all. In addition, many students have shared with me over the years that they have difficulty with their aural skills. They find it hard to focus on work, really hear, really remember, and really be able to respond effectively if they don't have a copy of the piece in front of them to look at during the reading and to review during the subsequent discussion. Likewise, they cannot *hear* the syntactical, punctuation, spelling, and other grammar problems. I knew I had to find yet another way. However, the simple solution of making copies of the material for the students did not quite resolve all my reservations.

Another concern, as articulated by Kass Fleisher (2002: 109) in 'Scenes from the Battlefield', is that the current workshop model of teaching 'actively suppresses both feminist radical writing and avant-garde writing and therefore is complicit in the more general tendency of academic institutions to perpetuate the . . . status quo'. I am not necessarily advocating one form of writing over another, but her point is well taken. Certain personalities react to certain other personalities with pre-programmed ideologies, a fact that can restrict student creativity. In other words, some creative writing workshops act much as society does, sanding edges to make writing (and students) conform to ordained genres, forms, and interests. Small groups can inflict this constriction with more frequency than large groups, which tend to carry a broader range of opinions, feedback, worldviews, and values. In full class workshop, instructors can also intervene to encourage this 'broader range'.

In addition to Fleisher's concerns, Chris Green (2001: 154) worries in 'Materializing the Sublime Reader', that he 'could only help students write poems that looked good in workshop'. Mulling over poetry written by both death row inmates and revolutionaries, Green reminds us 'to construct a workshop where the class readership acts to represent the rhetorical circumstances of interpretive communities *outside* the university' (p. 154, emphasis mine). Although Fenza (2000) seems to disagree, he does cite Andrei Codrescu and Charles Bernstein as they rue the fact that 'younger poets all write in the same confessional, Midwestern, middle-brow, middle-of-the-road, 'Iowa' lyrical style.' As the editor of *Review Americana*, I have watched my Advisory Board readers (and myself) struggle to find, what Jack Epps Jr (2006) calls 'original voice' in poetry submissions (he is referring to screenplays, but his call, I believe, applies to all genres). I have even had students come to my office hours and privately complain that a certain course or a certain instructor seems to be teaching and conforming student work to one style. Certainly, none of us wants to admit that course is ours or that teacher is us.

Similarly, Katherine Cole (2006: 11) argues that conventional workshops teach students 'to steer clear of the kinds of risks that might result in catastrophe' – and, I would add, that we may inadvertently be steering our students away from the kinds of risks that might result in genius. As Epps (2006) further argues, 'Writing students must learn to take chances, to push their writing beyond their comfort zone. Good writing is original, provocative, takes a position, and challenges the reader to take a fresh look at life and the world around them' (p. 102). The point I am trying to illustrate by citing from these five articles is that we need our students and our workshops to be as free and open as possible. Larger groups tend to contribute more diversity and thus broaden the workshop experience. But the argument for full class workshops is not the central argument of this essay. Many others have made this case, and many of us have already bought into its necessity. Rather, the central argument of this essay extends *from* the full class workshop. From within it, we, like the parents of our undergraduates, need to let go.

But before I move on to a description of this method, return with me, if you will permit the indulgence, to the spring of 2006 when I decided to break from my tread-wearing, wall-staring ways, and distributed a questionnaire on the first day of class. Among other questions, I asked the following: What did you like least about other writing classes you have taken? After students filled out the form, I went around the circle in which I had arranged them and asked them to address the topics they most wanted to share from what they had written. Almost every student discussed her or his answer to this question. Both the written responses and the oral discussion of those responses included comments such as the following:

> 'I don't like workshopping'; 'Why do I *have* to workshop my work if I don't want to?'; 'I don't like being forced to workshop'; 'Sometimes my writing isn't ready for workshop, but I have to do it anyway, and it's embarrassing'; 'I don't like workshopping in small groups'; 'Workshopping in small groups only works if you get with good students'; 'I'm not really good at workshopping other people's work. I don't know what to say. That's why I'm taking this class in the first place'; 'Some students don't take workshopping very seriously'; 'Some people are good at workshopping and some people aren't'; 'I don't like what some people want to do with my work. They don't get me'; 'I'm taking this class to get a professional's feedback, not feedback from other students at my level'; 'Some of us are good at workshopping, but others just don't know what to say.'

After hearing these comments from so many students, comments that echoed some of the complaints I had heard in my office hours over the years, I realized that most of these comments were tied to issues of format, strictures, rules, procedure, and control, so I decided to try something completely different (or, in some ways, I guess you could say I decided to try *nothing*, as you will soon see). Again, although the students were not explicitly stating it, their comments also revealed their inner instinct that another format, or lack thereof, would be more fun, more interesting, more rewarding, and more beneficial to their writing. Thus that semester I developed what I call the Anonymous Floating Workshop for my beginning creative writing students working on short forms within a multi-genre classroom in Introduction to Creative Writing. (I should state that I don't see this workshop style as appropriate for single genre/ building a longer work all semester, advanced, or graduate classes.)

But before explaining this workshop style, I must address one last issue that had haunted me for some time. Many beginning creative writing students will not fully engage in the workshop process because they don't want to hurt the writer's feelings. I have found this to be especially true for the students I often teach – undergraduates in a small, liberal arts institution. Raised in certain genteel traditions, they have been trained to believe that it is better to be liked than to tell the truth. As Fleisher fears, they felt their response should enforce normative practice; as Green fears, they felt their notes should contribute to an excellent 'workshop piece'; as Cole and Epps fear, they were not taking enough risks – either as writers or as responders. These factors were barriers I felt I had to break through in order for my students to have a rigorous, exceptional workshop experience.

In sum, I saw the major issues I needed to contend with as the following:

(1) Many students don't like small group workshops for a variety of reasons, including the fact that they instinctively believe their work would progress more rapidly by other means.
(2) Many students want instructor involvement and feedback in the workshop process. They believe instructors have more training and expertise to offer than do peers.
(3) Some students are better at workshopping than others.
(4) Many students have difficulty being honest in workshops because they don't want to hurt the writer's feelings.
(5) Some students are trapped within certain ideological systems. A larger group offers broader perspectives.
(6) A few students prefer not to have their work workshopped.
(7) Sometimes students don't feel their work is ready to be workshopped on the scheduled workshop day.
(8) Work is often trapped within a box called 'workshop', rather than being 'free' to find its own 'original voice' and a subsequent audience.

(9) Writers and responders – especially at the introductory level – don't take enough risks.

With these issues in mind, I decided to try the Anonymous Floating Workshop model which operates as follows: we have no scheduled workshop days; instead, students are invited to attach their work and email it to me anytime they are ready to workshop it – in other words, the workshop 'floats' throughout the semester; when they email their work to me, I make copies for the entire class; we examine the work as an anonymous submission – much like the blind review process used by *Review Americana* and most academic journals and literary reviews. Thus we workshop all work as an entire class. The work is anonymous, which eliminates many of the ties that bind and constrain work within the workshop process.

After having used this technique for several semesters with beginning creative writers, as I have previously stated, in the short form, multi-genre, introductory classroom, I have found that the benefits include the following:

(1) Rather than three or so other people thinking about and commenting on work, every brain in the class concentrates on each submission. Students leave the class with a broad array of commentary on their writing.
(2) Anonymous workshopping brings out more honest and thorough commentary from students and frees students from some personality and ideology constraints.
(3) Students can submit work when they are ready. They are not forced to workshop anything at anytime which I have found to be much more compatible with the creative process. (I might add that my students were very conscientious and sent work regularly.)
(4) Some students *are* indeed better commentators than others when it comes to workshop feedback – we might say that 'workshop commentating' is a gift. These students are always involved in the workshopping of all material.

Admittedly, however, this technique has several drawbacks as well: The instructor needs a hefty copying budget although this problem may be ameliorated if the university has Blackboard, Elmo, or classrooms that are equipped with a projection system or if the instructor is teaching in a computer classroom. Likewise, some universities have wireless internet and require students to purchase laptops. Students can post the work online, and the class can read it from the class computers, their own laptops, or the projection system from the classroom computer. Of course, electronic media has its own set of problems – many of my students prefer hard copy. As I stated earlier, they have a different 'relationship', if you will, with paper, and they can write on hard copies. Sometimes, if they feel their notes are particularly useful, they will give the work back to me, and I then return it to the student author. Lastly, students often tell me they cannot *see* problems on computer screens.

Another problem is that not all work will be workshopped. First, there simply is not time for the entire class to workshop every work (our class size is 20). Second, some students will never submit work to be workshopped. If an instructor feels that all work should be workshopped or each student should workshop at least once, this model would not be ideal. It puts the responsibility for workshopping in the hands of the student. Indeed, in order for this technique to be successful, students must be mature and serious to ensure that work is submitted and workshopped on a regular basis. Thus, the instructor who embraces this model will be the instructor who believes less in control over students, a point to which I have been alluding for some time, and more in the student's personal responsibility in terms of growth. The instructor must also have faith that the students will participate fully in this model. (As I mentioned above, I never had any problem in this regard. Students were very conscientious and submitted work regularly.) This model can be modified without adding too many strictures and controls. For example, the syllabus can state that all students must workshop each genre at least once or something to that effect.

At the end of every class, every semester at Pepperdine, students fill out an anonymous evaluation form for every course, school wide. Among the questions on the form, students are asked what they liked best about the course. Since I have instituted the Anonymous Floating Workshop model, students have not offered a single negative response. On the contrary, their comments both on the forms and to me personally have been overwhelmingly positive, such as the following:

> 'I like that we can workshop when we're ready'; 'We're not forced to workshop stuff'; 'I like workshopping as a class and getting 20 perspectives on my work instead of just a couple'; 'I like that the professor participates in all the workshops'; 'Anonymous workshopping makes everyone more honest'; 'Even though we know the author is in the class, taking the name off the story makes it easier to talk about it for some reason'; 'Taking the name of the stuff makes me freer to say stuff.'

Indeed, this model allows students to be 'freer' in every way.

In closing I would like to return to some earlier points I made and add just a few more. If Stephanie Vanderslice (2006: 156) is right and workshops are 'sacred space', we must persistently remind ourselves that our concern should not be restricted to the physicality of workshopping alone. I hope we will remember, as yet another example, James Alan McPherson's call in his 1999 essay 'Workshopping Lucius Mummius.' Similar to Green, Codrescu, and Bernstein, McPherson asks the following question: 'Just how much are the many writing workshops, with their heavy emphasis on technique over passion, contributing to an aesthetic that celebrates the outside, the surface of things, while obscuring the essential inside world, the subjective world that is essential to good fiction?' (p. 185). One of the benefits of working as a class, with instructors involved in all exchanges, is that we can redirect and thus ensure that our students are not falling into the surface-technique well but are always mindful of the inside world, the 'passion ... essential to good fiction' – or poetry or drama for that matter (McPherson, 1999: 185). I believe this can be done without being too controlling.

Likewise, Stefan Beck (2006: 116) in 'Learning from Tools' worries that 'there are many ways in which the workshop system is rigged to yield books that primarily appeal to – I hesitate to say *speak to*, though it does suggest the one-sidedness of the transaction – other writers and would-be writers'. '[W]e have met the Workshop,' the essay concludes, 'and the Workshop is us' (p. 118). Conducting workshops that nurture the development of the students' individual styles and publishing interests, a concern close to Fleisher's heart, rather than the production of one MFA, literary-fiction style – even at the undergraduate level in which many of us teach – not only respects students' personal interests but also enriches the publishing marketplace. Another benefit is that audiences have a wider variety of styles and experiences to choose from and read about; hopefully, then, they will find texts that resonate for them especially in terms of their needs and life experiences.

Walt Whitman reminds us to be sensitive to these issues. We don't want to be dry and statistical like his 'learn'd astronomer' with 'proofs,' 'figures,' 'columns,' 'charts,' and 'diagrams'. We don't want our students 'unaccountable', becoming 'tired and sick.' The frustrated narrator of the poem ends it thus:

> Till rising and gliding out, I wander'd off by myself,
> In the mystical moist night-air, and from time to time,
> Look'd up in perfect silence at the stars.

Who among us wants to be a kind of astronomer confining the creative imagination? No, of course, none of us. We, like Whitman, like the narrator, like our students, want to look, in perfect silence, at the stars. To do so, we must not become too mechanical, but allow a certain range of motion.

Toward the end of Melville's short story, the narrator visits Bartleby in prison. Both the narrator and Mr Cutlets offer the scrivener support, comfort, company, even dinner, yet Bartleby refuses all of these, preferring to 'move to the other side of the inclosure, and [take] up a position fronting the dead-wall.' My wish for myself, indeed for all of us, is that we might not ensconce ourselves in front of a windowless, doorless wall, but forever seek the methods and the substance that might help our students as they themselves learn, grow, and develop as creative writers and, I daresay, as human beings. As Epps (2006: 103) firmly believes, 'Students should be encouraged to write "naked" on the page'. Perhaps, then, we have to let go of our 'controlling' teacher and allow our students freedom to run, laugh, cry, even fall.

References

Beck, S. (2006) Learning from tools. *New Criterion* 25 (1), 114–218.

Boyle, T.C. (1999) This monkey, my back. In F. Conroy (ed.) *The Eleventh Draft* (pp. 1–21). New York: Harper Collins.

Coles, K. (2006) Short fiction. In G. Harper (ed.) *Teaching Creative Writing* (pp. 8–20). London: Continuum.

Epps, J. (2006) Writing for film and television. In G. Harper (ed.) *Teaching Creative Writing* (pp. 102–218). London: Continuum.

Fenza, D.W. (2006) Creative writing and its discontents. *The Writer's Chronicle* <http://www. awpwriter.org/magazine/writers/fenza01.htm>.

Fleisher, K. (2002) Scenes from the battlefield: A feminist resists the writing workshop. *Iowa Review* 32 (1), 109–215.

Garland-Thomson, R. (2004) The cultural logic of euthanasia: 'Sad Fancyings' in Herman Melville's 'Bartleby'. *American Literature* 76 (4), 777–206.

Green, C. Materializing the sublime reader: Cultural studies, reader response, and community service in the creative writing workshop. *College English* 64 (2), 153–274.

Henderson, G.E. (2006) Through the eyes of a scrivener. *The Southern Review* 42 (1), 144–252.

McPherson, J.A. (1999) Workshopping Lucius Mummius. In F. Conroy (ed.) *The Eleventh Draft* (pp. 181–297). New York: Harper Collins.

Melville, H. (1853) Bartleby, the scrivener: A story of Wall-Street <http://www. bartleby.com/129/>.

Meyer, J.M. (2006) Melville's 'Bartleby, The Scrivener'. *Explicator* 64 (2), 84–26.

Reed, N.C. (2006) The specter of Wall Street: 'Bartleby, the Scrivener' and the language of commodities. *American Literature* 76 (2), 247–273.

Vanderslice, S. (2006) Workshopping. In G. Harper (ed.) *Teaching Creative Writing* (pp. 147–157). London: Continuum.

Weinstock, J.A. (2003) Doing justice to Bartleby. *American Transcendental Quarterly* 17 (1), 23–22.

Whitman, W. (1900) When I heard the learn'd astronomer. *Leaves of Grass* <http://www.bartleby.com/142/180.html>.

Chapter 16

'A Space of Radical Openness': Re-Visioning the Creative Writing Workshop

MARY ANN CAIN

'Does it work?' To those unfamiliar with the commonplaces of creative writing instruction, this question would likely seem puzzling, if not troubling, inviting other questions: 'Work *how*, *for whom*, *when*, and *where*?' and perhaps even '*Why?*' Or perhaps not so much puzzling as presenting a puzzle: Figure out what the teacher thinks 'works'. In either case, one would assume that *someone* – student or teacher – would have an answer, would have some idea of what makes a piece of writing *work*.

Contrary to what common sense might suggest, this question, so much a writing workshop stock phrase, is not merely a solicitation of individual taste. For instance, in my experiences as a student (and now, a professor) of creative writing, an instructor rarely asks, 'Do you like it?' – this despite the fact that students often respond with an 'I like' or 'I don't like' preface to their comments. Instead, asking whether a text 'works' suggests some reference point not strictly personal, taste-driven, or uniquely individual. It calls forth a discourse of shared understanding, of 'craft', in which writers are encouraged to apply concepts and skills that distinguish their knowledge as something particular, disciplined, even, in some cases, professional.

Thus, to ask of a student's text, 'Does it work?' is to assume that students and instructors already know something about how texts 'work', that they have learned, or are in the process of learning, just that. However, as Joseph Moxley (1989) points out in his landmark book, *Creative Writing in America: Theory and Pedagogy*, creative writing students have rarely been taught such knowledge. He cites students as having little experience with invention, critical reading, revision, and editing, as well as overall understandings of composing processes (and, I would add, rhetorical contexts). Although Moxley's comments were published in 1989, creative writing pedagogy at both postsecondary and graduate levels often still organizes itself around a question that is seldom supported by the necessary knowledge or experience to address it, particularly when writing curricula focus on 'the workshop' as central to pedagogy. Furthermore, with the benchmark for professional teaching credentials as the Master of Fine Arts degree and/or 'success' as a publishing writer, instructors often rely upon practical knowledge or experience in the publishing world (literary and/or commercial) without critical awareness of what that might mean within an academic context.

In addition to craft, process, and knowledge of publication outlets, this question also assumes an ability to discern, as D.G. Myers (1996) claims, whether writing is 'alive'. As he notes in *The Elephants Teach: Creative Writing Since 1880*, creative writing instruction in the academy has been shaped around 'a *dissent* from professionalization' (p. 7). Such dissent assumes writing is taught neither for the sake of subject knowledge (as with literary studies) nor for any practical application (as with rhetorical and composition studies). Instead, creative writing came into being to foster writing as an end in itself: 'to be *lived*' (p. 7 – author emphasis). And here is where I locate one of the more significant contradictions of creative writing's academic existence, past and present. If the raison d'être of creative writing in the academy has been, as Myers claims, for writing to be 'lived,' then how does one know if it (and by extension, writing workshops) is, in fact, 'alive,' i.e. whether it 'works'? This question is especially problematic given that academe is not organized to answer the question of whether a text (or a life) is being lived well, i.e. whether it 'works.' Insofar as academic knowledge seeks to distance itself from individual experience and expression, this question is particularly problematic, as the academy privileges disciplinary and (increasingly) professional forms of knowledge and skills.

This apparent contradiction between the purposes of creative writing and those of its institutional locations has led some creative writing instructors to profess that they cannot, in fact, teach creative writing. Instead, instructors such as Ron McFarland (1993) claim to teach craft, skills, and, to a lesser extent, processes that might indirectly lead to an experience of 'working.' Others who have been influenced by studies in composition and rhetoric (Wendy Bishop, Stephanie Vanderslice and Kelly Ritter, and Timothy Mayers, to name a few), critical theory (Patrick Bizzaro), and (in my case, along with Nancy Welch, Katharine Haake, and Sandra Alcosser, among others) feminist theory and praxis, believe it is possible, even imperative, to teach writing, 'creative' and otherwise.

In light of creative writing's historical ties to writing and literary instruction, many of us view the distinction between creative writing and more 'practical' forms of writing (as taught largely in lower-division composition) as more an issue of economics and politics shaping the institution than any significant formal difference. Yet the problem of location within academe still exists, no matter which side of the 'Does it work?' fence one occupies. How can one even begin to address a question that has little legitimacy within academe?

However, my goal in this chapter is not to try to answer the question of what makes writing, or writing workshops, work. Instead, I believe a better question to ask is what makes it possible for those in academe to keep asking 'Does it work?' without any real challenge or inquiry to the question itself. In addition, I will inquire into the possibilities of creative writing instruction by complicating, or, as theorist Edward Soja (1996) calls it, 'spacializing' that question so that our understanding of *how* it works within specific social, textual, and material spaces is engaged. To this end, I will discuss Soja's concept of 'spatialization' as it relates to the spaces of writing workshops in the academy. I will then show how the question of 'Does it work' both represents and creates particular kinds of spaces for writing, spaces that both enable and deny writers the ability to 'write for writing's sake.' Furthermore, I will describe how students at my institution and I engage in 'spatializing' the classroom (albeit with less theoretical terms) so as to better 're-vision' (after Welch, 1997 and Cain, 1995) alternative questions to ask of a text, a writer, and, too, of a life. Additionally, I will discuss how to create and take spaces for acting upon what is learned. Instead of keeping private, and thus unavailable for revision, how a writer experiences her own work, and perpetuating the fiction of subjective response as being consequential only to the person who experiences it, 'spatializing' the writing classroom instead seeks to address how writing and writers 'live' by inquiring into the spaces of writing and, in turn, provide necessary the imaginative spaces to construct alternatives to conventional representations of writers, writing, and writing lives.

Such inquiries, I argue, help writers better understand how writing 'works' and to imagine a greater range of choices involved in writing 'for its own sake.' Instead of pitting practical against scholarly considerations, 'spatialization' of the writing classroom critiques, even as it draws from, the existing spaces of writing toward the formulation of spaces that are neither opposite nor a synthesis but, as Soja, quoting bell hooks, claims, 'space[s] of radical openness' (p. 85), including an openness to and invitation to change, the experiences of writing for its own sake. Finally, by pursuing this line of inquiry, I also demonstrate the significance, even usefulness, of theory to academic creative writing classrooms, curricula, and programs.

'To Be Lived' – The Unrealized Radicalism of Creative Writing Programs

Creative writing entered the academy not as a means for producing 'professionals' or even to reproduce other writer–teachers in the academy, as it subsequently has done. Instead, creative writing originated as an instrument of teaching, in particular the teaching of literature, 'as a discipline of education, not a livelihood for creative writers' (Myers, 1996: 6). Unlike literature, creative writing early on eschewed formal research. Its status was defined not in terms of 'expertise,' but instead as writing for the sake of writing, for cultivation and appreciation rather than for making a living or pursuing specialized knowledge. Literature was, at the time, similarly aligned with the humanistic goals of reading for its own sake. Creative writing was understood as a way of bridging critical understanding with practice, thus completing the humanistic cycle of development.

However, as literature developed as a disciplinary pursuit, its focus shifted from humanistic understanding and appreciation of literary works towards a professionalization of research and scholarship. After WWII, the 'science' of literary study overtook the reading of literature as the primary focus of the discipline, ushering in the rise of criticism and later, of critical theory and cultural studies. Knowledge of literature from the standpoint of production, of writer rather than reader/critic, was cleaved off, and creative writing filled that void, while maintaining the separation from scholarship and research, of reading from writing, consumption from production of texts.

This 'dissent from professionalization' (Myers, 1996: 7) marks a unique space for creative writing, namely that of questioning and, at times, resisting, the social, economic, and cultural forces that have shaped and continue to shape English studies in particular, and academe in general. At the same time, creative writing has failed to fully explore this space as a site of resistance and struggle in relation to social, economic, and cultural assumptions about writers and writing. Questions about writers' identity, the value of writing along with its uses, as well as understandings of how writing is learned might be productively pursued as part of the inquiry that writing represents. Unfortunately, creative writing organizes itself around a significant opposition – between the humanistic 'writing for writing's sake' and the social/professional imperatives of writing for 'success,' i.e. publication. This tension is often represented in discussions about the ineffectiveness of workshop pedagogies. The criticisms about workshop efficacy tend to fall along these lines: either instructors set too low a standard (seduced by institutional imperatives to fill classes and expand programs), thus forsaking their own expertise by allowing students too much latitude in determining 'what works'; or instructors reproduce themselves, imposing their particular expertise upon students, whose only choices are to embrace or rebel against such models (Moxley, 1989).

My purpose in noting these oppositions and the tensions they (re)-produce is not to argue one position over the other. Rather, I wish to illustrate how these oppositions are illustrative of assumptions about writing, writers, and the writer's lived experiences that are taken for granted as 'reality' as opposed to constructed viewpoints. Such assumptions are enabled by the untheorized practices of writing workshops, in particular those that organize themselves around the question, 'Does it (i.e. a student text) work?' At the same time, I wish to describe how such spaces at times do enable individual writers to question and even resist the imperatives of both the humanistic model ('writing/reading for its own sake') as well as those of professional 'success' by seeking alternatives to received cultural, social, and economic understandings of the lives and works of writers. In short, I believe a 'third space,' to draw from Edward Soja's theories of social and geographic space, is yet possible even within an academic context that is increasingly tilted towards privatizing the subjective experiences of writers.

Such a space does not come without a struggle, nor does it come with clear standards of 'what works' that are reproducible from one situation, one space, to another. But to realize the 'radical' potential of creative writing into a more engaged public position, I believe such a struggle, if embraced by writers both within and beyond academe, would 're-vision' the early educational and humanistic goals towards the struggle for more engaged public spaces for creative writing to exist. In short, I think it is still possible for creative writing to matter in terms of how we live, not only individually but also socially, even collectively.

Third Space and 'Radical Openness'

One aspect of creative writing's academic history that is rarely, if ever, discussed is its debts to social justice movements of the 1960s. These movements, including civil rights, Black Power, women's liberation, and gay rights, along with massive student-backed protests against the Vietnam War, ushered in a wave of political and social consciousness that the academy had not seen before. Students themselves began to make demands upon the university for courses that were more closely linked to their own experiences, interests, and (in an age of rapidly expanding social consciousness) necessities. As women's studies, multicultural and ethnic studies, gay and lesbian studies, and other programs gained a foothold, in large part due to student demands, creative writing offered potentially radical spaces from which to question the cultural, social, intellectual, and aesthetic assumptions that shaped academic disciplinary and professional life.

In this new era, writing was figured not merely a vehicle for self-expression or a path for professional success. Instead, it provided a space in which to develop new kinds of knowledge, knowledges that, as Edward Soja describes, enabled 'a certain practical continuity of knowledge production' (p. 61). Creative writing was not simply based on some universal, unchanging knowledge, nor was it assumed to simply throw off the traditional knowledge of a previous generation. Instead, sparked by activism such as the Free Speech movement at Berkeley in the mid 1960s, students began to create and also claim spaces of knowledge production for themselves, to demand courses and curricula that served purposes that they defined, with social and political ends that complicated traditional definitions of academic work.

While creative writing was already following a trajectory of becoming, as Myers puts it, an 'elephant-making machine,' creative writing also shared in this 'radical' moment where the usual oppositions between academic and practical knowledges – the knowing 'that' versus the knowing 'how' – were disrupted. The 'thirding' force (to borrow Soja's term of 'thirding-as-othering') in this binary between academic expertise and student experience was that of the public. In this case, the public was a space created but at the same time claimed by students as well as political and social leaders demanding change and reform for the greater good. Don Mitchell (2003: 35) describes such spaces in terms of representation: 'The very act of representing one's group (or to some extent one's self) to a larger public creates a space for representation. Representation both demands space and creates space.' In this way, students' demands for representation, not simply as individuals but also in various forms of collective action, demanded and created space for the kinds of courses and curricula that would disrupt their relationship to the academy, specifically the binary social relationships (teacher–student, expert–novice) that structure institutional hierarchies.

Creative writing was poised to help to create just this kind of 'thirdspace' within and beyond the academy. In such spaces, the knowledge and expertise of both academics and the conventional publishing world were 'thirded' by the collective demands and social visions of those 'others' who sought a significant role in the production of knowledge and expertise. The usual choices for students – to either embrace the conventional constructs of knowledge and expertise, or to rebel against them – are, in this way, 'spatialized,' allowing for other viewpoints, other choices, the either/ors of these binary social relations.

This is where Edward Soja's theory of thirdspace, as a re-visioning of social, as well as textual and material spaces, provides some insight into the possibilities for a 'radical openness' within and beyond the creative writing workshop. According the Soja, thirdspace begins with disrupting categorical oppositions that structure social relations, thus affecting their resulting social practices. In academic workshops as well as self-sponsored social writing groups, 'what works' is defined by an assumed, often unarticulated understanding of the social that tends to reproduce itself along dominant images of gender, race, class and other under-represented identities (Cain, 1995). The dominant discourse of the workshop, asking what 'works' and what 'doesn't work' calls forth these binary relations between readers and writers, critics and artists, masters and apprentices, without having to challenge or otherwise re-vision them. As a result, the larger social and political project – of making creative writing available to more than the presumed 'gifted and talented,' to those who 'successful' writers deemed worthy of their attention and nurture – tends to collapse. Yet, just as earlier moments in creative writing's history sought to make literature available to more than the privileged few, creative writing in the 1960s took on similarly progressive attitudes, with real potential for not simply liberalizing creative writing (i.e. making it more 'inclusive') but radically re-visioning its place in the social, cultural, and political life of people from across the social spectrum. Soja is careful to note that thirding 'is an antidote to the hyperrelativism and "anything goes" philosophy often associated with radical epistemological openness' (p. 61). In other words, thirding is not a liberal, 'democratic' position that advocates inclusiveness for its own sake, forsaking 'standards' of 'expertise.' Instead, it is about creating space for questioning and eventually re-visioning the whole enterprise of knowledge-making and expertise, in particular that of writers.

It is important to note that Soja's theory of thirding, borrowing heavily from Henri Lefebvre, a French 'metaphilosopher,' is distinctly different than the traditional dialectical synthesis of thesis/antithesis/synthesis. In other words, the potential radical space of creative writing is located not in a synthesis or compromise between standpoints held by readers and writers, critics and artists, masters and apprentices. Instead, it comes from 'a disordering, deconstruction, and tentative reconstitution of their presumed totalization producing an open alternative that is both similar and strikingly different' (p. 61). As Soja states, 'Thirding produces what might best be called a cumulative *trialectics* that is radically open to additional othernesses, to a continuing expansion of spatial knowledge' (p. 61). For the creative writing workshop, this means that instead of assuming that the binaries that inform the question of 'what works' are either stable, universal conditions or subjects of rebellion, the work of the workshop is, instead, to 'disorder,' 'deconstruct,' and 'tentatively reconstitute' these totalizing assumptions. Such assumptions inform not only the social hierarchies of academic knowledge but also those of writers' social, cultural, political, and material conditions, their identifications, as well as their sense of agency in the production of social and cultural knowledge. In short, such thirding enables writers to demand and claim a different, re-visioned representation of themselves in social, cultural, and political – in other words, public – spheres.

Re-visioning Workshops as Thirdspaces

What, then, would a 'spacialized' creative writing workshop look like? What would it do that isn't already being done, both within and beyond the academy? Moxley, drawing from process-oriented theories of composition, notes that workshops tend to ignore the full range of composing processes, most notably invention, assuming that students already know how to go about generating texts as well as revising them. From Moxely's standpoint, the correction to workshops is additive – to supply what is lacking. However, while I agree with Moxley that workshops tend to operate under these assumptions (to the detriment of student writers, particularly those whose social positionings mark them as 'other' to the academy), I would take Moxley's argument one step farther. To this end, the focus in my classrooms is on revision.

One important reference point for how I approach revision is Nancy Welch's (1997) *Getting Restless: Rethinking Revision in Writing Instruction.* From this perspective, revision is more than a step in the linearly conceived model of either process pedagogy or classical rhetoric, as Moxley suggests. To be clear, I agree with Moxley that revision is often not taught, and that it needs to be taught. However, Welch's and my views of revision are more overarching. What gets revised is not simply the textual product, but also the writer in relation to the textual, social, and material spaces assumed by specific genres. The genres in question include not only those of the writing workshop (short story, poem, essay, etc.) but also the modes of discourse that shape the discussion of 'what works.' Revision, then, is not so much a process of adaption and refinement of a specific text to 'what works.' Instead, it is a 'disordering' 'deconstructing' and 'tentative reconstitution' (to quote Soja) of what Welch identifies as 'too socially adapted.' In short, revision is about identifying places in the text that suppress or otherwise cut out the 'excesses' that a writer brings to the text but also to the enterprise of knowledge-creation. Such 'excesses' are often marked by what *doesn't* 'work' – a 'faulty' narrative arc, a 'wordy' passage, an 'unruly' poetic line, an 'unrealistic' character. But besides the craft-oriented terms, other excesses are marked by moments where some aspect of the writer's experience is struggling to find form, struggling in the face of applications of form and genre that are a bit too well adapted to unexamined assumptions about 'what works.'

One method I employ in most of my writing classes, whether 'creative' or rhetorical studies, is geared towards re-visioning the question of 'what works,' to make the resulting comments, written and spoken, more dialogical, and thus more 'open' to other, previously unthinkable alternatives. I call this method 'Observation, Interpretation, and Evaluation' (OIE). Depending on the class, I spend a fair amount of time orienting and illustrating what each of the three OIE elements is and also how to best employ them when responding to peer drafts (see appendix for class handout). I borrow this method from poet Marie Ponsot and co-author Rosemary Deen's (1989) *Beat Not the Poor Desk*, in which Ponsot and Deen begin with the premise of treating student writing (in this case, freshman composition) as literature. Students and I write letters to writers in which we 'spacialize' the question of what works by grounding all evaluations in specific observations and interpretations of the work. In this way, I seek to help students identify those places in the text, as well as in our interactions with each other, that mark a space that resists social adaptation, a space usually signaled by a sense of error, of something 'not working.' But instead of addressing this 'error' as something to 'fix,' I try to 'spacialize' such errors in terms of choices being presented, of 'excesses' seeking representation. Such excesses are often disruptive, not only to readers but in particular to writers who may resist any alternative 'vision' of their work, especially if such visions are not initiated by themselves.

By way of describing how OIE works, let me offer some examples. I typically begin by presenting a student draft, either from a current student or from a previous semester, just to get the hang of how to apply the OIE method. I explain that it is a method that requires some practice, even though some aspects of it may at first seem rather obvious. Depending upon whether the class is comprised of general education students unfamiliar with responding to writing, or experienced, self-identified writers in advanced courses, I emphasize to greater or lesser extent the difference between OIE and merely offering opinions about a draft in progress. I explain that, unlike the critical responses to published works, their task is not merely to offer an opinion. Instead, as they develop their critical capacities as readers, they are also expanding their creative understanding of how texts 'work' as texts. To that end, I often ask them to only offer observations and interpretations of a draft, a conscious effort on my part to derail their inclination to lead with a (typically unreflective) opinion. For instance, I might go around the entire class and ask for each student to provide one observation of the text. I list these on the board so that we can see the accumulated responses. Observations can include single, localized examples such as 'The main character is not named until page three' (see Appendix for handout on OIE). But they can include broader patterns observed; for instance, one might note that the color red is used ten times throughout the draft and that other colors are used less, if at all. Another example would be how all characters have first names but none have last names.

Sometimes just offering a single observation can spark creative dissonance for the writer. For instance, the observation that an introductory paragraph is replete with poetic devices such metaphor, simile, alliteration, consonance, and so forth, while subsequent pages offer less embellished prose might lead to the question of why the stylistic shift? Was the writer even conscious of this shift, and if so, to what ends is it being used? If the writer was unaware of this stylistic shift, then pointing it out might be enough for the writer to reconsider the effects of her style. If she was aware, continuing with some interpretations of the style might generate some useful dissonance in terms of understanding how other readers construct meaning around that stylistic shift. For instance, one reader might offer how the introduction implies a more tranquil, reflective tone of voice, as if much time has passed from the event narrated versus the narrator's present circumstances. This would locate the narrator in a present moment that the rest of the narration subsequently ignores. Such interpretations might generate some useful questions – why this glimpse into the narrator's present time? What meaning might this shift in style suggest? Another question might be whether there are, in fact, other, less obvious references to the narrator's present time in the past time of the story that readers have overlooked? Still other questions might arise regarding the narrator's present circumstances and the need for referring to them, however briefly? Is there a contrast and/or continuity implied with the past? Or is there more of a break implied? What else in the text might help address these questions? As interpretations are raised and discussed, it may be that some readers generate some new interpretations and observations: the narrator is searching for something in his past that he has lost; it has to do with the natural world that is now under threat of commercial development. The scenes from the narrator's past are a way of searching for the key for how to live in the present, how to either resist the loss or accept it.

In this way, a great deal of discussion comes simply from observing and interpreting the student's draft, along with observing and interpreting the list of observations on the board. This can all occur without reference to a single comment as to whether the draft 'works.' Instead, the question on the table is *how* the text 'works,' that is, what meaning-making it generates and where those meanings converge and diverge from each other. Instead of assuming readers already know what the 'ideal' text is, discussion focuses on generating 'thirdspace' alternatives, a plethora of possibilities for what a draft *might* mean, given its contradictory impulses as identified in the listing of observations and interpretations. Instead of ignoring these contradictions or otherwise trying to smooth them over, readers are invited to engage these differences for the sake of deepening their own readings as well as to mirror back to the writer, 'something else, something different?' (Welch, 1997). When evaluations are, finally, introduced into the discussion, participants have a frame of reference for the competing and conflicting meanings offered by this and any text instead of unreflectively stating opinions that tacitly support one version of a story without consideration of possible alternatives.

So, for instance, when a writer is confronted with the stylistic dissonance between a lyrical, nostalgic opening paragraph and a grittier, past tense narration of a childhood memory, instead of being instantly presented with the suggestion to cut the one paragraph that doesn't 'fit' the rest, a discussion might ensue as to how to best explore that stylistic dissonance and its potential significance for revising the story. More carefully considered readings could help short-circuit facile responses, ones that would quickly edit out textual anomalies in favor of the perceived dominant style of the piece for the sake of consistency or, in a similar vein, lobby to make the 'minority' style the 'majority' style. Thirdspace considerations fostered by the OIE method would ask the group to collectively explore the multiple possibilities for how this draft might be reconstituted; not one style over the over but how the relationship between various styles might be reconstituted in a revision. In addition, such Thirdspace considerations helps readers understand how style is less a unified, singular 'voice' and more a range of various styles, registers, and 'voices' contained within a given text. Authorial style, then, has more to do with how a writer employs any number of stylistic devices, not as a smooth, singular 'voice' but within a skillful navigation among the competing and conflicting discourses that co-exist within a given text.

The myth of individual style and voice is a powerful one, however. For some students, exploring alternative visions of a draft can become a struggle for control and power over their work. To accept someone else's vision of one's own work, to see it in light of alternative meanings and possibilities, can violate social adaptations about writers' autonomy, individual voice, and artistic integrity that one has developed, sometimes with great effort, over the years. Yet this is a dialogue that matters more than asking, 'Does it work?' I see my task, then, not to make students 'better' writers, at least not in terms of making their stories 'work,' i.e. adapting them to uncritical acceptance of writers' conventions and identifications. Instead, I construct my role as helping writers re-vision textual choices so that the either/or dynamic of their (rightly) perceived struggle with 'author-ity' might be opened up. I don't expect students to revise in a way that would please me, the teacher, and thus compromise their own sense of integrity. Nor do I expect them to only write to please themselves, and risk a lower grade. Instead, I expect students to take the risk of 'messing up' their original vision and explore some of the 'excesses' that their 'sealed tight' (as Welch calls it) draft was concealing.

While it is not uncommon for students to construct my insistence on revision as a power struggle, I keep referring to how revision isn't simply a choice (although on some levels it is true that we do choose it). Instead, I argue that revision is something that we are always doing, often on a tacit basis, at every turn of the writing process. Similarly, collaboration is something we don't simply accept or deny (although again, on some levels we do choose with whom we will collaborate). Language itself requires that we 'collaborate' with meanings that we have not created and cannot in any final sense control but that we must instead work both within and against. Thus, the 'otherness' that I bring in by way of 'thirding' the writing classroom is language itself. Language carries meanings, shapes itself into discourses, collaborates with and revises not only our texts but ourselves, in particular our social identifications, including those that 'exceed' those of writers, exceed what seems to be possible to represent as a writer. It is always already at work in shaping who writers are, what they do, and what difference they make to anyone else.

Sometimes, I admit, it does feel as if I am 'forcing' students to go against strongly developed 'instincts' of adaptation, asking them to revisit identifications as well as skills many have worked hard to acquire and for which they have received praise and encouragement. Who am I, after all, to question 'what works'? But because I want to live in a world where writers matter, not for the 'star power' (and enrollments) they bring to the academy, nor for liberalizing access to writing classes that keep the 'elephant machine' running, but instead for our ability to re-vision the texts and the social relations that define who we are and what we are capable of doing and being. Such a world depends upon Thirdspaces where knowledge is produced, not by the few but by the many, in a dialectical tension that is constantly moving and shifting in light of the 'excesses' that our too successful adaptations would have us ignore. By inquiring into the conditions that give rise to the question of 'what works,' we have a chance to re-vision the classroom in light of differences that have yet to be named.

References

Cain, M.A. (1995) *Revisioning Writers' Talk: Gender and Culture in Acts of Composing.* Albany, NY: SUNY Press.

McFarland, R. (1993) An apologia for creative writing. *College English* 55 (1), 28–25.

Mitchell, D. (2003) *The Right to the City: Social Justice and the Fight for Public Space.* New York: Guilford Press.

Moxley, J. (ed.) (1989) *Creative Writing in America: Theory and Pedagogy*. Urbana, IL: NCTE.

Myers, D.G. (1996) *The Elephants Teach: Creative writing Since 1880.* Englewood Cliffs, NJ: Prentiss Hall.

Soja, E. (1996) *ThirdSpace: Journeys to Los Angeles and Other Real-and-Imagined Places.* Cambridge, MA: Blackwell.

Welch, N. (1997) *Getting Restless: Rethinking Revision in Writing Instruction.* Portsmouth, NH: Heinemann.

Appendix: Responding to Drafts: Observation, Interpretation, and Evaluation

As readers, each of us is responding to particular details and patterns of details in our texts and assigning meaning to them. We are also forming a sense of how we value what we read – whether we like what is being portrayed and how it is written. In addition to these three main strategies of readers, we experience a host of impressions or associations that the writing triggers in our memories. These may or may not have much to do with the text at hand, given that they turn our attention away from the text itself and towards our own experiences.

Separating out these three main strategies that we employ as readers is a way of making them more apparent and thus more consciously applied. Any information that a reader gives is potentially useful, even impressions or associations. However, at other times, when only these aspects are reported, it is difficult for the writer who receives such comments to revise from then, since those kinds of responses focus on the reader more than on the text.

Here are the three main strategies we will be employing in our responses this semester. See if you can start to separate them out in your spoken and written responses. You can start with any of the strategies then work your way towards the other two.

OBSERVATION: Describe details and patterns of details in the text. These can be about any aspect – style, punctuation, diction, form, characterization, etc. You don't necessarily have to know what they mean or why you noticed them. Also notice anomalies or other disruptions to patterns you notice.

For example, you might observe that the main character isn't named until page three. Perhaps all the other characters are named right away. The main character's name is then an anomaly in the pattern of how characters are named.

INTERPRETATION: Say what certain details and patterns of details mean. For instance, the main character is not named because she is a drifter who is seeking to escape her former identity. She does not identify with the name she has been given.

EVALUATION: Say how you value what you have observed and interpreted. For instance, you may like that the character goes unnamed for three pages because it draws a sense of mystery around the character. You experience a sense of 'drifting' that parallels the character's own experience. On the other hand, you may not like not knowing the name because when the name does come, it doesn't seem to come for any particular reason, doesn't fit the previous 'pattern' of meaning. The two patterns, then, seem in conflict.

Afterword
Disciplinarity and the Future of Creative Writing Studies

JOSEPH MOXLEY

Back in the early 1980s, I was fresh out of a master's program in creative writing and a doctoral program in composition and rhetoric. Having taken numerous writing workshops for the BA (Utah) and MA (SUNY Buffalo) in Creative Writing, I appreciated the flow – the give and take – of the writing workshop, yet I wondered why creative writing teachers didn't experiment with alternative pedagogical approaches, why my academic training included so little literature, particularly contemporary fiction. The standard approach of the writing workshop – the teacher leading a critique of a work while the author remained silent and the alpha students fought for the class' attention or teacher's approval – seemed like loads of fun to me yet ultimately weak if more than social entertainment was the goal. I yearned for training in specific genres of fiction, wanted to learn to conduct research for future fiction, and hoped to learn craft moves from modern literature. How could I best develop ideas for new work? What could I learn from the practices of successful novelists? Then, as now, creative writing pedagogy seemed limited 'to put raw pain on the page, with the only substantive critical questions asked being those concerning imagistic clarity' (Andrews, 2009: 248). In contrast, from my doctoral studies, I was inspired by writing process research, and I wondered why the creative writing faculty or RhetComp faculty didn't research the creative processes of established writers or research the efficacy of the workshop model. As a result, hoping to stimulate research and scholarship in the field of creative writing – and hoping to take the first step in my career – I edited *Creative Writing in America: Theory and Pedagogy* (1989c: 25). In this book (as well as a related essay in *The AWP Chronicle*), I argued 'the general segregation of creative writing from literature and composition corrodes the development of a literary culture.' Ultimately, I was hoping the book would inspire more interdisciplinary work, more talk among faculty in creative writing and RhetComp:

> Although the walls in English departments that separate creative writers, literature professors, literary critics, and composition scholars are not easily scaled, we must tear down the arbitrary boundaries and firmly establish professional writing programs that are informed by the dynamics of the creative process. After all, without theory for teaching writing, we have no compass to direct or evaluate our activities, no way to understand why some exercises succeed while others fail ... In order to meet the myriad needs of writing students, we need to inform each other, rather than retreat from each other's disciplines. We are, after all, a family dedicated to language, creativity, self-expression, and critical thinking. Together, we carry the treasures of the humanities, the keys to the mind. We must remember that narrow-mindedness discourages that spirit of eagerness, of creative play, that is essential to creativity, learning, and development. Greater interdisciplinary communication among our related disciplines will invigorate our practices, our students, our culture. (Moxley, 1989c: 42–23).

At the time I was (as I'm sure you can tell from the above) extremely optimistic, and I opined that 'there is evidence that our discipline is preparing to undergo a paradigm shift, a period of self-reflexiveness in which we question our theories and practices' (Moxley, 1989b: xi). Now, over 20 years later, my belief in the need for greater collaboration among literature, creative writers and composition specialists remains resolute, yet I have a much stronger appreciation for the enduring power of the status quo. As an assistant professor I didn't have an understanding of how slow disciplines are to evolve. But now, as I look back on the limited scholarship in this area over the past two decades, I can see that contemporary creative writing theorists (Stephanie Vanderslice, Tim Mayers, D.G. Myers, Patrick Bizzaro) are faulting creative writing teachers for not reflecting on alternatives to the writing workshop method, for avoiding questions about creative writing theory and pedagogy, just as my colleagues (Wendy Bishop, Eve Shelnutt, Stephen Minot) and I did back in the 1980s. Here, for example, are three sample passages to illustrate the enduring nature of these critiques:

> **Moxley, 1989:** [Q]uestions about teaching creative writing have been virtually ignored. At present, no debate rages in professional journals as to whether creative writing programs are providing students with necessary writing skills, knowledge of the composing process, or background in literature needed to write well. Although professional writers frequently have criticized the workshop method, few have recommended viable alternatives (1989a: xi).
>
> **Bizzaro, 2004:** 'It might be an understatement to say that most teachers of creative writing are not particularly enthusiastic about inquiries into their classroom practices (and many still may feel such inquiries are meaningless . . . the mere mention of *theory* or *praxis* sets off alarms in the brains of most creative writers' (p. 295).
>
> **Vanderslice, this volume:** '[M]any creative teachers *still* do not avail themselves of the growing body of scholarship on the teaching of creative writing' (p. 4).

After 20 years of criticism, one wonders why MFA programs are still characterized as 'anti-intellectual' (Bizarro), 'anti-professional' (Cain), 'anti-academic' (Ritter), why the writing workshop method remains unrevised after 100 years (Bizarro). In response, today's creative writing theorists have offered a number of explanations. Kimberly Andrews (2009) thinks she knows the answer. She suggests, it seems to me, that the anti-intellectual, anti-professional stance comes down to laziness:

> My own suspicion is that teaching lore – this set of mystical principles, this idea that the only thing that matters is the raw (or slightly refined) product of the heart – is fundamentally *comforting*, because the handing-down of 'tried and true' writing tips and tricks is an endeavor requiring little maintenance: no pedagogical trends to follow, no debates to become embroiled in, and, fundamentally, no critics (well, except some of us, and only recently) knocking on the classroom door. Teaching lore further comforts creative writers who are intimidated by the enormous body of literature and criticism that encircles them; it is much easier to speak of the genius of creative writing, to say, like a bad infomercial, 'you, too, can cultivate this genius in yourself!' (p. 247)

As an alternative to the rather harsh criticism that creative writing teachers are lazy, Randall Albers suggests creative writing teachers ignore praxis and theory because they 'would rather spend that time writing their own work than taking on the extra reading, thinking, experimentation, and training that new models would take' (qtd in Donnelly, 2010). Alternatively, Mary Ann Cain (2009) questions whether universities appreciate the anti-professional, anti-establishment persona of the creative artists because it can serve as a countermeasure, a gratuitous symbol of the gadfly for the otherwise entrepreneurial university. When it's the humanities, art for arts sake, then it lacks value except as a symbol for creativity, the symbol of Good Academic Housekeeping:

> The corporate university values creative writing precisely insofar as it produces figures of freedom for the business-oriented, skilled laborers of the captive new class that it trains. We are thus figureheads, beings of leisure, of no real use at all ... [I]t is no wonder that creative writers are loathe to examine the field in detail (Andrews, 2009: 251)

Gerald Graff (2009) has yet another explanation for the lack of rigor in creative writing programs. He points to the general dysfunctional nature of English departments, and suggests the notion of an 'English Department' is a 'euphemism or polite fiction,' (p. 273) that the 'separatist dynamics of the university' (p. 275) are to blame, that not only do faculty across programs fail to communicate, but that faculty within programs are too self-centered to do more than swap stories about kids' sports teams:

> I've been teaching for more than forty years and have never heard of an English department meeting to discuss the philosophical relationship between its creative writing program and the 'regular' literature program. (p. 271)
>
> But not only is there little communication *between* creative writing and literature (or between linguistics and minority literatures), there is also little communication *within* these programs, which is a way of saying that there's a certain element of wishful thinking in our very use of the word 'program' – which rarely means anything more than a set of unconnected courses that happen to be on roughly the same topic. (p. 273)

Now, looking back 20 years, I realize my personal experience supports Graff's argument as opposed to the argument that solipsistic self interest or laziness reinforces the lack of rigor in creative writing programs when it comes to questions of praxis or theory. As I try to account for why I didn't follow up on *Creative Writing in America* with additional research and theory, numerous excuses come to mind, particularly my efforts to help build a doctorate program in Rhetoric and Composition. Plus, there was the goal of seeking tenure. Then full professor. And then, somewhere along the line I became someone else. I no longer had reams of rejections from *The New Yorker*, SAR Agents, or top publishing firms. Instead, I found myself writing academic essays in composition and rhetoric, various academic books, and directing dissertations in RhetComp. Looking back, I can see the bread crumbs leading away from who I used to be, that is, a writer with one foot in creative writing and a scholar with the other foot in RhetComp.

Perhaps, even back in the 1980s, when my department chair at the time (a poet) warned me that the NCTE collection would not count in my tenure package because it wasn't firmly grounded in Composition Studies, I should have had a greater appreciation for the constraining force of the existing faculty reward system. 'You can't earn tenure by conducting research in creative writing,' he warned. A large, formidable man, he scowled at me and muttered, 'Focus on composition or pack your bags!' Looking back on these more rigid times before English departments rebranded themselves as departments of cultural studies, before the world was a text, I realize he meant the best for me. Then as now the pursuit of new knowledge is most reliably found by pursing academic specialization. Hired and tenured because they can write the publishable poem, short story or novel, creative writing stars perpetuate their standards, offering narrow reading lists, praising the same top-tier publishers, and leading the same writing workshops – the workshops with the authoritative teacher directing the conversation, silencing the author from the discussion of the work, the politics of peer review, and the clichéd workshop piece. This is good work if you can get it: roll into class, have a student or two read work out loud, and then direct a discussion about the submissions, suggesting ways for the work to be improved. Otherwise, no homework; just free time to hone one's craft. In turn, composition faculties specialize in their discipline, conducting qualitative and quantitative research or theorizing works that can be published in RhetComp journals. When tenure or academic promotion is the goal, interdisciplinarity remains the exception to the rule. Then, as now, poets are tenured for poetry; creative writers, for fiction; and rhetoric and composition faculty, for research and scholarship. To break this cycle and question the dominance of senior faculties and the publishing processes of research universities, younger faculties would need to reject their training and reject the values of the senior faculty who will judge their tenure cases. Alternatively, senior faculties would need to embrace new values and standards for academic promotion. Morton

Winston (1995) has written eloquently on the ways the academic reward system reinforces the status quo:

> The power that the disciplinary elites exercise within their academic communities depends essentially on their ability to perform 'certification function.' According to the dominant ethos, since only members of these elites can authoritatively lay claim to being real 'experts,' only they possess the authority to certify what counts as knowledge. Disciplinary elites use their control over epistemic certification to maintain their hegemony within the academy by deciding which practitioners will be certified as 'professional experts,' whose works will be published, and, what other activities of professors will be rewarded within academic institutions. (p. 55)

In addition to the comfort of story swapping around the workshop text, the symbolic value of hosting a few creative writers on staff, and the confining nature of the academic reward systems, there are other pressures that support the status quo. Popularity is certainly a factor. While 40 years ago there were only about 40 programs in creative writing registered with the Associated Writing Programs, now there are over 400 programs to choose from, including MA, MFA, and PhD options (Bryne, 2009). Perhaps in response to postmodernism, neocolonialism, and every increasing layers of jargon and theory that characterize modern scholarship in literature – or maybe it's just the small size of the writing class – people love workshopping poems, fiction, and creative nonfiction. While English departments have been crushed since the 1960s by diminishing enrollments – down 18% overall in contrast to disciplines such as communication that have grown exponentially (Modern Language Association, 2009) – other than service courses like first-year composition, creative writing programs have been the darlings of the department.

Given growing enrollments in creative writing programs, the self-gratification of our personal efforts to craft fiction or poems, and the rigidity and conservatism of the scholarly reward system, can we identify any pressures that could motivate creative writing faculty to seek alternatives to the writing workshop? In brief, do I still believe 'our discipline is preparing to undergo a paradigm shift, a period of self-reflexiveness in which we question our theories and practices?' (Moxley, 1989b: xi).

Emphatically yes.

On the surface creative writing programs may be evolving at a pace that makes plate tectonics seem positively speedy, yet deep beneath the surface, subduction is at work. The steady pressure of four disciplines – Creative Writing, RhetComp, Literature, and Professional and Technical

Writing – grinding away against one another will surely result in eruptions here and there, transforming the local ecologies, if not the planet. Eventually, I'm certain that the ecologies of whole universities will be transformed, resulting in interdisciplinary programs that will be remarkably different from the staid authoritarian writing workshop of our grandparents. While, academic time may not take the eons of geologic time, eventually – if not in the next 20 years – we can expect creative writing programs to embrace pedagogy, research, and theory. Below, I elaborate on some of the factors that are likely to motivate these innovations:

(1) Consensus seems to be building in published literature that the MFA is not a terminal degree except for the occasional well-published writer, that MFA programs don't properly prepare students to be creative writing teachers or theorists, that the PhD is a superior alternative given that most creative writing students will fail to become published poets or novelists. More specifically, critics now seem to agree that a new discipline is evolving: Creative Writing Studies. Originally articulated by Tim Mayers as a compromise move, the idea that we should divide the discipline of creative writing into two models – the traditional **MFA Model** (which can continue to ignore praxis and theory and focus on the studio approach) – and the **Creative Writing Studies PhD Model** (which can be more interdisciplinary and academically rigorous) – is gaining widespread support (Ritter, Mayers, Bizzaro, Donnelly).

So what would creative writing studies look like? As Patrick Bizzaro has suggested, creative writing studies could include coursework in research methods from composition and rhetoric (especially qualitative methods) and courses in historiography to better prepare students for historical fiction. Programs in creative writing studies could also have teaching training courses for faculty. In addition, these programs could add courses in Intellectual Property, Social Networking Systems, Desktop Design, and New Media. As Dianne Donnelly reports in the introduction to this book, important new media work is being pioneered by a number of institutions, including the University of Massachusetts Amherst, George Mason University, Texas A & M, College at Santa Fe, Adelphi University.

(2) As suggested by many of the chapters in this book (see Donnelly, Bizzaro, Abbott, Haake, Perry, Wilson), the hegemony of the traditional writers' workshop is under attack as creative writing teachers develop new pedagogical approaches such as courses that combine

reading literature and criticism with the workshop, courses that dedicate classroom time to listening to recordings and YouTube videos of poets reading, and courses that work with drama students to perform students' works.

(3) At the undergraduate level, many creative writing courses fall under the auspices of General Education programs. Given the move toward accountability and outcomes assessment efforts in response to external accrediting agencies such as SACs, faculty may be inspired to develop more fine-tuned outcomes than 'students will write publishable fiction and poetry.' Indeed, the MLA's 2009 'Report to the Teagle Foundation on the Undergraduate Major in Language and Literature' calls for 'empirical research to assess the successes and shortcomings of the program' (2009: 2). Once we truly quantify success on the part of students – perhaps, for example by measuring their publications – we will have important evidence that can guide our writing programs.

(4) Technology matters. Finally, and to my mind most importantly, we would need to have blinders on not to notice the major changes that are redefining writing and reading practices. Just as Shakespeare was a pioneer in drama, so will tomorrow's creative writing students be pioneers in new media. Interactive gaming environments, video, wiki poems, and wiki fiction, hypertextual texts – these are the new genres that we should be teaching. Organizations like the Electronic Literature Organization (http://eliterature.org/), the Interactive Fiction Archive (http://www.ifarchive.org/), and the ACM Conference on Hypertext and Hypermedia (http://www.interaction-design.org/references/conferences/series/Acm–conference–on–hypertext–and–hypermedia.html) provide students with extraordinarily large audiences. If impact is a chief measure of success, then we can expect our students to seek access to the millions of online users as opposed to the one hundred or so people who might read an obscure literary print journal published by a university. Eventually, innovative English departments will develop their own interactive writing environments to support the excellent works of their students. With students leading the way our disciplinary identity will be substantively revised. It's just going to take a little time.

References

Andrews, K. (2009) A house divided: On the future of creative writing. *College English* 71 (3), 242–255.

Bishop, W. (1990) *Released into Language: Options for Teaching Creative Writing.* Urbana: National Council of Teachers of English.

Bizzaro, P. (2009) Reconsiderations: Writers wanted: A reconsideration of Wendy Bishop. *College English* 71 (3), 256–270.

Bizzaro, P. (2004) Research and reflection in English studies: The special case of creative writing. *College English* 66 (3), 292–209.

Byrne, E. (2008) Creative writing programs: Brief observations and advice. *One Poet's Notes.* Valparaiso Poetry Review: Contemporary Poetry and Poetics. 7 March 2008. Web. 10 September 2009.

Cain, M.A. (2009) 'To be lived': Theorizing influence in creative writing. *College English* 71 (3), 229–241.

Graff, G. (2009) Opinion: What we say when we don't talk about creative writing. *College English* 71 (3), 271–279.

Mayers, T. (2009) One simple word: From creative writing to creative writing studies. *College English* 71 (3), 217–241.

Minot, S. (1989) How a writer reads. In J. Moxley (ed.) *Creative Writing in America: Theory and Pedagogy* (pp. 89–26). Urbana: NCTE.

Modern Language Association (2009) Report to the Teagle Foundation on the undergraduate major in language and literature. New York: Modern Language Association, 2009. Web. 9 Sept 2009

Moxley, J.M. (1989a) The future of creative writing programs. In J. Moxley (ed.) *Creative Writing in America: Theory and Pedagogy* (pp. 47–21). Urbana: National Council of Teachers of English.

Moxley, J.M. (1989b) Preface. In J. Moxley (ed.) *Creative Writing in America: Theory and Pedagogy* (pp. xi–xxii). Urbana: National Council of Teachers of English.

Moxley, J.M. (1989c) Tearing down the walls: Engaging the imagination. In J. Moxley (ed.) *Creative Writing in America: Theory and Pedagogy* (pp. 25–25). Urbana: National Council of Teachers of English.

Moxley, J.M. (ed.) (1989) *Creative Writing in America: Theory and Pedagogy.* Urbana: National Council of Teachers of English.

Myers, D.G. (2006) *The Elephants Teach: Creative Writing Since 1880.* Englewood Cliffs: Prentice Hall.

Ritter, K. (2001) Professional writers/writing professionals: Revamping training in creative writing PhD programs. *College English* 64 (2), 205–277.

Shelnutt, E. (1989) Notes from a cell: Creative writing programs in isolation. In J. Moxley (ed.) *Creative Writing in America: Theory and Pedagogy* (pp. 3–24). Urbana: National Council of Teachers of English.

Winston, M. (1995) Prospects for a revaluation of academic values. In J.M. Moxley and L.T. Lenker (eds) *The Politics and Processes of Scholarship* (pp. 53–26). Westport: Greenwood Press.